Love, Heterosexuality and Society

Heterosexuality is a largely 'silent' set of practices and identities – it is assumed to be everywhere and yet often remains unnamed and unexplored. Despite recent changes in the theoretical understanding and representation of sexuality, heterosexuality continues to be socially normative.

Love, Heterosexuality and Society forges a new agenda for the study of heterosexuality, presenting an empirical study of the construction, negotiation and enactment of heterosexual sexuality. Using in-depth, interview data from a sample composed of men and women of disparate ages, the book investigates how heterosexuality, as both an identity and a set of practices, is accomplished through love relationships. Rather than assuming that romantic love is an outcome or expression of a pre-defined sexuality, Johnson explores how sexuality is brought to life through love. Situated in the ongoing theoretical debates concerning the relationship between gender and sexuality, the work shows how ways of loving are interwoven with the construction, practice, regulation and government of heterosexuality.

Paul Johnson is Research Fellow in the School of Applied Social Sciences at the University of Durham.

Routledge advances in sociology

This series aims to present cutting-edge developments and debates within the field of sociology. It will provide a broad range of case studies and the latest theoretical perspectives, while covering a variety of topics, theories and issues from around the world. It is not confined to any particular school of thought.

1 **Virtual Globalization**
   Virtual spaces/tourist spaces
   Edited by David Holmes

2 **The Criminal Spectre in Law, Literature and Aesthetics**
   Peter Hutchings

3 **Immigrants and National Identity in Europe**
   Anna Triandafyllidou

4 **Constructing Risk and Safety in Technological Practice**
   Edited by Jane Summerton and Boel Berner

5 **Europeanisation, National Identities and Migration**
   Changes in boundary constructions between Western and Eastern Europe
   Willfried Spohn and Anna Triandafyllidou

6 **Language, Identity and Conflict**
   A comparative study of language in ethnic conflict in Europe and Eurasia
   Diarmait Mac Giolla Chríost

7 **Immigrant Life in the U.S.**
   Multi-disciplinary perspectives
   Edited by Donna R. Gabaccia and Colin Wayne Leach

8   Rave Culture and Religion
    Edited by Graham St. John

9   Creation and Returns of Social Capital
    A new research program
    Edited by Henk Flap and Beate Völker

10 Self-Care
    Embodiment, personal autonomy and the shaping of health consciousness
    Christopher Ziguras

11 Mechanisms of Cooperation
    Werner Raub and Jeroen Weesie

12 After the Bell – Educational Success, Public Policy and Family Background
    Edited by Dalton Conley and Karen Albright

13 Youth Crime and Youth Culture in the Inner City
    Bill Sanders

14 Emotions and Social Movements
    Edited by Helena Flam and Debra King

15 Globalization, Uncertainty and Youth in Society
    Edited by Hans-Peter Blossfeld, Erik Klijzing, Melinda Mills and Karin Kurz

16 Love, Heterosexuality and Society
    Paul Johnson

Love, Heterosexuality and Society

Paul Johnson

Routledge
Taylor & Francis Group
LONDON AND NEW YORK

First published 2005
by Routledge
2 Park Square, Milton Park, Abingdon, Oxon OX14 4RN

Simultaneously published in the USA and Canada
by Routledge
270 Madison Ave, New York, NY 10016

Routledge is an imprint of the Taylor & Francis Group

© 2005 Paul Johnson

Typeset in Garamond by Wearset Ltd, Boldon, Tyne and Wear
Printed and bound in Great Britain by MPG Books Ltd, Bodmin

All rights reserved. No part of this book may be reprinted or
reproduced or utilized in any form or by any electronic, mechanical,
or other means, now known or hereafter invented, including
photocopying and recording, or in any information storage or
retrieval system, without permission in writing from the publishers.

British Library Cataloguing in Publication Data
A catalogue record for this book is available from the British Library

Library of Congress Cataloging in Publication Data
A catalog record for this book has been requested

ISBN 0-415-36485-X

For my mam

Contents

Acknowledgements x

Introduction: making love, doing heterosexuality 1

1 The essence of love 23

2 Making love and regulating sex 47

3 The lack of love: producing heterosexual subjectivities 76

4 Haunting heterosexuality: homosexuality and the borders of desire 103

5 The escape of desire, the constraints of love 120

Conclusion 135

Appendix 139
Notes 143
Bibliography 148
Index 154

Acknowledgements

A shorter version of Chapter 4 appeared as 'Haunting heterosexuality: the homo/het binary and intimate love' in *Sexualities*, 7, 2, pp. 183–200, 2004 © Sage Publications, 2004). Permission is kindly granted by Sage Publications Ltd.

My grateful thanks to the people who took part in the research on which this book is based; without their generous contribution I would have very little to say.

My colleagues and friends at the University of Durham and the University of Newcastle have always been happy to discuss and comment on this work. At Newcastle I must single out Erica Haimes and thank her for both the academic support she provided and for her friendship. Similarly, Lesley Hall contributed invaluable advice and insight as well as being a constant source of fun. At Durham, Andy Nercessian is a great source of practical help. My thanks to Margaret Bell, Nicki Carter, Sarah Dawson, Les Gofton, Andrew Law, Diane Richardson and Brad Robinson, for their invaluable help and assistance. I owe a great deal, academic and otherwise, to Steph Lawler and I often try to tell her as much. And I am equally indebted to Robin Williams who would only be embarrassed if I tried to tell him. I am very grateful to Stevi Jackson at the University of York for the encouragement she has given me to get this work done.

The following people have provided enduring friendship over many years, for which I am very thankful: Pamela Alexandrou, Veronica Crooks, Tony Holland, Jonathan Kent, Alice Malpass, Brian Statham and Susan Williams. I am very lucky to have David Pringle as my close friend. And I am indebted to David Lown for the kindness and generosity he has shown me. My family provide me with so much support: Terry Bedford, Doreen Bogdanyi, Janos Bogdanyi, Evelyn Johnson, James Johnson, Audrey Palmer. A special thanks to my brother, Stephen. And to Marilyn Bedford I owe far too much to express.

Love to Yevgeni Sheshenin.

Introduction
Making love, doing heterosexuality

This book is about love and heterosexuality. It is an empirical study of the ways in which intimate *loving* is related to the practices of *doing* heterosexuality. Succinctly put, the whole work is concerned with how intimate love is interwoven with the construction, practice, regulation and government of heterosexual sexuality. The book therefore turns on two central concepts: first, the social construction of 'romantic' love, from 'falling in love' and 'being in love' to the long-term 'relationship'; and second, the social construction of sexuality and the delimited constitution of what we mean by a particular *hetero*sexuality. What I seek to do with these two central concepts is to use one to explore the other. Thus, this is not a book about what love *is*, but an attempt to show what love *does*. I look at how intimate love is the basis for the production and enactment of a particular form of sexuality and how it is linked to a whole sexual ontology. So this is not a work that seeks to explore the ritual practice of the romantic experience but, rather, is concerned to show how *loving* is enacted through a socially mediated set of beliefs and practices that reproduces a particular set of conditions – the conditions of heterosexuality.

It is important to make this disclaimer at the outset because, although I am concerned to show how a specific form of love which we commonly call romantic is related to heterosexual sexuality, I do not focus on how romance is enacted or constructed through specific rituals. Romance is a particularly codification of love (Bell and Binnie, 2000; Luhmann, 1986) which has received sociological attention in recent years (Stacey and Pearce, 1995) and, whilst the data I present in this book strongly corroborates the view that romance is a highly scripted practice (Jackson, 1999), built around particular configurations of consumption (Illouz, 1997), I do not consider this phenomenon explicitly. Whilst I want to hold on to the notion of romantic love as a historically specific set of ideas, experiences and actions, I am not concerned with the elaborate detail of romance – such as 'dating', the status of romantic gifts or music, or the broader economy of such practices (see Illouz, 1997, for an extensive analysis of such matters). My aim is to explore how romantic love is enmeshed in the construction of a particular way of 'being': specifically, how love forms a dynamic process for producing practices and identities deemed heterosexual.

2 Introduction

There is always slippage between the terms 'love', 'sex' and 'sexuality'. Whilst these terms can remain analytically separate they are, in practice, extremely difficult to tease apart. Heterosexual intimate love is, in modern Euro-American societies, constructed as sexual and sexuality is organized around expressions in relationships usually premised on love. The monogamous ideal of the heterosexual couple ties these three terms into an interwoven set of ideas and practices where they become indiscernible. Whilst I want to separate these terms, I took advantage of the slippage between them in order to facilitate the research because, in talking about love, we inevitably talk about the way that such a process is inscribed in relations of sexuality. In this sense, we can separate love from sex and sexuality for analytic purchase but it is their interconnection that allows us to understand them more fully. It is precisely because love and (hetero)sexuality are normatively inscribed together that we can understand them through each other.

In one sense, love and heterosexuality seem 'natural' partners in social and sexual practice. In biological science, for instance, the condition of falling in love is often seen as the essential basis for the ultimate goal of heterosexual reproduction. As Marazziti *et al.* argue:

> Since falling in love is a natural phenomenon with obvious implications for the process of evolution, it is reasonable to hypothesize that it must be mediated by a well-established biological process.
>
> (1999: 741)

This way of understanding the process of falling in love is diametrically opposed to the critique I am making in this work. In this biological model, love is an *essential* human process that forms the foundational principle for a directional sexuality which, manifest in the particular configurations of a relationship (the heterosexual couple), is the basis for a distinctive type of social and sexual practice. Although Marazziti has a complex explanation of the 'biology' of romantic love – he suggests that the serotonin 5-HT transporter (the mechanism which controls the level of serotonin in the brain at any one time) is activated, much like in obsessive–compulsive disorder, because of the 'need' for individuals to become fixated to one another – much the same argument can be found in some evolutionary psychology (see, for example: Miller, 2000) where love is imagined as a process which facilitates reproductive activity. It is rare to find any explicit question of 'heterosexuality' in such work because it is implicitly taken for granted that heterosexuality is foundational to sexual and amorous practice (and this, we might note, is a good definition of how 'heteronormativity' operates). Love, in this sense, forms the basis from which a whole trajectory departs: the 'well-established biological process' creates a chain of events that impels people to form monogamous relationships, have sex, and produce children. Love, therefore, is an innate and forceful premise from which a form of practice, which is inscribed as normatively heterosexual, proceeds. Love, we might conclude, is something that is a residual essence of biological humanness, an essence which is the basis for sex, desire and sexuality.

One would expect to find, in sociology, a critique of such assertions. In a discipline which is turned towards producing understandings of human practices based on accounts of social processes (through whatever theoretical frameworks) one would hope to find several (if not many) critiques of the essentiality of love. And yet, surprisingly, we have few accounts of how ideas about love might act as the socially constructed vehicle for normalizing heterosexual practice. One reason for this is the way that 'heterosexuality' and 'love' remain analytically separate concepts in sociological work. Considerations of love often fail to account for how it actually constructs heterosexuality and, vice versa, critiques of heterosexuality rarely consider the love relation. Where love and heterosexuality are considered together is usually in an analysis of the *gendered* dimension of 'intimate practices' such as marriage, domesticity, divorce, reproduction and so on. What I want to do in this work is to look at how love and sexuality 'work' together to authorize and naturalize the configuration of *hetero*sexuality.

To naturalize love, as in biological science, is to reify a socially constructed mode of existence but it is also to inscribe it within the construction of sexuality. Love *must* have a biological basis, claims Marazziti (1999), because heterosexual practice is *natural*. But what if heterosexuality wasn't natural and neither was love? What if love was a socially constructed and cultural process which, although seeming to express the most natural ontology of human beings, was actually only an expression of the historical construction of the 'intimate' relations in which it was founded? And what if love was felt to be natural, not because of the serotonin it released, or the biological process on which it was founded, but because it offered ways of being, ways of existing, ways of becoming which were compelling? Then, if that were the case, we would need to think about how that compelling mode of being related to the heterosexuality in which it is normatively expressed. Of course, this is not to suggest that love is not the basis for non-heterosexual relationships because clearly it very often is. The proposition I am making is not that love *causes* heterosexuality but that the social construction of love is bound up with, and legitimizes, a range of heterosexual practices. This is the opposite of the biological model where we 'read forward' from love, because I am proposing that we 'read backwards' from sexuality, to see how love is invoked as the basis for a way of being, rather than being a natural basis for that way of being.

Love itself can be conceptualized in various ways, as 'romantic love', 'intimate love', 'confluent love', 'sexual love', and it is important to look at how these differences are expressed. But, however named, these types of love are underwritten by a set of beliefs which express a common essentialism. In other words, whilst 'doing' romantic love may take various forms (from the process of falling in love, to falling out of love, to producing relationships, to getting married), these ways of behaving circulate around an essential belief that love itself is natural, universal and ahistorical. In understanding how such an 'essence of love' is constructed and reproduced it seems important to relate it to its meaningful and tangible expression in normative modes of heterosexuality.

Heterosexuality can be thought of in various ways: as sexual practices, a sexual identity, an institutionalized form of social organization, and a set of conditions through which family and kinship are constructed. As Beverley Skeggs sums up: 'Heterosexuality is institutionalized, reproduced in material practices, regulated and normalized through signification, consolidated through links with other forms of capital and enacted in performance' (1997: 135). And, of course, 'the heterosexual' is also a modern individual, a person imbued with specific characteristics, and a gendered individual who is inscribed with a biological sex. This book considers how this heterosexual subject is 'brought to life' through the discursive construction of love; how love facilitates a *mode of becoming* heterosexual; and how the construction of *compelling* love provides a mechanism which secures *compulsory* heterosexuality. In looking at love I work towards an answer to the question: how does one *become* heterosexual and how does one sustain this mode of becoming?

Why study heterosexuality?

We live in a time of profound contradiction in the social organization of sexuality. The second half of the twentieth century witnessed enormous and significant changes in the social and political constitution of both sexual identities and practices. Central to this has been: reforms in divorce law, the Sexual Offences Act 1967 and the Abortion Act 1967; the availability of new contraception methods; the discourses of sexual 'permissiveness' and the prevalence of HIV and AIDS; the new social movements of gays and lesbians; the transformation of the family and of parenting; and the wider changes in the industrial mode of production which has facilitated women's greater involvement in the formal economy. Myriad changes have resulted, some might say, in a profound transformation of intimacy and a pluralization of sexuality (Giddens, 1992). In sociology we have witnessed a movement away from, or a lack of engagement with, notions of 'compulsory heterosexuality' (Rich, 1980) towards more 'fluid' conceptions of sexuality which celebrate diversity (Weeks, 2000). Yet, whilst it is true that the social construction of heterosexuality has undergone significant changes, is it right that we lack a broad-based, ongoing study of its 'compulsory' nature? Neither the visibility of homosexuality, nor any of the social or political changes in the last 50 years negate the essential normativity of heterosexuality and, indeed, may even compound its construction as 'original'. Homosexuality still remains 'other' to heterosexuality and therefore appears as a departure from a norm (it is still 'bent' from that which is 'straight'). And social changes have not significantly altered the belief that heterosexuality is 'natural'.

To analyse heterosexuality is to study one of the most fundamental axioms of our contemporary social organization. It is to look at how human beings engage in a process of 'being' which orders not just sexual expression but is the foundation of gender difference (which connects, in modern contemporary societies, with class, ethnicity, disability and so on). Heterosexuality is, because sexuality is, the foundation of *who* we are and therefore *what* we can be. To study heterosexuality we must therefore account for the ways in which, even amidst the continual and processual changes in the social construction of sexuality, it retains its status as normative, privileged and *compulsory*. To say that heterosexuality is compulsory means, as Diana Fuss notes, that 'it must present itself as governed by some internal necessity' (1991: 2). This book aims to explore the *social* context of this 'internal necessity' in order to explicate the continued reproduction of normative heterosexuality.

To study heterosexuality is to turn directly upon heterosexuality and not treat it as an effect or outcome of some other social process. Keeping heterosexuality as central, but exploring other substantive issues, means that we can look at how forms of commonality and difference intersect in the construction and experience of a monolithic category which, because it is divided by gender, class, age, ethnicity and so on, might rightly be talked of as 'heterosexualities' (Smart, 1996). There are a number of ways that one might study heterosexuality. One could, for instance, choose not to study heterosexuals at all but to look at homosexuality and homosexuals as a way of understanding the relational construction of sexualities. So the question of *how* to study heterosexuality is a key issue. Another is how to study heterosexuality *empirically*. Whilst one can theorize heterosexuality in a number of ways, it is very difficult to 'get at it' through empirical work. Unlike studies of homosexuality, where 'sexual identity' is a visible and available 'concept' which can be discussed, heterosexuality is a largely silent principle of social organization (Wilkinson and Kitzinger, 1993). One could not investigate heterosexuality by simply asking someone questions about their experience of 'it' because such questions would be unlikely to facilitate meaningful answers. Therefore, empirical research of heterosexuality needs to study an *expression* of heterosexual practice and identity in order to make it visible.

I use love as the basis from which to look at how heterosexuality is consolidated and I do this for two reasons. First, because the desire to love is often translated into delimited sets of heterosexual arrangements – what we commonly call 'relationships' – and, second, because love is often felt as essential, natural and compelling. I could have chosen to use experiences of marriage, or reproduction, or the family – all of which have been used in studies (not necessarily with the focus on the construction of heterosexuality per se) – and this might have seemed more appropriate since these things are, normatively, expressions of heterosexuality. Intimate love, on the other hand, we might say cuts across sexuality and can be experienced by everyone. How can love, then, be related to compulsory heterosexuality? Put simply, love is more fundamental to heterosexuality than any of its 'manifestations' in social institutions because ideas about love, as I argue throughout this book, are connected to fundamental notions of personhood that function in relation to ontological ideas about innate sexuality. Again, at no point do I argue that love *causes* heterosexuality, but what I do maintain is that love legitimates forms of heterosexual practices and identities because love itself is felt to be natural. To love, and be loved, is often felt to be absolutely essential but it is the ways in which that essentiality is satisfied which become of crucial significance. So, to study heterosexuality from the point of view of the construction of love is to ask how, through engaging in love, we negotiate the construction of sexuality.

But is it legitimate to talk of 'compulsory' heterosexuality in what some might call a post-heterosexual society? Why study *hetero*sexuality specifically at all? The answer to both these questions can be found in the almost hegemonic invisibility of heterosexuality within social life.[1] To say that heterosexuality is invisible is, some might say, oxymoronic because heterosexuality is everywhere. *But is heterosexuality everywhere?* What we observe in the world may be the manifestations of heterosexuality but what we call it is not 'heterosexual'. We call what we see in the world 'marriage', 'the family', 'reproduction', 'relationships', but we rarely prefix any of these things with the word 'heterosexual'. Far more visible, in relation to sexuality, is homosexuality. Homosexuality is, in social life, what sexuality *is*. Much like ethnicity, where whiteness remains normative and invisible (and yet is, of course, everywhere) heterosexuality is everywhere and nowhere.[2] Use any library online catalogue and search for the word 'heterosexual' and the list will show, if lucky, ten books; type in 'homosexuality' and the list will multiply to hundreds. Heterosexuality is, ironically, the poor relation in sexuality studies but this reflects its privilege in social life. In the next section I consider some of the key issues which have been raised within the still significantly small body of sociological research concerned with heterosexuality.

The history of het: sex, gender and sexuality

The linchpin of the sociology of heterosexuality is Adrienne Rich's now classic 1980 intervention into, what she regarded as, the 'shoal' of feminist work which took heterosexuality for granted, considered women's heterosexuality as normative 'sexual preference', and ignored the historical and contemporary viability of 'lesbian existence'. Whilst there was work on heterosexuality before Rich's intervention (for example, in Gagnon and Simon's (1973) research and in Freud's work more generally), it is Rich's account of sexuality (and particularly lesbianism) that contains the first forceful critique of institutional heterosexuality, as a social and political construction, rather than as a personal, psychological or biological preference. Summed up by Catharine MacKinnon's idea of women's sexuality being 'that which is most one's own, yet most taken away' (1982: 182), Rich's account attacks heterosexuality at the core of the sex/gender system where 'compulsory heterosexuality' imposes institutional constraints upon women to deny them legitimate and 'free' sexual expression. Central to her thesis is a critique of the assumption that sexual preference is a natural and innate quality of human beings which needs little or no explanation: 'This assumption of female heterosexuality seems to me in itself remarkable: it is an enormous assumption to have glided so silently into the foundations of our thought' (Rich, 1980: 637).

Rich's use of the word 'silent' is crucial. Heterosexuality remains silent in social life, in most sociological work, and in much of the available literature on sexuality. Even where relationships between men and women are most forcibly critiqued (for example, Dworkin, 1987) often there isn't an emphasis on the social construction of heterosexuality per se but rather the patriarchal relations of gender inequality which structure, and reproduce, heterosexual relationships. The emphasis, in this sense, is placed firmly on gender. But the point of Rich's work was that it argued explicitly against this emphasis because it sought to think about how gender relations were themselves *produced* through the social relations of heterosexuality. In invoking what would become the long debate between essentialist and constructivist theories of sexuality (see Stein, 1992), and by undermining the idea that we are innately sexualized in particular ways, Rich's argument opened up new conceptual horizons by asking the most basic question: what is heterosexuality and why does it exist in its present form?

However, as Debbie Cameron (1992) notes, there are certain problems in Rich's thesis which stem from a contradictory duality in her conceptualization of how heterosexuality 'works': there is both an implicit voluntarism around lesbian sexual identity and an instatement of heterosexuality as a pervasive method of ideological control. Rich's heterosexual woman is denied legitimate and authentic sexual expression by contemporary heterosexual relations but *could* find the possibility for a 'way out' of such constraint. On the one hand we find heterosexuality as a totalizing form of power, one that attempts to 'colonize the consciousness' of women; on the other, she describes a historical form of resistance which is made possible by lesbianism. What is problematic here is the essentiality of the gender categories that such resistance invokes and relies upon. Whilst feminism has consistently engaged with the essentiality of the category 'woman' (see Spellman, 1990, for a considered analysis), and has attended to the complex interrelationship between gender and essentialist/constructionist conceptions of sexuality, the need to hold on to sex categories as way of providing an adequate critique of gender inequalities remains crucial: something which has led Spivak (1996) to argue for the necessity of 'strategic essentializing'. But this, as Linda Nicholson (1995) argues, is inherently problematic:

> One of the weaknesses of a difference-based feminism is that it cannot account for the phenomenon of such societies having produced feminists – that is, beings whose genitals, by virtue of the account, should have

made us completely feminine but whose actual political skills and/or presence in such previously male-dominated institutions as the academy must indicate some masculine socialization.

(1995: 57)

And this is essentially the problem with Rich's conceptualization of both power and resistance: exactly how do *some* women resist? Nicholson identifies several important problems with foundational claims about biological sex difference. If, for example, gender forms the socially constructed attributes which become socialized onto the pre-social ontological configurations of biological matter (like, as she says, a coat hanging on a coat-stand) then how do we account for, even with the types of power differentiations elaborated by Rich, the ways in which some women simply do not 'conform'? How can, as Cameron (1990) believes possible, some women access a continuum of sexual pleasure outside of patriarchal structures and escape the 'hegemony' of heteronormativity?

Such questions take us to the heart of the problem of theorizing heterosexuality and show how sexuality is always framed by wider ontological issues of biological sex and gender. Since de Beauvoir's famous intonation that one *becomes* a woman, feminism has been left with the residue that becoming a woman, that gendered feminine being, is built on an inherent truth, what we might call the 'facts of life': 'Males and females are two types of individuals which are differentiated within a species for the function of reproduction' (de Beauvoir [1949] 1997: 35). What we often find is an implicit belief in the axiomatic biological principle of sex difference around which all social attributes of sexuality and gender circulate. It is a view which Monique Wittig (1981) has powerfully challenged by claiming that the term 'woman' can be applied only within the parameters of heterosexuality (lesbians, she famously claimed, were not 'women' because that category of sex is a political foundation of heterosexuality). Yet the usefulness of biological sex difference remains analytically pervasive precisely because we need it in order to make tangible critiques of the gender relations on which heterosexual constructions rely. And getting away from notions of absolute difference leaves us with a problem, especially in considering heterosexuality, because we are left with the wild card of 'reproduction' which can be thrown up at any time: surely, it might be claimed, heterosexuality is natural because reproduction is natural?[3] Aren't men and women *really* different?

The problem we have is that sex difference often remains intact even where heterosexuality is critiqued. In Sue Wilkinson and Celia Kitzinger's (1993) seminal collection, the question of biological sex is never far from the centre of analysis but, throughout the book, it is rarely questioned. Whilst this volume is invaluable for its constant attention to the silent and organizing principles of heterosexuality, and assumptions made around heteronormativity, it is striking in its lack of consideration of the way in which biological sex itself might function as a corollary of heterosexuality. Wilkinson and Kitzinger are preoccupied with the concerns of many feminists regarding heterosexuality: the construction of power differences in penetrative sex (see Smart, 1996, for a consideration of this issue), the use of sexual violence in heterosexual relationships (see Kelly, 1988, for an understanding of sexual violence as a continuum), the often painful and unequal nature of marriage (see VanEvery, 1995). But one central aspect emerges in Wilkinson and Kitzinger's book, and from most (but not all) of their contributors: 'heterosexuality is not very good for women' (1993: 12).

Whilst this may, from their point of view, be true, it implicitly reiterates a problematic vein within theorizing heterosexuality because it introduces a simultaneous understanding of sexuality as both absolute constraint and possible emancipation: 'women' can either be exploited in their relationships with men ('sleep with the enemy' as the Leeds Revolutionary Feminist Group (1981) once said) or become (political) lesbians. The latter is the preferred method of 'escape' for Denise Thompson (1993) who, in what might be seen as one of the most patronizing accounts, urges heterosexual women to love other women: 'Although heterosexual desire functions to keep women from each other, even to turn us against each other, women can love women in spite of it' (1993: 176). But who is Thompson invoking as this discrete personage 'woman' who could commit the 'act of resistance' which is lesbianism (Clarke, 1981)?

It is precisely this question which is axiomatic to Judith Butler's work and to a range of other theorists who we might, for convenience, place under the sign of 'queer' (for example: Fuss, 1991; Halperin, 1995; Sedgewick, 1990; Seidman, 1996; Warner, 1993). Whilst it is not true to say that queer theorists have 'invented' a new tradition which provides answers to questions of essentialism, they do offer a new way to think about some of the problems raised around power and constraint within the construction of sexuality. But it would be a mistake, however, to see queer as a radical break in sexual epistemology. According to Stevi Jackson, much of the work of queer is actually just a 'reinvention of the sociological wheel' (1999: 161). Whilst it is true that the type of critique which queer offers, usually influenced by the work of Michel Foucault, can also be found in the work of others, such as the anti-essentialist split between 'homosexuals' and 'homosexual acts' offered by Mary McIntosh (1968), or the critique of sexual identity categories found in Ken Plummer's work (1981), what queer offers is a radical shift in emphasis. No longer specifically concerned with a critique of gender per se, queer attempts to move the analysis to heterosexuality, or sexuality, directly.

The key principle of this theoretical move can be seen to be an explicit focus on the homosexual/heterosexual binary as the central point for analysing the contemporary configurations of gender and sex. Eve Sedgwick's seminal work *Epistemology of the Closet*, published in 1990, begins with an outline of this radical shift in emphasis. She proposes that:

many of the major nodes of thought and knowledge in twentieth-century Western culture as a whole are structured – indeed fractured – by a chronic, now endemic crisis of homo/heterosexual definition, indicatively male, dating from the end of the nineteenth century.

(1990: 1)

She goes on to state that, because of this, 'an understanding of virtually any aspect of modern Western culture must be, not merely incomplete, but damaged in its central substance to the degree that it does not incorporate a critical analysis of modern homo/heterosexual definition' (1990: 1). This radical shift in emphasis from a study of gender relations, to a reconfiguration of the conceptual apparatus for understanding gender (notice, however, that she holds on to the concept of a 'male'-defined knowledge), places the homo/het binary at the centre of analysis. The reason for this is, as Sedgewick states, because this modern binary, roughly 100 years old (Halperin, 1990), has come to be the central axiom of how we define ourselves as modern human beings. It is a thesis which Jonathan Ned Katz (1996) takes to its logical conclusion by writing a history of heterosexuality's 'invention' in the twentieth century. As Katz states, some might think this idea 'crackpot' because, after all, isn't heterosexuality as old as time itself – the 'Adam and Eve' of sexual categories? 'Questioning our belief in a universal heterosexuality goes completely against today's common sense', Katz writes, '[s]till, I speak of heterosexuality's historical invention to contest head-on our usual assumption of an eternal heterosexuality' (1996: 13).

It is in the work of Judith Butler that we find this re-emphasis on heterosexuality taken to its logical conclusions. In *Gender Trouble* (1990) Butler attempts to deconstruct the unity between gender, sex and sexual desire by analysing them through the 'heterosexual matrix' which she argues is the normative framework through which sexual ontology is produced. The central feature of her analysis is that it is not simply gender which is reproduced within heterosexuality but the categories of biological sex – in short, bodies – something she goes on to explore in *Bodies That Matter*:

the regulatory norms of 'sex' work in a performative fashion to constitute the materiality of bodies and, more specifically, to materialize the body's sex, to materialize sexual difference in the service of the consolidation of the heterosexual imperative.

(Butler, 1993: 2)

For Butler, sex and gender are the subservient categories of 'compulsory heterosexuality' because, through their constant reiteration and performative citation, they consolidate and naturalize themselves as the basis for heterosexuality. What heterosexuality brings into being, Butler argues, becomes imagined as the eternal necessity on which 'natural' heterosexuality is based.

The sex differences which some feminists would wish to protect as 'real' ontological differences should be re-thought as performative imitations of the regulatory framework through which they come into existence: 'what they imitate is a phantasmatic ideal of heterosexual identity' (Butler, 1991: 21). There is no 'proper' sex or gender, she argues, only the endless chain of signification which is put into operation by the compulsory nature of heteronormativity. And what *forces* subjects to incite sex and gender (and what places them in relations of interpellation which fixes them to an identity) is that they are continually haunted by the spectre of the homo/het binary which regulates their identities as gendered and sexed beings. It is the compulsion to re-enact the *normative versions* of masculinity and femininity, to materialize standard ontological configurations of sex–gender–desire, which maintains heteronormativity. In short, heterosexuality directs and conditions all of us (regardless of how, or whether, we ourselves enact it).

In the empirical work we have available to us on heterosexuality, there is nothing which attempts to directly apply a Butlerian or queer analysis to the study of 'real' lives and, consequently, the preoccupations of queer have remained a largely theoretical area of work. Because of this, Butler and others often attract the type of criticism made, for example, by Stevi Jackson:

> I sometimes wonder whether the theoretical hyperreality inhabited by some of these writers, where the representations they have constructed come to constitute the only 'reality' they acknowledge, might indeed be a separate 'queer planet'.
>
> (1999: 162)

Jackson has argued that a central preoccupation with sexuality ignores the materiality of gendered 'reality' and that by focusing on sexuality we lose the ability to theorize 'real' lives. For Jackson, understanding how heterosexuality is operationalized in terms of a homo/het binary is inadequate because it does not engage the central issues which feminism should address, namely, the conditions of gender which *create* heterosexuality. For Jackson, it is gender which we should attend to in order that we can than understand heterosexuality. The privileging of sexuality by queer theory is an 'obscure and elitist post-modern language' which ignores the 'facts' of gender (Jeffreys, 1996: 89).

In view of this, we find claims that empirical sociology should become more 'grounded' and attend to the 'real' lives of individuals (Plummer, 1998). And yet, with a handful of exceptions, there is very little empirical work on heterosexuality. Where there is empirical work it is usually concerned with relations of gender within heterosexual relationships (for example: VanEvery, 1995; Dryden, 1999) rather than heterosexuality per se. Ironically, these works do offer an analysis of how heterosexuality is performatively reiterated through gender, how it is 'done', but this is offered implicitly because the authors are concerned with the reproduction of gender 'roles'. What we have is a conceptual difficulty because, although these works tell us how gender is enacted, they do so without addressing the social construction of sexuality. The question remains: why do people enact *hetero*sexual practices and consolidate *hetero*sexual identities? Studies of gender relations within heterosexual relationships do not automatically tell us anything about the social construction of heterosexuality.

These conceptual difficulties are addressed in the work of Holland *et al.* in their book *The Male in the Head* (1998) where we find, not only an explicit empirical analysis of the gender relations set up by heterosexuality, but also an analysis of the ways in which gender is consolidated relationally within the social construction of sexuality. In this work, heterosexuality is understood to be performatively reiterated through the enactment of normative forms of gendered behaviour. For instance, writing about young men's masculinity, the authors conclude that there is a 'particular concept of hegemonic heterosexual masculinity at work' which is operationalized through a 'separation from effeminacy, and homosexuality' (1998: 162). Beverley Skeggs (1997) has similarly argued that the reiteration of heterosexual convention, through the take up of the position 'woman', is always structured through both relations of gender *and* sexuality. In a rare empirical application of such ideas, Skeggs looks at how heterosexual femininity is constructed in relations of disidentification with 'the lesbian'. In understanding heterosexuality as a normalizing discourse, built around the conventions of gender, Skeggs argues that heteronormativity retains its privileged position because it makes the homosexual 'other' seem so unattractive, so unrespectable, so 'different'. Skeggs' work is a good example of empirical sociological work which takes the concerns of Rich's conception of 'compulsory heterosexuality', Butler's idea of heterosexuality as a relational construction, and a broader commitment to a feminist analysis of gender relations, and constructs an account of 'real' lives.

Sociology in love: where did heterosexuality go?

In contrast to the small body of work on heterosexuality, there has been a significant movement towards addressing 'intimacy' in sociology and theorizing on the related subjects of romance, the experience of falling in love, monogamy, and the relationship between sex and love. Yet, one thing is characteristic of much of this work: its neglect of a critical engagement with either sexuality generally or, specifically, heterosexuality. A good example of this is Ulrich Beck and Elisabeth Beck-Gernsheim's sustained analysis of intimacy found in *The Normal Chaos of Love* (1995), a text which builds on Beck's work on 'risk society' and the transformation of the industrial mode of production (1992), where there is no significant analysis of the historical construction or deployment of sexuality. Their thesis is, as Bell and Binnie note, 'relentlessly heterosexualized' (2000: 127). Whilst Beck and Beck-Gernsheim have an elaborate understanding of the ways in which intimate love, that 'longing for salvation and affection' (1995: 12), is structured by broad changes in the 'public' sphere which comes to affect the constitution of the 'private' intimate domain – a concept formulated by Max Weber (1948) – they never tell us why, or indeed if, the 'private sphere' is normatively inscribed as heterosexual.

Anthony Giddens' (1992) work attempts to avoid this blindness to issues of sexuality but, ironically, only serves to compound it. For Giddens, intimate love relations are axiomatic to the social transformation of modern societies. Central to his thesis is the belief that 'romantic love' has been replaced by the intimate democracy of confluent love, or the 'pure relationship'. This pure relationship, Giddens suggests, is not restricted to heterosexuals because, as a consequence of social changes in sexual politics, engendered by the 'disembedding mechanisms' of high modernity which 'lift' individuals out of traditional social arrangements, a new 'plastic sexuality' is socially pervasive. Axiomatic to the establishment of new intimate practices are the relationships which gay men and lesbians are consolidating because, on the one hand, gay men have been instrumental in developing the type of episodic sexuality free of the institutional structures of romantic love whilst, on the other hand, lesbians have pioneered the intimate democracy of the pure relationship. Regardless of the (il)legitimacy of this conceptualization of homosexuality, Giddens never significantly engages with the constitution of sexuality itself; he accepts that 'plastic sexuality' operates along a pre-established heterosexual/homosexual axis without questioning how such a binary is produced and sustained.

In Giddens' work the interrelationship between love and the social constitution of sexuality is never addressed. In Wendy Langford's (1999) recent work, which is a direct attack on Giddens' thesis of democratization, and which presents empirical findings from a study of 15 women, we also find no significant analysis of the social construction or regulation of heterosexuality. Langford's work might be seen to take the theoretical split between love and sexuality to its logical conclusion because she is concerned only with the gender inequalities found in intimate relationships and not the regulation of sexuality per se. Whilst *Revolutions of the Heart* provides an analysis of the inherent dynamics of gendered power and its reproduction through romantic love, focusing on the ways in which 'romantic love, the most intimate of relationships, is at the heart of the mechanism by which contemporary society reproduces itself' (Lindholm, 1999: 244), it never directly questions why society is reproduced in a *heterosexual* way.

The omission of a consideration of the social construction of sexuality is common to most human science work on love. For example, in Niklas Luhmann's (1986) wide-ranging study of the historical transformation of love into the symbolic codification of romance we find no significant mention of heterosexuality. Luhmann is concerned to construct a genealogy of love that charts its development through the transition from 'traditional' to 'modern' societies – a process driven, he suggests, 'primarily by means of the differentiation of various symbolically generalized media of communication' (1986: 5). Like Giddens, Luhmann attempts to situate the historical conventions of love within a wider sociological framework in order to understand why particular forms of amorous practice arise under certain conditions. And yet, there is no question of why such practices would be inculcated in the modern configurations of sexuality in which we currently find them. There is never any question of how love is enmeshed with what we now consider to be 'sexual preference'.

What 'love' stands for in most sociological work is 'heterosexual love'. To say 'love' is just a shorthand which hides the heteronormativity which it reproduces; an intimate nomenclature for a range of heterosexual practices which are performed by men and women. This split between an analysis of love and heterosexuality reiterates a certain heterosexism in sociological work. Although we find many different analytic insights in published research on love – such as the relationship between love and the family (Beck-Gernsheim, 1999), the constitution of what might be called 'post-modern' love (Illouz, 1999), love as a modern 'ideology' (Evans, 1999), or love and gender (Hepworth, 1999) – we find no significant study of the relationship between heterosexuality and love. Again, this is always ironic because all of these authors are concerned *only* with heterosexual love.

The sociological blindness to heterosexuality has also been reproduced in the substantial body of research on emotion. For example, Eva Illouz's (1997) work is concerned to understand how romantic love is experienced as a form of emotionality which is fashioned in relation to the cultural context in which individuals are situated. The social world, she argues, frames emotion and produces it in particular ways: culture provides meaning to physiological arousal; it labels and attaches meanings to particular bodily sensations; it provides evaluative criteria for embodied existence; and it offers a whole range of symbolic media through which to situate one's own experience (1997: 4). Illouz introduces a way to think about how emotions are themselves produced through the interrelationship between individual embodiment and cultural context (something which has become a site of concern within sociological work more generally: see Bendelow and Williams, 1998; Hochschild, 1983; Lupton, 1998; Williams, 2001; and which has been considered in terms of its place within heterosexual relationships: see Delphy and Leonard, 1992; Duncombe and Marsden, 1993). This opens up new ways of thinking about how 'emotional individuality' is itself an active construction, an aesthetic and reflexive operation, which takes place through the enabling constraints of sociality (as, for example, in Foucault's conception of the self, 1988). Yet there is no exploration in any of the available research of how relations of sexuality may influence or shape emotions.

Rather than consider the normative status of heterosexuality in relation to intimacy, recent theorists have tended towards characterizing heterosexuality's authority as diminished. Whilst Jeffrey Weeks' (1999, 2000) work on the changing patterns of intimacy places an analysis of sexuality as central, he argues that we are witnessing a redeployment of intimacy which is transforming the institutional parameters of heterosexuality: 'It is in this context that we can begin to understand the significance of the new stories about non-heterosexual families of choice' (2000: 216). Weeks uses the term 'families of choice' to show that the relationship between the social relations of sexuality and the production of intimacy is no longer configured by 'compulsory heterosexuality'. Of course, this is, in one respect, very difficult to deny: homosexual intimate relationships *do* take place (for a consideration of homosexual intimacies, see Weston, 1991). But 'choice' is a problematic term when considering sexuality. Who is this subject who 'chooses' ways to love and through what frameworks is their choice negotiated?

Weeks argues that the production of new frameworks for intimacy allow individuals to appropriate new forms of relationships (love, family, friendship) which, in turn, weaken the normativity of institutionalized and hegemonic heterosexuality. This view is also expressed by Bell and Binnie who, in attending to 'the dominant scripting of love in terms of long-term monogamous pairing' (2000: 125), argue for the need to 'reformulate what love means' outside of heteronormativity (2000: 140). Much like Weeks' work, Bell and Binnie are persuaded by Giddens' account of social changes in the transformation of intimacy. Whilst they would seek to account for the ways in which the discourses of institutional heterosexuality still exert a normative force over intimacy they are persuaded that love relationships are being manufactured at other sites, outside of delimited heterosexuality.

In view of these claims, Stevi Jackson, one of the few sociologists who has attempted to relate the construction of romantic love to heterosexuality, argues that these theorists 'frequently overestimate the changes which are occurring' (1999: 120). 'What may be happening', argues Jackson, 'is that the contradictions of romantic love are becoming more apparent with the partial erosion of its institutional supports' (1999: 121). But, whilst changes in heterosexual relationships are taking place, and whilst homosexual intimacies are a possibility outside of heteronormative ideals, expressed through 'new' discourses such as those concerned with gay and lesbian marriage (as both an intimate practice and a political demand), we cannot conclude that this has significantly affected the social constitution of normative heterosexuality. In its cultural representations, love is hegemonically expressed heterosexually and still draws on the 'traditional' scripts of marriage and heterosexual domesticity (Ingraham, 1999). Yet we have so little work available to us which attempts to discern the interrelationship between romantic love (in all its manifestations) and heterosexuality.[4]

Whilst all of the work outlined above attends to the multi-faceted experience of romantic love – from falling in love, to being in love, to

16 *Introduction*

romantic conventions – it does not significantly address the ways in which these cultural expressions of human life are organized in relation to the principles of (hetero)sexuality. Of course, one could argue that cultural formations of love are detachable from those of sexuality; that love is a discursive formation that is separable from its expression in the arrangements of sexuality, sex and gender. Whilst it is true that love is indeed a separate construction (in the sense that it is expressed in a distinct set of discourses), and this is something I wish to hold on to (and address in the next chapter), it is impossible to think of it outside of the rubric of the conventions of modern (hetero)sexuality. Nor is it adequate to cite gay and lesbian love relationships as evidence of the end of heterosexuality's hegemony in the social organization of sexuality. Whilst it cannot be denied that social changes (well documented by Jameson, 1998) have significantly altered the ways in which 'intimacy' can be experienced across the binary of homosexual/heterosexual, this is not a sufficient condition to argue that the binary itself has been altered. The homo/het binary is implicated exactly at the moment when individuals practise intimacy precisely because they operationalize love within the historical conventions of sexuality. It is not as if there is, on the one hand, 'sexuality', and then, on the other, ways of loving. How could ways of loving ever be separated from the relations of sex and gender and the construction of sexuality which frames them?

Doing the research

Whilst this book is situated within the context of the debates discussed above and, therefore, draws on theoretical work already available to interpret and understand the interwoven construction of love and heterosexuality, it is, throughout, based on the empirical accounts of social actors. The data presented here are taken from semi-structured interviews that I conducted with a sample of 24 heterosexual men and women, drawn from a wide age range, and differentiated by social class. The interviews focused on the participants' experiences of love, relationships and sexuality and covered a wide range of topics. Interviews lasted between one and three hours and were open-ended in relation to the individual's own experiences and interests. I wanted to talk primarily about experiences of love and whilst, as in all social science interviewing, I needed to focus upon key questions (outlined in Appendix 1), participants were willing to talk in detail about aspects of their life which, in most contexts, they would no doubt deem personal and private.

My methodological commitment to qualitative interviews is based, ironically, on Michel Foucault's (1979) observation of the ways in which we incite sexuality into discourse. In using Foucault's 'method' for understanding how discourse provides the structural resources through which people relate to each other, to themselves, and through which their action is mediated, it seems to me that the qualitative interview is the best place to start. For Foucault, individuals are the *products* of discourse:

there are not on the one hand inert discourses, which are already more than half dead, and on the other hand, an all powerful subject which manipulates them, overturns them, renews them, but that discoursing subjects form a part of the discursive field – they have their place within it (and their possibilities of displacement). Discourse is not a place into which subjectivity irrupts; it is a space of differentiated subject-positions and subject functions.

(Foucault, 1991: 58)

There is a tension in Foucault's work between the subject who is 'within' discourse but who can also manoeuvre inside of it. This is why qualitative interviewing is consummate with a Foucauldian understanding of discourse because we can use interviews to discern the ways in which discourses are apprehended, understood and deployed by individuals. This is axiomatic to Judith Butler's ongoing consideration of interpellation and performativity. Central to her conceptualization of agency and subjectivity, as emergent properties of the performative translation of discourse (via speech) into ontological effects, we find a continual preoccupation with 'compulsory discursivity' (1997a: 136). Butler's concern is with the ways in which certain discourses are rendered compulsory through both their normative status and the 'threats' which maintain such normativity. Such threats work to ensure that the subject incites specific discourses in particular ways to reproduce ontological effects within normatively delimited parameters. Butler has worked towards producing a theoretical framework capable of accounting for the ways in which convention can be incited in non-conventional ways but this has the tendency to dislocate speech acts, or the ability to deploy discourse, from the social context of the individual speaker. This is something which Bourdieu (2001) chastises her for doing because, he contends, it introduces a voluntarism into social life which ignores the constraints experienced by social actors who inhabit specific social contexts.

I think there are weaknesses in Butler's theoretical framework because she does undervalue the ways in which social context will significantly affect performative possibilities. However, I use Butler's work throughout this book because it extends Foucault's conceptualization of discursive fields by accounting for their enduring and repetitive nature whilst avoiding the unilateral tendencies of an over-bearing conception of power. For Butler, the active subject emerges through a continual and ongoing tension between the 'rules' of normative intelligibility which precede it and the reiteration of those norms. As in Bourdieu's work (which is not often considered in relation to Foucault's (see Fowler, 1997), we find that the subject is the nexus between an oscillating sociality and a sense of uniqueness. I want to hold on to both Butler's and Bourdieu's theoretical frameworks in this work because, along with the work of Michel Foucault, I think they offer a useful combination for considering the ways in which individuals utilize, re-enact and re-work the discursive formations in which they find themselves.

The divide between 'discourse' and the 'individual' introduces the perennial sociological dichotomy between structure and agency but, in considering questions of discourse, Foucault was clear in his aim: 'I try to answer [these] questions without referring to the consciousness, obscure or explicit, of speaking subjects' (1991: 59). Such a 'method' is, for a humanist sociologist like Ken Plummer, 'dangerous' because 'analyses of discourse overtake the analyses of real world events' (1998: 605). On the one hand we have a type of analysis which would favour a genealogy of 'knowledge' (in its most general sense) and on the other a form of inquiry which would seek to be grounded in the 'real' lives of individuals. Heterosexual intimate love, we might say, is at the 'coal face' of these methodological and epistemological issues because it is one of the most subjective, most individually felt, forms of sociality. Yet to begin with the 'individual' is not to dismiss the discursive constructs through which heterosexuality operates. Indeed we may even claim, as Bourdieu would, that 'the true object of social science is not the individual' (in Bourdieu and Wacquant, 1992: 107) but the social field in which that individual is situated. But this assertion, enshrined in the methodological principles of Durkheimian sociology, engenders a crucial question: can we understand the social cosmos without recourse to speaking subjects? The answer is, for Bourdieu, 'no' and the solution is a 'total sociology' that operationalizes a 'submission to the singularity of a particular life history' whilst producing 'knowledge of the objective conditions common to an entire social category' ([1996] 1999: 609). What we need is something akin to a 'structuralist phenomenology' which can resist an arbitrary separation of individuals from the social relations in which they are situated.

Most importantly, we need to do justice to the real lives of the individuals we study. The data we produce do not speak for themselves and we construct 'knowledge' through the theories we use, the ontological beliefs we have, and the epistemologies we employ. In other words, we interpret the social world. In writing this work I have faced another act of interpretation because I needed to order the testimonies of 24 people – disparate and distinct accounts of individual lives – into the areas which, now forming chapters, I believe to be the most salient. Sociology, we might say, attempts to make the 'whole' from the sum of the 'parts'. To turn what takes place in an interview into this type of edifice is, beyond any reasonable argument, an act of the greatest construction. The result is this book: a consideration, albeit partial and perspectival, of individual experiences of heterosexual love and the conditions under which these experiences are shaped.

Outline of the book

Chapter 1 introduces the empirical data and, as a starting point for analysis, seeks to define, by asking the much overlooked question, 'what is love?', the ways in which love is constructed. In looking at how 'romantic' love is delimited from love generally, and in examining the various ways in which such an experience is constituted, I argue that when we speak about love we do so by reproducing the belief in an 'essence' of love which is profoundly asocial. Romantic love (much like sex and sexuality) is an experience that is perceived as biological, powerful, natural and compelling. This chapter attempts to begin to relate this specific construction of love to heterosexuality.

Chapter 2 examines the construction of romantic love in relation to heterosexual sexual expression. I look at how 'intimacy' is constructed around the interconnection of love and sex and how, in attempting to separate sex from love, fundamental constraints are revealed. The construction of heterosexual sex, I argue, puts sex consistently at the service of love because love is imagined to be more important, more intrinsic, and more essential to human happiness, than 'casual sex'. The constraint which love exerts over sex also reveals how sexual expression within heterosexual relations is gendered in particular ways and how forms of feminine and masculine sexual expression are produced. Ultimately, I argue, love exerts a normative force over sex that cannot easily be escaped.

Chapter 3 looks at how, through engaging in the processes of love, particular types of gendered subjectivity, anchored within a heterosexual matrix, are produced. In examining the way that subjectivity is both enabled and constrained through love, I argue that heterosexuality is consolidated into selfhood through an approximation of specific ways of being which are infused with the categories of gender. In producing subjectivity in relation to the organizing principle of 'lack' (in the positions of feminine and masculine) the process of love operationalizes specific ways of being which reproduce modes of selfhood anchored within heterosexuality. Love is experienced, by both men and women, as a way of producing and reifying a particular type of being but such a process, structured in dialogic engagement between self and other, anchors them in relations of constraint whereby without the 'other half' they can never be 'whole'.

Chapter 4 asks *who* can we love? In looking at heterosexual identities I argue that the most important way such identities are secured is through a relational rejection of homosexuality. Ways of heterosexual desiring, and expressions of heterosexual love, are intimately bound up with ways of *not* loving and desiring – ways of maintaining the parameters between a distinctly heterosexual form of practice and the homosexual 'other'. In this chapter I focus upon how, in maintaining a heterosexual identity, subjects are forced to continually police their own practices and monitor their own sense of self. It is primarily through the homosexual/heterosexual binary, I argue, that heterosexual identity is secured and that this binary is controlled around 'borders' instituted through delimited intimacies.

In Chapter 5, continuing with the theme of Chapter 4, I explore how forms of desire often exceed the constraints of heterosexual identity. I look at how forms of ambiguous desire often seem incongruous with the heterosexuality of the subject and how, in light of these desires, the subject negotiates

20 *Introduction*

the parameters of heterosexuality. A central question emerges: can love and desire 'escape' the delimited nature of heterosexuality and, if not, what is the cost of a defined heterosexual sexuality which reproduces delimited forms of love?

The participants in the study

All of the participants identify as heterosexual and all, except where indicated, identify as White–British. Class is based on self-identified categories which were supplied by the participants during the interview. A 'significant relationship' is one which the participants identified themselves. These details reflect the life of the participant at the time that I interviewed them.

Alex is 22 years old and is currently working part-time in an unskilled job and studying part-time at university. He is currently single and lives with his parents. He has no children. He identifies one significant partner with whom he formed a brief relationship. Alex did not self-identify with social class.

Barry is 59 years old and works part-time in a clerical/administrative role. He lives with his wife whom he married over 30 years ago. His relationship with his wife is the only relationship he identifies as significant. He has three adult children, none of whom live with him. Barry identifies as middle-class from a middle-class birth family.

Barbara is 51 years old and works full-time in a professional role. She is currently single, lives alone, and has no children. Barbara identifies three significant partners in her life, most notably her previous partner from whom she has recently separated. Barbara identifies as middle-class from a working-class birth family.

Carl is 27 years old and a full-time university student. He is currently single and has no children. Carl identifies one significant partner who he formed a relationship with. He identifies as upper-middle-class from an upper-middle-class birth family.

Catherine is 23 years old and works full-time in a clerical/administrative job. She is currently engaged and is planning to marry very soon. She has been in a relationship with her partner for two years during which they have lived together for one and a half years. Before her current relationship Catherine identifies one other significant partner. She has no children. Catherine did not self-identify with social class.

Dorothy is 80 years old and is retired. Her working life was spent mainly in the home after she married. She is married to Jack (see p. 21) and they have lived together, since their wedding, for 54 years. Dorothy views her current relationship as the only significant one in her life. She has two children. Dorothy identifies as working-class from a working-class birth family.

Douglas is 22 years old and works full time in a clerical/administrative role. He has been living with his partner for five months and they have been together for a year. Douglas identifies one other significant relationship previously to the one he is involved with. He has no children. Douglas identifies as middle-class from a middle-class birth family.

Elizabeth is 17 years old and is a full-time student at a sixth-form college. She began a new relationship very recently and identifies, previous to this, one other significant relationship. She has no children and lives with her parents. Elizabeth identifies as middle-class from a middle-class birth family.

Ellen is 56 years old and is retired, due to ill-health, from her job as a training manager in a large company. She is currently in a long-standing relationship with a man who is married and living with his wife. Ellen lives alone and, having been widowed after ten years of living with her husband, is unmarried. She identifies four significant relationships in her life of which her current partner is one. Ellen has one step-daughter from her marriage and no other children. She identifies as middle-class, from a working-class birth family.

Gary is 41 years old and is employed full-time in a clerical/administrative role. He lives with his wife of seven years whom he met three years previous to their marriage. This is his second marriage and he identifies his first wife and a girlfriend before that as two other significant relationships. He has two children, both of whom live with him. Gary identifies as working-class from a working-class birth family.

Heather is 43 years old and is currently studying part-time for a professional qualification. She is in a new relationship which she began one month ago. She has been married, and divorced, and has three children, all of whom live with her. Heather identifies as middle-class from a working-class birth family.

Jack is 80 years old and is retired from his job in catering. He is married to Dorothy (see p. 20) and they have lived together, since their wedding, for 54 years. Jack views his current relationship as the only significant one in his life. He has two children. Jack identifies as working class from a working-class birth family.

Jackie is 36 and is a part-time student. She is currently single and has no children. She has been married previously and is divorced. She identifies two significant relationships in her life. Jackie identifies her ethnicity as Asian–Indian. She does not self-identify with social class.

Margaret is 50 and is employed full-time in retail management. She is currently single and lives alone. She has one child from a previous marriage from which she is divorced. Margaret identifies three significant relationships in her life. She identifies as working-class from a working-class birth family.

Mark is 35 years old and works full-time in industrial manufacturing. He is currently having a relationship and lives with his partner of two years. He has two children from a previous marriage of which he is not divorced. Mark identifies these two relationships as the only significant relationships in his life. He identifies as working-class from a working-class birth family.

Martin is 27 years old and a full-time university student. He has been married to his wife for one year and they have been together for two years. They do not have any children. Previous to his marriage, Martin identifies one significant partner. He identifies as middle-class from a middle-class birth family.

Patricia is 55 years old and is a retired professional. She married her husband two years ago after they had lived together for 19 years. Patricia has one child from a previous relationship. She has been married twice before and cites four significant relationships throughout her life. Patricia identifies as middle-class from a working-class birth family.

Peter is 24 years old and is a full-time university student. He is currently single although has recently had a relationship which he identifies as the only significant relationship in his life. Peter does not have any children. He identifies as middle-class from a middle-class birth family.

Phillip is 56 years old and is not employed due to long-term sickness. He is divorced from his only marriage and, currently single, he lives alone. He identifies two significant relationships in his life, of which his marriage was the latter. He has two children. Phillip identifies as middle-class from a middle-class birth family.

Ruth is 52 years old and is self-employed in a professional role. She is currently having a relationship which began four years ago. She lives alone and has one grown-up child. She has been married, and divorced, and identifies this as her only other significant relationship prior to her current partner. Ruth identifies as middle-class from a working-class birth family.

Scott is 31 years old and works part-time, and with a temporary contract, in an unskilled job. He is currently married from which relationship he has two children (one of the children is from his wife's previous relationship). Scott has only recently returned to living with his wife and children after a period of separation. Scott has previously been married, and divorced, and has a child with his first wife. Scott identifies as working-class from a working-class birth family.

Susan is 31 years old and works full-time in a professional role. She is currently single and lives with her two children. She identifies two significant partners in her life, her husband (who recently died) and a previous boyfriend. Susan identifies as working-class from a working-class birth family.

Victoria is 18 years old and is employed full time in a clerical/administrative role. She is currently having a relationship which began six months ago after the end of her previous relationship and these are her two significant relationships. Victoria has no children and lives with her parents. Victoria does not self-identify with social class.

William is 36 years old and is employed in a clerical/administrative role. He currently lives with his partner of four years. He has two children from a previous marriage, from which he is divorced, and which he identifies as the only other significant relationship in his life. William identifies as working-class from a working-class birth family.

1 The essence of love

> No wonder everyone wants it – as if they have known such love before and can barely remember it, yet are compelled ever after to seek it as the single thing worth living for. Without love, most of life remains concealed. Nothing is as fascinating as love, unfortunately.
>
> (Hanif Kureishi, *Intimacy*, 71)

> Love is only an explanation of the whole thing.
>
> (Dorothy)

Love, writes Erich Fromm, '*is an active power in man*' ([1957] 1995: 16, italics in original): 'I love from the essence of my being – and experience the other person in the essence of his or her being. In essence, all human beings are identical' ([1957] 1995: 44). Is love, and the process of loving, essential to all human beings? Is it, as Fromm suggests, a residual 'power' which is inside every 'identical' human being? Is it a need which, perhaps like eating and sleeping, requires no explanation other than it is vital to our lives? We might conclude that this is the case given that sociology has paid little attention to actually explaining what romantic, passionate or intimate love is (Jackson, 1999). Even though romantic love has a highly stylized and coded language through which it is spoken, represented and communicated (Goode, 1959; Luhmann, 1986), and is recognized to adhere to distinctive discursive parameters (Barthes, 1990), there is very little *empirical* work which seeks to elucidate how people define love or how they experience it.

In this chapter I want to explore how people understand love and, furthermore, begin to sketch out how constructions of love are interwoven with, and delimited by, heterosexuality. I want to begin with a common assertion that love is one of the most natural and requisite forms of human experience and that it represents a basic human ontology. bell hooks (2000), for example, argues that all human beings *yearn* for love. Such a yearning is produced because every human being is a 'wounded child' who, in order to repair the 'first banishment from love's paradise', must 'find the love our hearts long for' (hooks, 2000: x). 'The light of love is always in us', argues hooks, 'the life force inside a dark place waiting to be born – waiting to see the light' (hooks, 2000: 68). When I began to look at how people talk about love I found that this view was pervasive: love is often conceived as a universal property of human existence, a force or power inside the body, which is natural, innate, and struggling for expression.

This idea of love is exemplified in most 'self-help' books or 'manuals' on the subject where instructions, plans and programmes promise to aid us through the negotiation of this most complicated of all human cosmologies. This is not absent from academic work where a whole tradition of 'radical Freudians' attempted to show us how we may love 'properly' (Fromm, [1957] 1995; Marcuse, 1955; Reich, 1961). Even Shulamith Firestone, an arch critic of romantic love, would like to hold on to an essentiality of love which becomes distorted by power: 'when we talk about romantic love we mean love distorted by its power context – the sex class system – into a diseased form of love' (1972: 139), 'it becomes complicated, corrupted, or obstructed by *an unequal balance of power*' (1972: 124, italics in original). Yet what such work achieves is a reification of love. Rather than analyse the social construction of love, the emphasis is placed on the analysis of the social organization of human relationships. What this affects (and this can be seen in the beliefs which hooks and Fromm outline) is an idea that the ability to fall in love, and the desire to be in love, are natural or human essences which, although subject to social forces which direct them in certain ways, remain the 'truths' of humanity.

In hooks' and Fromm's work, armed with the language of psychology, love is often posited as that which all humans *could* do if only they could do it free from external constraint. Love is conceived of as a 'stubborn drive' (much like Foucault described our view of sexuality) denigrated by the impersonal forces of capitalism and patriarchy. And yet, as Nikolas Rose points out: 'What humans are able to do is not intrinsic to the flesh, the body, the psyche, the mind, or the soul; it is constantly shifting and changing from place to place, time to time, with the linking of humans into apparatuses of thought and action' (Rose, 1998: 182). If the capacity to 'do' love is therefore historically specific and, as Rose points out, relies on certain apparatuses of thought which both enables and constrains what humans are and what humans can do, then we must problematize ontological assertions which claim love (as both desire and practice) is simply the result of being human. Instead we must consider how such assertions are constructed and maintained through the discourses which constitute them. As Jackson (1999) argues: 'Emotions are not simply "felt" as internal states provoked by the unconscious sense of a lost infantile satisfaction – they are actively structured and understood through culturally specific discourses' (1999: 119). In the following sections I want to explore how these culturally specific discourses construct love as an essence of humanness and, as an effect of our continuous incitement of them, how we 'make love' the basis for particular ways of being and acting.

What is love? Finding the words...

I want to begin with one of the most striking features of our language of love, which is the lack of a clear way to describe what love 'is'. Given that romantic/passionate love is one of the fundamental facets of our social existence, we might expect that most people would be able to define it. Yet when I asked people the questions, 'what is love?' or 'how would you define love?', I was presented with a range of answers which all demonstrated how love appears difficult to render into language:

PHILLIP: It's a mutual thing [...] and you can sense it. You can feel it building. It's hard to describe, I don't think I could put a description on it.

HEATHER: There isn't a word that encompasses it, just, I don't know [...] it's almost as if there's something beyond love. As if love isn't a big enough word to encompass the unconditional aspects of it.

CARL: It's intangible [...] well it can mean all kinds of things can't it?

RUTH: It's difficult, it's hard isn't it, [...] it's hard to put it into words.

DOROTHY: It's a thing you can't really grasp, you can't really say to anybody what falling in love is, it's not something you can get hold of, it just seems to . . . blossom. Doesn't it?

CATHERINE: I think it is something extra, there's something a little bit extra that you just can't quite explain, you can't quite put your finger on it but you know that there's something there that's extra, definitely, something you can't describe [...] there are lots of different elements that make love up, there must be, there must be [...] but I don't think there are many people that can explain things.

What is common to all of these accounts is that love, both conceptually and experientially, appears resistant to descriptive language. There is, as Catherine says, something 'extra' which resists reduction to a simple description. This extra dimension of love, something 'intangible' that 'you can't really grasp', and a thing which one can only 'sense', is the language of love personified. These are descriptions which attempt to capture love in language, but serve only to recount love as something which 'you can't put your finger on', a state of being which mysteriously 'blossoms'. Freudian psychoanalysis would account for the inability to explain love in rational description as one aspect of a form of human desire which is a largely unconscious process. As Wendy Langford argues, in her psychoanalytic analysis of love's compelling nature, our desire for love is based on an original childish narcissism, the 'knowledge of which has been lost from consciousness' (1999: 143). 'The whole point of love', argues Langford, 'is that our actions are motivated by what we are *un*aware of' (1999: 149, italics in original).

Much like psychoanalysis, biologically deterministic explanations often describe love as the result of innate human drives which result from biological impulses derived from the foundational need to reproduce. The conflation of love into sexual desire and, further, into a reified model of reproductive sexuality is *the* normative explanation of why human beings love. As Ellen explained to me during an interview, love can be understood as a biological process which results from 'this hormonal, physical thing, this mating urge'. Mike Featherstone notes:

> The need to reproduce sexually is something we share with other animal species, along with most plant species [...] animals always copulate in the same way, whereas human beings have woven around this act a wide range of practices, institutions, rites and representations.
>
> (1999: 1)

In this sense, Featherstone's argument is clear: 'sexuality is clearly the primordial source with eroticism and love the derivative forms' (1999: 1). What this elaborates is a commonly held belief that all sexual and amorous practices have a distinctive genealogy which can be read back to an original need to reproduce (the seemingly indisputable state of nature). But is sex an authentic real to love's socially constructed ritual? The fact that both psychoanalytic and biological accounts reduce love to some more 'fundamental' feature of existence means that they fail to tell us what love 'is' outside of a mechanistic description of what love 'does'. And, in leaving the issue of love being something 'you can't really grasp' unexplored, affect a certain 'naturalness' around love.

The central problem of an untheorized essentiality of love has continually found direct expression in social science. If individuals find love difficult to 'put into words' so too has sociology.[1] But the descriptions of love outlined above present intractable philosophical problems within the language of social science because they appear, by convention, outside of the rubric of the rational analysis which sociology delimits as the criteria for its own business. Since falling in love appears, as Jackson notes, as 'indefinable, mysterious, outside rational discourse', it often seems sociology concludes that it is 'knowable only intuitively, at the level of feeling' (1999: 100). Such a conclusion has often relegated love to a realm of an incommunicable set of emotions that are beyond the reach of a social science which cannot pervade the 'inner' life of the individual. Thus, love remains the domain of philosophy, of psychoanalysis, of psychology and biology, and of poetry. The problem seems one of language; the language of the heart seems to resist the rationalist descriptions of any activity which attempts to impose explanation upon it. As Catherine says, there is a belief that there are few people who could actually explain love. And Catherine would be right if she turned to science for the answer. The causal language of science is, as Charles Lindholm argues, no use because it 'tends strongly to reduce romantic attraction to something else, that is sexual desire, the exchange of pleasure, the maximization of the gene pool and so on' (1999: 247).

As Jackson (1999) notes, social science has frequently studied the institutional expression of romantic love whilst leaving love itself as an unspecified object of inquiry. In doing this, social science has reproduced the perennial subject/object problem of its own domain of inquiry, specifying the 'objective' manifestations of romance, marriage, kinship and domesticity as its site of study whilst relegating the 'emotion' of love to the personal sphere.[2] Perhaps this is because love, as a set of emotions, has no materiality outside of the relations which it inspires. Yet this is no reason to conclude that the construction of love itself is not important. On the contrary, it is precisely the ways that love appears mysterious and elusive which is of central significance to the material relations to which it becomes attached.

As we see above, love presents difficulties for analysis because it is premised on a belief that it cannot be precisely communicated in language. Yet, what is more easily and more frequently communicated is how love 'feels'. When we say we are 'in love' with someone we have a particular lexicon of associated feelings (sensations, emotions, bodily metaphors) to describe it:

CATHERINE: [being in love is] being very very happy, being very very comfortable, being able to trust somebody.

DOROTHY: It's just we felt comfortable and warm with each other, you know, it just seemed, you know, nothing at all, we never argued about anything.

CARL: [love is] profoundly emotional, being very close to someone.

VICTORIA: Like a warm blanket. Well you know when you're in the bed and you're all curled up in your blanket and you just go to sleep and you're in a deep sleep and nothing can disturb you. You don't want to get up, you don't have to get up. It's just like that.

These quotations illustrate that, even though people often have difficulty answering questions about what love 'is', they find it far easier to talk about how love 'feels'. Words such as 'comfortable' and 'warm' are extremely common in the accounts about how it feels to be in love. Love is often represented in specific metaphors that relate to temperature and bodily condition (see Lupton, 1998, for a detailed description of how language metaphors are employed to materialize emotions within corporeality). These metaphors are tangible ways of describing love and constitute a definite descriptive language which employs our body at the centre of delimiting how love feels. More importantly they constitute a way of describing, through expressing the feelings that being in love produces (as opposed to the feelings and sensations we associate with our other social relationships) what romantic/intimate love 'is'.

So there are two central tropes in the language of love: the first is that love is constructed as beyond description and the second is that it produces certain common 'feelings'. A question arises: is love resistant to language or is language productive of such resistance? In other words, might language, instead of being a stuttering and gasping movement towards unearthing a truth, be performative in its practice? Might the way we speak about love be, as Stevi Jackson argues, a process which 'contributes to the cultural construction of emotions' and provide 'a means by which we participate in creating a shared sense of what emotions are' (1999: 101)? And, in creating this shared sense of emotions, might we also construct love as something which resists our description? As Martin commented during an interview:

MARTIN: I'll tell you what it's like, it's like that fucking Eskimo thing where you've got five hundred words for different kinds of snow, do you know what I mean? It's like the same kind of thing, and everyone knows it's kind of the same kind of thing, but it's kind of different in different contexts.

Love, as Martin explains, both exceeds language and is not reducible to it. It is something which is spoken and written about endlessly, appearing in many different manifestations, yet is not reducible to a simple description. As Martin says, there is an element of love that is the same and which everyone knows. For Martin there is something essential to love, something we all recognize, but something which retains its multiplicity and resists reduction. This duality, of multiplicity and sameness, is the foundation for the social construction of romantic love where the indefinable is reduced to understandable and common experience. There is no singular answer to the question 'what is love?' and there is no way to define what love is in formulaic terms. Despite bell hooks' (2000) wish that we could all share a common definition of love and speak about it in a kind of Esperanto of the heart, the process of falling in love resists such practices. 'Love', argues Niklas Luhmann, 'solves its own attendant communicative problems in a completely unique manner [because] love is able to enhance communication by largely doing without any communication' (1986: 25). But if romantic love resists a reduction to language, if we cannot communicate exactly what it is, then what remains? As Jonathan Rutherford argues: 'The words might not be there for me to use, yet I know the feeling is real' (1999: 4).

'Butterflies': individuality, embodiment, and the uniqueness of love

A common understanding of romantic love (and, in particular, falling in love) among the people I interviewed was the belief that everyone has a unique sense of what it feels like. Even in view of the similar ways that people talk about how love makes them feel 'warm' and 'comfortable', and the fact that we speak to each other repeatedly about such feelings in everyday life, the belief that love is individualized in its experience is trenchant. As Elizabeth explained:

ELIZABETH: Everybody's got their own definition of what love is and so I [...] don't know if you can actually define love.
PJ: Right, OK. Do you think everybody has a different idea?
ELIZABETH: Well I think everyone interprets their own emotions in different ways. Probably you can't really say, I don't really know because I've never actually asked someone what they think it is. And I think everyone would probably see it in a slightly different way.

The individuality of love, in Elizabeth's account, stems from the fact that she thinks that everybody has different criteria for interpreting their own emotions. However, when we analyse the responses that my interviewees provided about these emotions, and how they understand them, we can find considerable similarity in their accounts. Interpreting emotions is not something which is highly diverse; on the contrary it is something which is highly standardized. Yet such standard experiences retain uniqueness because they take place within our bodies, at the level of our nervous system:

CATHERINE: [Being in love] gives you butterflies in your tummy, and when you're sitting there in a room on your own and you think about something, or like that person, and it just puts a smile on your face for no reason. [It] gives you a really nice warm gut feeling, it's that sort of thing that you can't explain.

MARK: It was like every time we saw each other there was a 'yes'! There was like a tingle inside. You know, it was nice. And just a tingle, you know, a sort of, I don't know, a fuzziness took over me head.

DOUGLAS: I'd see her and there'd be this over-whelming rush of, I mean it's chemical yeah, it is chemical, but that doesn't make it any less spiritual really. This sense of becoming light on your feet and, I guess I get a tingle around the back of my legs or something like that, and my heart starts beating faster.

MARTIN: I personally get a very strong feeling in my [...] solar plexus area, do you know what I mean, it's quite intense [...] There's a chemical called endorphins that you have, that's kind of your biological equivalent of morphine, or opium heroin, and it gives you these kind of euphoric feelings, and you get, apparently you get, release lots, large amounts of it when you're in love. So maybe it's just drugs [laughs].

As these examples show, love is understood in remarkably similar ways as a type of experience that produces particular bodily sensations. Whilst these neurological sensations appear as distinctly personal, because of their containment as innate biological experiences, we can see that they are experienced in a fairly stable way as 'tingles', 'butterflies' and 'fuzziness'. Understanding these embodied sensations often departs from the belief that they are chemical reactions to particular external stimuli, the result of a biological process which takes place when we fall in love. As an explanation for such embodied emotionality a biological understanding retains its primacy in people's accounts through recourse to the notion of bodily 'chemicals'. Yet if we are to argue that love is socially constructed we need to problematize the essentialism of biological accounts which reduce the experience of love to the workings of our bodies. This is not to negate the body and its experiences, but to suggest that the bodily sensations we experience are socially ordered and produced through specific discursive constructions. The debate between an absolute biological understanding of the experiences outlined above and a constructivist one is multifarious and complex (for a full discussion, see: Williams, 2001, Chapter 3), but one of the essential disputes in this debate is the relationship between language and embodiment. When we speak of our embodied emotions, are we elaborating feelings that pre-exist their expression in language? Are feelings felt because of the well established biological process which biological scientists, such as Marazziti *et al.* (1999), would explain as the result of the release of serotonin in our bodies? Or are such feelings produced through the construction of language as it exists at that moment in time and space? How could a feeling be 'real' if we could not elaborate that feeling in words?

Such questions problematize the bodily sensations associated with romantic love because they dislocate the simple causal link between innateness and sensation. They question the relationship between an initial feeling and an expression of that feeling, not by negating the feeling, but by asking how the expression of emotion is negotiated through discourse. The relationship between embodied sensation and emotional understanding provides a crucial point at which to understand the reflexive interchange between the discourses of love and their subjectively experienced effects. As Hochschild (1998) argues, we each have an 'emotional dictionary' which we employ to understand our own embodied sensations. Such a dictionary allows us to understand what particular forms of embodied feeling mean and under what circumstances they might arise. These understandings are reliant on the discursive constructs under which we negotiate the minutiae of our own bodies which, in turn, produce historically and culturally specific readings of ourselves. We can see this when we look at the above quotations. People do not reinvent language every time they speak of their embodied sensations; on the contrary, they draw on a range of conventional linguistic frameworks to render themselves understood.

This still leaves the question of whether embodied sensations pre-exist the social construction of the terms by which they are named. Consider the following quote from Elizabeth:

ELIZABETH: It was, I felt sort of elated and, not dizzy, that's the wrong thing to say, but sort of like you were swimming a little bit. And sort of stomach pains all the time, I couldn't actually eat much at the time [laughs]. [...] You get butterflies in your tummy and you know you just want to be with them. I don't think anyone can really describe it. [But until I was in love] I just thought I wonder what it's actually like. And it wasn't until I actually experienced it that I knew.

For Elizabeth, it is at the moment of feeling the sensations of love that she knows what love is. In this sense, love is rendered understood by measuring it against the way her body feels. Of course, it is quite possible to suggest that under different cultural circumstances the feeling of being in love would not produce the types of bodily sensations described above[3] and it may be the case that one would know one was in love by a different set of bodily criteria. Even so, it is clear from Elizabeth's account, when we contrast it with the accounts above, that the set of emotions and feelings associated with romantic love are, whilst experienced inside the body, also socially ordered outside of it. Emotions are 'outside' the body because they are rendered legitimate and recognizable in language and language is, if we follow a constructivist understanding, limited by how, and of what, we can speak (Foucault, 1991). We would render ourselves unintelligible if we connected certain sensations of the body to types of emotions in an illegitimate way. But the crucial point is that the 'outside' construction of love becomes incorporated and inscribed to form an 'inside', a bodily corporeality which becomes an interiority of the sociality in which it is situated.

As Nikolas Rose (1998) suggests, this process involves an invagination of exterior social relations into the constitution of a bodily depth. The result is that:

> depth and its singularity [...] is no more than that which has been drawn in to create a space or series of cavities, pleats, and fields, which only exist in relation to those very forces, lines, techniques, and inventions that sustain them.
>
> (Rose, 1998: 188)

In this sense, the depth of the body, with its 'tingles' and 'butterflies', is the effect of social relations which are enfolded into the self. But the effect of this transfer of discourse to corporeality is that the latter appears to be a 'natural' depth of selfhood, the result of 'urges' which spring from a bodily interiority of the subject who feels it. This depth seems to express something entirely profound about our individuality and our innateness.

If the interiority of the body corresponds, as Rose argues, to the inventions which sustain it, then we have a causal link between discourse and innateness which is mediated, in the case of speaking, through language. And yet, what if we cannot appropriate the required discourse to speak about the innateness which we feel? Can feelings be real if there are no words to describe them? There is a hiatus between the embodiment of love – as Elizabeth says: 'I don't think anyone can really describe it' – and the discourses we use to understand it, and this is one explanation of why love remains compellingly mysterious to us. Because we often rely on 'biology' to explain romantic love, there is always a gap between our own biological embodiment and the 'expert' knowledge of biological science of which most of us know very little. As Elizabeth told me, she cannot explain what love 'is' because she 'doesn't know much about the chemicals in people's bodies'. The body itself becomes the site at which the mysteries of love unfold but it remains a process that cannot be wholly known or explained (except, perhaps, by biological scientists). The body is a nodal point in operationalizing an essentialization of love because love is reduced to an 'indescribable' set of bodily sensations. We become enmeshed in a circular causality whereby sensations confirm emotions and emotions confirm love. The neurological becomes its own truth, an inside biology which, resistant to our control, appears as 'natural'.

The power of love

One of the most compelling aspects of how we experience love is the way in which it is often felt as something outside of our control. Love is often felt as a 'force' that is outside of our will. For example, one of the most trenchant beliefs about love is that arrives, overpowers us, and changes our state of being:

CATHERINE: It was just out of nowhere, it just came from nowhere, absolutely, I've never felt anything like that in my entire life, ever, and it was just the strangest thing.

JACKIE: I mean you are not planning to fall in love with them [...] it just happens. And it doesn't happen with everyone, does it? [...] There is something isn't there, you just can't put your finger on it but it is something there which doesn't go away, even if you're not with him or her, it's still there if you meet a person you think you like or you grow fond of them or whatever. Even if you are a strong person and say you are a married man and you say 'I know I want to do this but I'm not going to', right, and you may succeed in that. But I don't think, I feel that I am going against nature if I am doing that. If something is happening to me and another person and it's gone to such an extent I do feel that it's meant to happen.

PJ: Right, and you can't do anything about it if it's meant to happen?

JACKIE: Well, yeah, I mean, yeah you see, that's another enigmatic kind of question really. You can if you want to but I feel powerless in that situation.

For Catherine and Jackie, falling in love is both mysterious in its arrival – 'it just came out of nowhere' – and compelling in its effects. To go against the feelings of love is, as Jackie argues, to go against *nature*. Although one can attempt to resist falling in love, it is imagined that such a struggle is against a form of power so compelling that one is bound to fail. This is because love is 'meant to happen' and that it constitutes something that cannot be subject to rational intervention. A certain space for resistance is opened by Jackie when she states that one can resist the powerful nature of falling in love 'if you want to'. Yet Jackie herself, even with this belief, feels powerless to intervene in the process and sees the question of agency as 'enigmatic'. Jackie's description shows the power we attribute to love to create relationships between people but also to change and disrupt them. Although love is fundamental to institutionalized heterosexual relationships (such as marriage), the act of falling in love can actively destabilize such relations because, as Jackie argues, love is 'nature'. And why would we want to resist 'nature'?

Perhaps we might want to resist the power of love because it can produce feelings of subjection and fear. As Peter explained to me, falling in love felt to him like 'something I had no control over' and was a very 'obsessive feeling'. Falling in love, he said, 'definitely constituted a sense of powerlessness' and 'was something I couldn't step outside of'. The power of love is all-consuming, it compels us to recognize it and is not something we can easily dismiss. As William described to me, when you're in love 'you've lost your facilities of reasoning' and falling in love is 'like a bit of insanity' because it 'affects your judgement'. Such a view is common in the way that love is described by both the men and women in this study, and this sense of powerlessness is encapsulated by the most overused phrase in the language of love: that falling in love produces a battle between the 'head and the heart'. For many of the people I interviewed, this represented something which was both pleasurable *and* undesirable. One of the most common experiences was that love instigated a sense of desperation and 'need':

WILLIAM: I suppose you would just say you needed them. Because it is like that. It's a feeling like you're going to die if you're not with them. That you're so miserable and unhappy that you can't see a way out to feeling better again, feeling good. I think that says it all because at the time you really do feel you need that person. It's not an option, you have to have that person. And I can understand how some people do commit suicide or something if they lose the partner they want to be with.

Such a desperate need to be with the beloved love-object is common in accounts of falling in love and the feeling that one would do anything to obtain, or keep, that love-object is trenchant. Such obsessiveness and desperation also delimit, as Catherine explains, a type of 'real' love from more casual acquaintances:

CATHERINE: The difference between being properly in love with [my boyfriend] was that I would have done anything and I'd have gone to any lengths to have kept him, literally, completely and utterly. And with other people I just didn't feel like that at all, I never cared really.

Catherine is describing something which is extremely common in the accounts of both the men and women I interviewed: the ways in which powerful needs are invoked by falling in love. For Catherine, the obsessive and compulsive process of needing to keep that person is complemented by the idea that if that need is not satisfied it will result in a self-destructive process. Several people expressed experiences of feeling suicidal which resulted from a failure to satisfy their need of love. Others described feelings about not being able to get the other person out of their mind, thinking about them all day, doing anything to see them, not wanting anything else, not being able to imagine life without them, and wanting to go to any lengths to secure the person. Yet, such a need, whilst powerfully felt, is also understood to be transitory. As Margaret explains: 'you feel that you would die without them, probably feel that it was the end of the world if you didn't have them, but it never is.' What Margaret draws attention to is both the profound feelings of desperation and emotional instability which falling in love can produce and the ability to recognize those feelings as themselves associated with particular situations. It may seem as if the world has come to an end but, as Margaret suggests, it never has. The process of falling in love is imbued with some of the most profound emotional expressions we have at our disposal. Because of this, love is something which is centrally important to our lives and something which produces the most tempestuous of our passions. These passions, although temporary, are felt as natural and real. Feeling the need for love, experiencing the desperate urge to be 'in' love, produces moments of profound desire and times of deep unhappiness. Love is felt as an essentiality that is difficult to overcome because it engulfs, totalizes and transfixes the individual to its power.

'You would think,' suggested Ellen during an interview, 'that your intellectual life would find ways of overcoming your emotional [life] but it doesn't seem to work.' The difficulty with love is that it cannot be subjected to the type of control we are used to applying to other aspects of our life. Because, as Mark suggests, 'you lose all sense of logic', the experience of falling in love seems dislocated from both explanation and intervention. Such a lack of control over love expresses a fundamental dynamic in the hermeneutic relationship we have with our selves. Love is understood as both an abstract force and something which resides inside of us; it is a power which engulfs us but it does so because it seems so natural to us. The passions aroused by love are felt to be something which we must control within ourselves. One of the clearest ways to see this is through a consideration of age. Age is a mediating factor in the negotiation of love for the people I interviewed because they often had a belief that, the older one is, the more 'in control' one can become of the process of falling in love. As Phillip explained to me, when he was younger he felt that when he fell in love he wasn't in control of his emotions, but as he grew older he learned to control himself and his feelings. The experience of love for Phillip is therefore mediated primarily by 'learning' how to manage his feelings:

PHILLIP: The feelings have been more or less the same but I have been in greater control and not gone overboard and, you know, [I have thought] 'think this through'. I've certainly been more responsible in my attitude to it. And I suppose that's part of growing up isn't it?

In Phillip's accounts we see that there is a dichotomy between the power of love and the ways in which that power can be managed. When we manage our feeling and emotions we believe that we are applying our own rational judgement to the irrational force of feelings which come either from inside us or overwhelm us from outside. Thus, we believe that, if we learn the best ways to express or control feelings, we can subject them to a more rational set of conditions. Yet, as Hochschild argues: 'In managing feeling, we partly create it' (1998: 11). In this sense emotions are not independent of the types of management we create to order them; rather, the management of emotions itself creates ways of feeling. It is at the moment we attempt to control the emotion, which we feel to pre-exist that control, that we create the feeling itself. Rather than the 'head' attempting to 'control' the heart, it creates what the heart feels.[4] In this sense, a fundamental relationship is instigated between the feelings inside our bodies and the way that we manage those feelings in social interaction. Importantly, we come to relate to ourselves through experiencing 'powerful' emotions which we believe we can, or cannot, control in certain ways. In doing this, we imbue love with a power which instigates a particular orientation towards self-control, self-expression and self-management.

The heterosexualized language of love's chemistry

We can see that ideas about love draw upon, and replay, a number of discourses which emphasize the mysterious, the biological, and the powerful nature of falling into, and being in, love. Romantic love is not experienced as a rational way of selecting a partner but as a highly charged process which exceeds rational explanation. Yet this compelling and mystical process is also delimited by the forms of heterosexual practice which it engenders because the 'natural' and 'powerful' force of love produces particular kinds of relationships. When we look at the ways in which the discourses of love are expressed, they often underwrite naturalized conceptions of sexuality. One of the most common points at which love and heterosexuality are normatively inscribed together is in the language of 'chemistry'. When people talk about love, they use metaphors, such as 'chemistry', and an associated lexicon of words such as 'spark' and 'click', as frameworks in which to explain their own heterosexual experiences. An example of this is Jackie's description of love as 'some kind of chemistry which works between two people' which, once established, 'it is very difficult to deny'.

In view of Jackie's description, Helen Fisher's (1995) account of the 'evolution of romantic love', in various geographical and cultural contexts, is interesting. Fisher argues that 'chemistry' between two people is the result of basic human physiology through which chemical systems, such as the production of endorphins in the brain, serve to induce a form of subjective compulsion which is most conducive to 'bonding'. These 'natural opiates', she argues, are the basis for a 'primitive' form of sociality between men and women because they ensure the relationships necessary for the reproduction of the species (her account owes much to the ideas found in biological science and evolutionary psychology). Fisher would not like to rule out the 'social' altogether and does believe that 'culture' plays a mediating role in shaping biological experiences. In a somewhat confusing account, we find biology and culture mixed up together in an amalgam of theoretical claims which range from reproduction to marriage:

> Cultural forces play a powerful role in directing behaviour, as does one's idiosyncratic perspective – what philosophers call 'free will'. But marriage is a cultural universal and divorce is common in societies around the world. Any therapist would maintain that long relationships require work. And worldwide data on the duration of marriage and timing of divorce suggest that the brain physiology for human attraction, attachment, and detachment evolved in conjunction with our primary human reproductive strategy.
>
> (Fisher, 1995: 29, references omitted)

What Fisher demonstrates is the ease with which any critique of 'culture' can be reduced to the simple and (seemingly) indisputable state of nature: love is just the chemicals in our brain which ensure our reproductive strategy. In this perspective 'free will' is possible but the 'primary' chemistry of *heterosexual* reproduction is innate, fixed, physiological and timeless.

Regardless of the merit of the academic debate, the language of 'chemistry' serves as a constant discursive framework in accounts of love. For Catherine, it is a 'spark' which is crucial:

CATHERINE: I met a really nice guy, [...] lovely, lovely guy, very kind and thoughtful, bought me flowers, lovely looking guy, took me away for weekends, but if there's nothing there, then there's nothing there and you can't do anything about it and, well I finished with him because you just, no, I would never be with anyone if I didn't love them. No I couldn't do it, at all.
PJ: Was it love that wasn't there?
CATHERINE: Definitely, there was nothing there, no spark, no nothing, so no, I couldn't be with somebody if I didn't love them.

The 'spark' is the mechanism which would both produce love and verify it. It is a crucial element in the social construction and experience of love for a number of reasons: first, it denotes the existence of forms of emotions which are different to those found in other social relationships; second, such feelings are described within a framework which explains them as existing outside of will or choice; and third, the existence of such feelings provide a way to verify 'real' love. Despite all the criteria being in place which Catherine might use to select a partner – he was a 'nice guy' who bought her flowers, took her away for weekends and was good looking – it is the absence of that 'chemistry' which overrides any form of utilitarian partner selection. This is not to say that we do not enter into relationships which are not founded on that 'spark' because, of course, we do. But, for the people I interviewed, they overwhelmingly thought that if the 'chemistry' is not there then there is something essential missing from the relationship. As Patricia explains: 'there is no point in getting into a situation whereby there's no spark [...] there's just no point.' But Patricia is also critical of the way that such a 'spark' becomes the basis for love relationships: 'I think that is a very stupid thing to base an idea of love on but I think that is true, that is what happens.'

This is why relationships which are not founded on 'chemistry' are seen, by everyone I interviewed, to be worth less. For instance, when I asked people for their views about arranged marriages, I found that they expressed disdain at the idea that love should be anything other than that based on the 'free' experience of the 'spark'. Although this connects a metaphysical view of love's extra-human dimensions with a political view of forms of social organization – the process of falling in love is positioned outside of the control of any social or political force and, as such, is constructed in a realm of 'freedom' – arranged marriages are seen to be less valuable essentially because they do not rely on a 'natural' process of 'chemistry'. A common response to the idea of arranged marriages was Victoria's: she argues that it is 'artificial', 'unfair' and that the two people 'might not click, and you're forcing them to click'. The 'click' is a similar metaphor to the notion of 'chemistry', it is something which might happen between two people but cannot be planned. If such relationships are planned then they are, as Phillip argues, 'business relationships' because they exclude the special quality of love, which cannot be appropriated at will. This is expressed most succinctly by Martin when he argues that arranged marriages constitute 'a human imposition on a more kind of biologically driven relationship'.

The language of 'chemistry', 'fusing', 'clicking', and 'spark' are extremely common in the language of love. They are seen as the pre-requisite ingredients for a romantic relationship based on 'true' love which is natural and not 'artificial':

VICTORIA: Love [is] a harmonious balance between a man and a woman where everything else around you doesn't matter as long as your life with him is cosy and it's comfortable and it's exactly how you've dreamed of and you wouldn't want to change a thing [...] You fuse together as one.

DOUGLAS: It's lock and key isn't it, it's when people fit together, and everything fits you know. Not just those parts of the cogs but you know, not just ratcheted together. I mean you either match or you provide so much polar sort of energy, in terms of being different, that it's the opposites attract as well, you know. [...] It is like two halves coming together and if something doesn't fit right . . .

This 'harmonious balance between a man and a woman' is seen as the outcome of two different people 'fusing' together. It is the way that two people, who fall in love, become so closely integrated that they become 'one'. And this process is described as a 'lock and key' whereby two 'halves' come together to make a whole. These descriptions of love are highly heterosexualized. They rely upon a number of gendered descriptions about a 'polar energy' which, much like magnets, causes 'opposites' to attract. It is not simply a case of *any* two people being 'ratcheted' together but a process in which, propelled by an 'energy', men and women fuse together.

The generative mechanism which causes the 'spark' of chemistry in heterosexual intimate relationships is fundamentally, for both men and women, conceived through ideas about sexual attraction and desire which, in turn, often draw on discourses of human biology. Douglas, in describing the 'real magnetic pull' between two people told me about why the 'vibe' of chemistry is so important to a relationship:

DOUGLAS: I mean, you can love someone and be in a solid relationship, but if you don't feel that, that pull to someone, if you don't feel that looking at someone and thinking, you know, if you don't get your motor running, if you don't feel that instant kind of like, you know, stirring in your loins and testosterone flowing around your body, I don't know, that smouldering look where you can feel your brain fizzing up, if you don't feel that it's not really there.

This is a common type of description of the experience of chemistry. It is a profoundly biological account which draws on the imagery of bodily flows and chemical changes to describe what happens once the spark of chemistry is ignited. It is what Elizabeth described to me as the 'sexual chemistry' which is experienced between two people. For both men and women it is not *simply* the desire to have sex but 'the whole package' of compatibility. As Elizabeth explains: 'I mean, you can be sexually attracted to someone you pass in the street but you know when you actually click with somebody on all levels.'

To 'click on all levels' is to successfully combine 'sexual chemistry' with feelings of 'warmth', 'rightness' and 'comfort' in a long-term, companionable, monogamous and intimate love relation. It is not simply a question of 'having sex' because, as the older people in the study told me, they felt sex became of less significance within a relationship as it progressed. Sexual chemistry, and the practice which departs from it, is imagined as the *basis* for a love relationship and this, as Martin describes, is built around heteronormative ideas about species reproduction:

PJ: How does love change as you get to know someone? Does it change?
MARTIN: Yes, I think so. I think sexually it changes. Like you're not so sexually motivated in your relationship.
[...]
PJ: How does that change?
MARTIN: Well, you don't want to shag them all the time [laughs]. Do you know what I mean, not *all* the time.
PJ: Why do you not want to do that?
MARTIN: I don't know, why do you not want to do that. Well, that's an interesting question Paul. I think, coming at it from a scientific view, I tend to think ... I mean this is the biology of sex, procreation, you know everyone's genetic biases. You know, they're trying to spread their genes, this Darwinian stuff, which you know I would go along with quite strongly although I have chosen not to do that in my life, [I have] gone against the biology. But I think it plays, from how I understand it, plays an important role in bonding you.

This process of bonding which Martin is describing begins, he goes on to tell me, with 'a flurry of sexual activity at the beginning of a relationship' which later 'settles down': 'you can't be bonding all the time'. What is interesting about Martin's account is that, despite the normative weight accorded to the 'scientific' explanation of sexual desire and activity, a process anchored around heteronormative views of sexuality and reproduction, he claims to have 'gone against the biology'. So although he invokes Darwin as a justification for an essential and universal biological imperative that propels men and women into sexual relations which consolidate their love (it bonds them), Martin claims to have abstracted himself from this process. As a practising Christian, Martin was determined to make his first sexual 'act' take place, *after* he was in love, on his 'wedding night'. What Martin highlights, therefore, is the normative model of heterosexual love and sex, based on 'scientific' ideas about reproduction, which frames his experience but does not conform to it.

I want to explore the complex relationship between love and sex in the next chapter. However, the salient point I am making here is that ideas about biology, and about reproductive instincts, circulate in relation to (and sometimes as explanations for) heterosexual love. The chemistry of love is imagined to result from an innate, biological interaction which underwrites the way in which 'two halves' come together within a heterosexual relationship. Combined with ideas about the body, with its mysterious power, and with conceptions of biology, the language of chemistry denotes a process which is distinctly sexualized because ideas of the 'spark' and the 'click' are constructed through heterosexualized conceptions of who one will fuse together with. I will go on to explore this further, but the point I am making here is that 'chemistry' is not seen as a social phenomenon but, rather, a factor of innate biology. It is this naturalness of love which comes to normalize heterosexuality because it appears to emanate from an unsocial body. As Jack explains to me, the chemistry of love is something which pre-exists its enactment because 'it's instinct, I think really it's in you'. It is a process waiting for realization, a biological 'fact' lying dormant which awaits the potential to realise itself once the 'spark' has ignited it.

Instating the essence: heterosexual love as timeless

Romantic love is compelling. It is constituted at the level of a 'gut feeling' (Alex), something which makes you 'high as a kite' (Scott) and is a 'whole body experience' (Gary). It comes out of nowhere, cannot be planned, and overpowers those who experience it. It constitutes a need, a desperate urge, and displaces 'logic'. It is not reducible simply to sexual desire, but contains sexual potential. Yet, this multi-faceted construction of romantic love is premised on one central idea: that love is a trans-historical 'fact' of human nature. In short, love is understood as an essential human process that, regardless of historical change, remains an ontological foundation of human existence. Love is imagined, by the people I interviewed, as a process which *never* changes. Because love is reduced to the language of 'chemistry' (which is the language of both biology and metaphysics), it operates through beliefs about love's trans-historical and universal nature.

This universality, or essence, of love is most visible if we consider the ways in which people talk about love historically. Although everyone I interviewed had sophisticated ways of understanding the social history of heterosexual relationships (for instance, everyone talked about changes in divorce and marriage patterns), *every* person expressed the view that the experience of love, and being in love, never changes. Consider the following extract from an interview with Douglas where he emphasizes the trans-historical nature of love:

PJ: Let me ask you how you think love might have changed over time? You've said that you think women's feelings about love have always been the same but they've changed perhaps over the last century.

DOUGLAS: No I didn't mean to say things have changed in *love*, I said things in *society* have changed. Things to do with attitudes towards sex and sexuality have changed. I don't think love has changed at all. I don't think it's ever changed.

PJ: No?

DOUGLAS: No it might have developed into a more complex emotional response as we evolved from whatever kind of primate we were before we became Homo Sapiens. But [...] I think a lot's been the same that was the same two thousand years ago. It was probably the same four thousand years ago.

PJ: Because it is a biological thing?

DOUGLAS: It's a biological thing and I suppose connected to spirituality as well, you know, which is the thing that no one had really flagged down yet, to do with you know ... I mean that raises all sort of philosophical and metaphysical questions about things, you know. But I mean I don't actually know that love is the same for me as it is for other people because I'm not other people. Do other people see colours the same, you know? [...] Now the way relationships have functioned that's different, that's entirely different. Relationships have been functional relationships and people have had their courtiers and courtesans, they've had their whores on the side, and they've had their mistresses and they've just had a functional relationship, Kings and Queens you know. And yet still through it all I think there was still two people in the village, the Robin Hood and the Maid Marion or whatever, that loved each other. It's dead cheesy that isn't it. There's still always this ... I still always think there has been couples in love. But I think nowadays it's actually because relationships make-up and break-up that people are actually looking for that love more. Because you can actually live on your own, you don't have to have a, you don't have to be dependent on someone, a woman doesn't have to have a partner. So I think that the relationships that stay together purely for economic reasons aren't valid anymore, they're not quite so necessary. Therefore people end up looking for that, they're looking for that spark, yeah, people are looking for that love,

> people are looking for the whole package and not just the being able to get on with someone in a social sense or something. And people are looking for the whole burning and yearning still. I know I am, even though I'm in a relationship. And I've tried to get it within that relationship and it never really happened.

Douglas reiterates various claims about love and relationships that rely on two central constructs. The first is that love is a trans-historical fact of human existence. The second is that the organization of relationships and intimate practices are open to historical change. Considering the first claim, we see that Douglas uses two explanatory devices in his elaboration of love: a biological model (the language of the brain) and a metaphysical model (the language of spirituality). In explaining love this way Douglas connects both the embodiment of love (in human biology) to its transcendental potential (the spiritual realm). The trans-historical nature of love is explained as a 'fact' of human existence because, whilst relationship practices change, there remains, throughout human history, real love (represented in the heterosexual figures of Maid Marion and Robin Hood – a type of historical representation which instates a timeless and seamless normativity of heterosexual love across history and one, it could be argued, for which there is no homosexual counterpart). Douglas therefore disconnects the idea of an essence of love from the social relations in which it is situated and expressed.

Yet, as we see at the end of the quotation, the *desire* for that love is understood as inculcated within sociality. For Douglas, it is precisely because of the *social* organization of relationships – because the social context of relationships has changed – that people want the 'burning and yearning' of love's passion. In terms of this argument, Douglas can be seen to express, almost exactly, Beck and Beck-Gernsheim's thesis that a desperate desire to love arises out of modern social fragmentation. 'Individualization', they argue, 'may drive men and women apart, but paradoxically it also pushes them into one another's arms. *As traditions become diluted, the attractions of a close relationship grow*' (1995: 33, italics in original). The 'burning and yearning' of which Douglas speaks is produced, according to Beck and Beck-Gernsheim, precisely because of how Douglas perceives social change: people do not *need* to live together for economic reasons; a woman does not *have to* live with a man. Two assertions therefore emerge from Douglas' account: the first is that love is an unchanging 'truth' of humanness and the second is that such an essence of being is affected by the social relations in which it is situated.

Douglas' account of love is interesting because it replays all of the discursive axioms which I have outlined above. Besides imbuing love with an essentiality outside of history, Douglas also reiterates several other key points: first, that love is a biological fact (reactive or proactive) of human beings; second, that love is an acutely individual phenomenon that is experienced uniquely (it's like colour, do we all see it in the same way?); third, that love functions through the sensation of the 'spark' between two people; fourth, that love's chemistry is something which cannot be created at will; and finally, love is represented in explicitly heterosexual terms. All of these ways of speaking about love all contain one fundamental theme: that love is an *asocial* property. Although these themes express that fundamental principle in different ways, they rely on a formula of an essence of love which is dislocated from sociality. Such a view is, as in Douglas' account, often situated in a broader understanding of how social relations, and relationships between men and women, alter without significantly affecting the belief that falling in love, and being in love, are facts of human nature.

When I interviewed Carl, who is a university student and is familiar with some of the concepts and debates of social constructionism, we talked about love as an essence and he drew on that academic discourse in order to elucidate his ideas regarding the relationship between love and the social world:

CARL: [...] it's interesting because I've been reading all this stuff about essentialism and social constructionism and stuff, and I'm quite aware that I'm a bit too cynical about [love] being a part of a wider system. But I think there is probably an essence to love. If I was trying to write about it academically I would probably try and 'poo-poo' that idea but, kind of, I do think in myself, I would like to think there was some essence of love that was unchanging.

PJ: OK.

CARL: But, none the less, all around it, the way it's supposed to form, it's very much pushed around by society, the way you seek it out, I guess. What it can mean, there's lots of things that can mean ... the institution of marriage has no doubt changed and the institution of relationships has changed, and the way that relationships have formed has changed. Maybe love wasn't in all of them, maybe love isn't in them now, but I still would very much hope that there is still some little kernel of what love is that hasn't changed.

The importance of the 'little kernel' of love that remains unchanged (even though it may be fashionable in the academy to deny it) is an 'essence' of love that Carl would like to believe exists. He is aware, like Douglas, that relationships change but he is also concerned to demonstrate that such changes are not necessarily related to alterations in love. In Carl's social constructionist model, it is the social organization of relationships which is seen as constructed, but love retains its essential quality. Although Carl has the language in which to elucidate love as part of a 'wider system', he doesn't do this. Rather, he is concerned to make clear that an essence of love remains a fundamental part of human existence regardless of the 'wider system' in which it exists. This is an extremely important discursive split and, although Carl expresses it in academic vernacular, it is something which is achieved by every person (without exception) that I interviewed.

What is expressed through the essentialization and universalization of love is that the 'chemistry' of love, which 'fuses' two people together, is an unchanging and fixed attribute of human life. That such a residual belief endures means that, even when placed within elaborate and sophisticated understandings of the changing patterns of heterosexual relationships, the ideal of love is reified as an absolute given because it is 'natural':

ELIZABETH: Well I think love ... I'm not sure whether love itself has changed, I think marriage has changed a lot because, I mean, I think in the past people would be desperate to get married as soon as possible and to settle down and I think that maybe when they did get married maybe weren't really in love with someone. And so, and also, it wasn't as easy to get divorced in the past and so people used to stay in marriages when they weren't happy. And also with the whole women's movement I think that women are a lot stronger now because we used to just be passive. And I think because of that a lot of marriages are breaking up because they're not really in love, or they fall out of love maybe [. . .] so I think the way it's expressed in marriage has changed.
PJ: Right, so the feeling of love itself has stayed the same?
ELIZABETH: I would say so yes.

MARGARET: Well love is love, it's not going to change but the things that go with it change. I mean, in the olden days they used to just stay together for the sake of the children, you know they didn't love each other. Things like that have changed, is that what you mean?
PJ: Yeah.
MARGARET: Yeah? Kids today think they're in love straight away don't they, they're sort of in love when they're 12 you know. Because there's more in the media isn't there, it's all love, love, love, all the time, where they never talked about it before.

ALEX: I don't know, in little ways I would say yeah, but in, I don't know, in general I would say it was all the same.
PJ: Yeah?
ALEX: Although society's changed it's probably still the same. It doesn't matter what generation.
PJ: Yeah. Same type of feeling and that type of stuff?
ALEX: Yeah.

Let us consider what people are not saying. They are not saying that love is a product of a set of social relations which produces a series of ideas about how men and women enter into a specific form of union which is then expressed in a biological and metaphysical language of 'love'. What they are saying is that for an unspecified historical period men and women have entered into a type of union – which we call love – and that such a type of union has been expressed and practised differently within particular historical contexts and situations. Love, they say, never changes because it has an essence which, although 'pushed around by society', is essential and common to humanity. What we find is that the socio-biological view is the most readily invoked explanatory framework in accounts of love; it is a belief in a residual innateness of human beings which underwrites any conception of the role of 'culture' which may be layered over it.

But ideas about romantic love and intimate practices do have a history and are not trans-historical facts. The idea of a continuous and linear belief in one form of love throughout history is fictitious. Romantic/intimate sexual love is a social construction that can be seen to be context-specific. The 'essence' of love, which we believe transcends history, may be the foundation on which our modern construction of love is built but we know that love has been expressed differently in our own society throughout modern history (see Illouz, 1997, for a discussion of the transformation of beliefs about love from Victorian society to modern capitalism). From that we can conclude that romantic love has operated according to different principles under certain relations (we may also consider this globally: see Jankowiak, 1995). My point is not to show how love has operated under different historical contexts, but to highlight how history itself is invoked at the moment that the language of love is spoken. The 'essence' of love that remains unchanging, this 'chemistry' that expresses an essential human experience, is one of the ways in which the social construction of love is legitimated as a human quality. Whilst 'relationships' come under scrutiny – from the questions we ask about them to the government policy which inform them – the 'essence' of love is rarely questioned. It operates within discourse as so normative, as a process so essential to human practice, that the ways in which it is expressed resist intervention.

Conclusion

My task in this book is to show how ideas about love and intimacy intermesh with the social construction of heterosexuality. As we will see from a consideration of gender, sexual practice and the consolidation of heterosexual identities, love intersects in the operation of heterosexual sexuality. I want to go on to argue that 'intimacies' are produced, regulated and enacted through the dual discursive functions of love and sexuality but, more specifically, through the ways in which loving is imagined as a natural, innate, biological and unchanging truth of human existence. It is precisely because love seems 'natural' that it retains its compelling power outside of those discourses concerned with the state of 'relationships'. But this is not simply an argument about how love leads us into heterosexual relationships or a claim that love is an ideological device for ordering heterosexuality. Rather, I am arguing that the social construction of love serves a legitimating purpose for heterosexuality because it connects the modern construction of sexuality to historical ideas of innateness and essentialism which are then experienced as a unique set of 'feelings'. What concerns me is the way that we situate ourselves within these discourses of love and how, in doing so, we produce ourselves in particular ways. As Stacey and Pearce argue, love 'is one of the most compelling discourses through which any of us is inscribed' (1995: 12) and, as we can see, it is compelling precisely because it 'works' in such a fundamentally 'natural' way. For these reasons we appeal to love. And when we appeal to love we invariably do so in relation to its essentiality. The next chapter explores how this essentiality configures particular modes of sexual expression.

2 Making love and regulating sex

In the previous chapter I argued that ideas about love are intimately bound up with conceptions of what can be described in general terms as 'nature': love is experienced as profoundly essential, as an innate property of personhood, it is constructed as ahistorical, it is placed beyond rational description, and it is implicated in ideas about natural sexuality. In this chapter I want to explore how these ideas about love mediate concrete heterosexual sexual practice and how the discourses of love and sexuality intermesh in the negotiation of heterosex. Specifically, I want to do this by looking at how love remains a *compelling* foundation for heterosexual sex and how the negotiation of sexual practice takes place in relation to certain axiomatic principles of love and intimacy. So the question I am asking here is: how do love, sex and heterosexuality 'work' together?

In the biological model detailed earlier, sex and love are positioned together in their most deterministic and naturalistic form: they are intrinsically linked through reproduction. In evolutionary psychology, for instance, love is understood as a functional relationship which frames the primary act of reproduction: 'sexual selection produced a two-stage defence against sexual infidelity: romantic love, and then companionate sexual love' (Miller, 2000: 333). Love is conceptualized as the cultural form which frames the natural and innate need to conceive and reproduce but, if the love relationship is a functionality which facilitates the production and nurture of children, then how would evolutionary psychology explain sexual infidelity or divorce? As Geoffrey Miller explains:

> Our sexual fidelity evolved as a compromise between two selection pressures. On the one hand there was sexual selection favouring high fidelity through romantic love and sexual commitment. On the other hand there were potential reproductive benefits of philandering. Especially for males, those reproductive benefits made it maladaptive to completely turn off their sexual attraction to everyone other than their partners.
>
> (2000: 334)

One could critique the biological determinism of this view in many ways – in terms of its essentialization of sexual desire or its gendered model of male and female 'drives' – but what interests me, in the context of this debate, is the causal relationship set up between love, sex and heterosexuality. Through the use of claims about reproduction, a chain of assertions are made to naturalize heterosexuality as *the* primitive and enduring truth of humanity. A preoccupation with reproduction centres a 'natural' heterosexual act (the act of species reproduction) after which all other 'social' rituals, such as love, seem derivative forms. Yet claims based on reproduction are built on certain inherent assumptions, constructed around a normative model of heterosexuality, which bear little resemblance to the ways in which contemporary Euro-Americans fall in love and have sex (which rarely has anything to do with reproduction). As Freud was apt to say: 'If you make the function of reproduction the kernel of sexuality you run the risk of excluding from it a whole host of things like masturbation, or even kissing, which are not directed towards reproduction, but which are nevertheless undoubtedly sexual' (Freud, in Brake, 1982: 53).

Arguments about 'biology', that tie love and sex to heterosexual reproduction are examples of how love becomes the servant of heterosexual sex aimed at reproduction. But this is a *theoretical* claim which appears as 'natural' because of its normative force. What I want to explore is how love and sex are *empirically* negotiated within heterosexuality. What we will see is that the discursive constructions of love and sex are deployed both separately and in conjunction to legitimate certain forms of heterosexual sexual practice under particular conditions. As Holland *et al.* argue: 'The split between sex and love lies at the heart of the dominant discourses of normative heterosexuality' (1998: 102). In negotiating intimate relationships, they argue, it is the ability to order sex and love in precisely the right way that is crucial. 'Scripting' sexual relationships, they claim, is a gendered process and the discourses of sex and love delimit the types of practices and subject positions which are available to men and women. Negotiating these constructs is certainly gendered but it is, as I will argue, too generalized to suggest, as Holland *et al.* do, that the split between sex and love 'is what can make sex so dangerous for women, and love so dangerous for men' (1998: 102). The negotiations around sex and love, as we shall see, are never so unilateral in their gendered dimensions.

The historical relationship of love and sex is complicated and multifarious. As two distinct, but intermeshed, discursive constructs, their interrelationship has undergone, even in recent history, certain changes. At its most basic level we can see one historical change as the disruption between the linear pattern of love–marriage–sex. A simple comparison between the experiences of the oldest participants in this study with some of the youngest reveals a dynamic shift. For Jack and Dorothy, who are both in their eighties, their sexual relationship, beginning on their honeymoon, signalled a ratification of their love for each other which they had expressed in marriage. For younger people, as we might imagine, such a linear trajectory is seen to have been problematized and debunked.[1] The sexual history of the twentieth century, if we read the claims of theorists like Anthony Giddens, is a movement of the institutional decoupling of sex from its regulatory shackles in romantic love. New forms of 'plastic sexuality' 'severed from its age-old integration with reproduction, kinship and the generations' has, claims Giddens, been the basis on which the 'sexual revolution' of the past few decades has been built (1992: 27). Now sex is not confined by the institutional regulation of 'romance', but the basis for manufacturing forms of confluent love: sex and love have been fundamentally separated out from one another. Yet Giddens' historical reading is inaccurate for two reasons: first, there was never a 'golden age' of a pure linear movement of love–marriage–sex (as several older people in this study told me, they are well aware that sex before marriage certainly did occur); and second, the relationship between sex, love and institutional heterosexuality has not disappeared in the accounts of younger people. Certainly for Martin, who was determined to wait until he was married before he had sex (at the age of 26), love, sex and institutional heterosexuality are fundamentally tied together.

My aim here is not to provide a historical overview of the relationship between love and sex or the ways in which they have been constituted relationally in different historical contexts. Patterns of social change need a different type of analysis and can be found in various existing studies (Jameson, 1998; Seidman, 1991; Weeks, 1989). Rather, my aim is to analyse the ways in which love provides a framework through which heterosexual sex is negotiated in the empirical practice of social actors. There are two distinct parts to this chapter. In the first instance I want to look at how love and sex remain distinct discursive formations which are employed in tandem by men and women as they negotiate their heterosexual relationships. This introduces the distinct concept of 'intimacy' which, as Lynn Jameson (1998) notes, is the nodal point at which contemporary forms of sex and love overlap.[2] Questions of 'intimacy' therefore frame the second part of this chapter, which is concerned with the ways in which sex and love can, in practice, be separated from one another. Although sex is analytically separate from love, it remains empirically difficult to extract from the wider issues of intimacy in which it is situated. Even where we confront differentiation around gender, we see that sex and love remain tied together. Love has a normative force in regulating, authorizing and proscribing types of heterosexual sexual practices and, whilst the linear heterosexual 'script' of falling in love/getting married/consummating a sexual relationship is not prominent in practice, I want to argue that normative ideals of love still exert a considerable force over sex.

Love, lust or 'a horrible ugly mess'?

One of the most prominent ways of relating love and sex together, for both men and women, is through the idea that sexual practice is an *expression* of love. Sex, in this sense, ratifies a feeling of love by operationalizing a certain type of intimacy in which love is expressed. At its most basic, sex is something that one does with someone that one loves. If one believes that this is true, then certain features of sexual life are conceptualized in distinct ways. First, sex outside of love is considered to be less valuable than sex within love because it does not function to express anything (although what sex might be outside of love, as we shall see, is gendered). Second, and consequently, a whole sphere of activity and desire is seen to be problematic: this is the sphere of 'lust'. For those people who wish to maintain the view that love is a 'pure emotion', which becomes ratified through sexual practice, a necessity to sublimate 'lust' is created. The relationship between love and lust is crucial in the mediation of heterosexual sexual relationships. As Cas Wouters (1999) argues, the 'love/lust balance' is a constantly shifting historical construction that becomes expressed in different ways under certain contexts. The analytic separation of sexual love from loveless lust is a powerful and mediating principle through which heterosexual sex functions in contemporary relationships.

Lust is often positioned as an animalistic expression of human biology which, whilst being an essential part of human behaviour, does not correspond to the 'higher' principles of love. This phenomenon is certainly gendered and its genealogy can be traced to early sexology where masculine and feminine sexual 'drives' are conceptualized in particular ways: men as predatory and promiscuous and women as passive recipients to these male 'urges'.[3] Yet these distinctions are not 'real' in any physical or biological sense – we cannot unproblematically accept that 'lust' expresses a libidinal drive which is subject to the social forces of relationship practice (although this would certainly be axiomatic for Freudian psychoanalysis). Rather we need to think of the concept of lust as itself a discursive formation which complements the construction of love and, in doing so, understand how these two discourses divide, compare and re-enforce each other.

Lust is often understood as a form of desire orientated towards the consummation of sexual activity and, as such, is seen to express a function of sex which need not take place within a relationship characterized by love. But sexual desire is also understood, at times, to be a fundamental premise on which intimate love is based. In this sense, there is a difference between sex as an expression of love and lust as mere sexual energy (often imagined to derive from the primordial urge to reproduce). But this difference is never *really* separate in empirical practice because it is used as a framework in which to negotiate sex. For instance, when I interviewed Carl we talked about love and sex in his experience of heterosexual relationships:

CARL: I'll tell you I think there has been an ongoing theme throughout, I think it happens to a lot of people, it's trying to work out which part is love and which part is lust, and where the line is, and maybe you need a bit of both, and it gets fuzzy.

The 'line' is the distinction that people make between love – that set of feelings, practices and beliefs which I outlined in the previous chapter – and the desire to have sex with someone. The 'line' becomes 'fuzzy' precisely because sex is so closely intermeshed with the way in which we image love to be operationalized. The point for Carl is that he wants to achieve an analytic and practical separation of love and sex in order to make sure that sexual practice expresses and consummates a feeling of love. In other words, love should not be, as Stevi Jackson argues, 'lust gift wrapped in romantic convention' (1999: 103). As Carl explains:

CARL: I made a commitment to myself that I would make sure that love comes first and then sex. Even in broader terms ... this is something in the last year, I decided that I needed to be really thorough about this. But the problem is that when I start feeling the lust it gets kind of confused and I get distracted by it and the next thing you know you're snogging the woman, or you're in bed with her [...] so, I actually, at the end of my last relationship I put this shell on my neck as a reminder that I should ... I made a commitment to myself that I should fall in love with them, be in love with them, before I even kissed them. And then I should be committed to them before I sleep with them.
PJ: Why?
CARL: Why? Because I think love's more important than lust.

Love retains, in Carl's account, its hierarchical position above lust as 'more important'. For Carl, lust is a distraction which results in a confusion of the way that he wishes to negotiate his intimate relationships. As he says, he decided that he needed to be 'thorough' about this and made a commitment to himself that he should love his partner before he kissed her and that he should be committed to her before they had sex. This is certainly not an expression of the institutional decoupling of sex and love described by Giddens because, on the contrary, sexual activity is banished from the intimate sphere until love is consolidated. Maintaining this separation is felt by Carl to be both important and extremely difficult. As he explains to me, about the shell on his necklace: 'it's funny because this has become almost like a little cross when you're faced with the vampire. You know I literally hang on to it for dear life, reminding myself of my commitment [...] be strong, remember love should come first.'

It is precisely the presence of the 'vampire' – that temptation of lust – which problematizes his model of love and leads him to conclude that sex and love are always 'mixed up' and that they form 'a horrible ugly mess'. The foundation of gender difference on which this process of negotiating sexual love is constructed is interesting because is reveals the ways in which the discourses of love and sex are tied to a specific framework of sexuality (in this case a generic understanding of male 'drives' which become operationalized by women). But why would Carl actually want to separate love so fundamentally from sex? The answer to this question lies in the ways in which love and sex must be organized in a specific way in order to establish heterosexual intimacy; or, more specifically, in order to establish the *best* type of intimacy. What is crucial is that, despite a range of social changes, the belief that sex should follow love, that it should express a form of monogamous and enduring commitment, has been retained. It is certainly not the case that the (Christian/institutionalized church) view of sex within *marriage* endures in practice, but we can argue that it still exerts a conceptual influence through the defined notion of 'good' *intimacy*.

For Carl, and for most people in this study, heterosexual long-term and monogamous relationships are seen to be founded on love rather than sex. Sex should express love in an intimate relationship and not simply be an expression of lust. As Carl concludes near the end of the interview: 'for me, sex is an expression of my intimacy and commitment to that person and if it's not there's something screwy going on.' A 'screwy' relationship would be one which did not proceed from the foundational premise that sex should take place within a relationship characterized by love. Yet we can see a central problem emerge in Carl's understanding of love, sex and intimacy. Whilst sex is seen to be an expression of love in an intimate relationship, it is also seen as the vehicle through which intimacy is consolidated. The central problem for Carl is the rogue notion of lust. Lust has to be negated in order for sexual intimacy to take place. But that cannot negate sex because sexual activity is needed to express love intimately. The problem is one of balance; of bringing sexual desire and love together in the 'correct' way and within the right context.

The discourses of love and sex present social actors with a set of problems to solve in the negotiation of heterosexual intimacy. One of the clearest ways we can see this negotiation is through the way that, in attempting to manufacture intimacy, a balance must be brokered in relation to sexual desire. At the heart of this balance are ideas about how sexual desire is fundamental to the process of falling in love:

PJ: So, just going back to something you said about sex. Does sex actually play a part in falling in love?
MARTIN: Absolutely. Well in my personal opinion, yes it does. To varying degrees, probably. Like obviously for people like it's a very driving factor, it's interesting ... there's probably some really interesting biological shit going on there which I don't really, I wouldn't like to guess at. But yeah, I think so, I wouldn't, I doubt, that I would fall in love with someone who I didn't have sexual attraction for.

PJ: I just wanted to ask you what part do you think sex plays in falling in love?
ELLEN: Very important part.
PJ: In what sense?

ELLEN: Well there is this, this innate physical drive, and in choosing someone intuitively, I think that involves some sort of feeling as to whether you are going to be sexually compatible.

For both Martin and Ellen, and for many other people in this study, a form of sexual attraction is seen as integral to falling in love. This sexual attraction is imagined to be installed as a discrete biological process which 'drives' the two lovers together (the 'biological' and 'innate physical drive' which work 'intuitively'). This biological and essentialized understanding is one of the most entrenched views of falling in love and is axiomatic to the principles of heterosexual intimacy. As Douglas told me, 'you've got to fancy your partner', 'you've got to look at them and want to jump their bones'. This form of sexual attraction is seen to be foundational for love because sex will, at some point, be the vehicle through which love is expressed. Therefore, 'fancying' a partner is absolutely central because it denotes an immediate potential for future sexual expression. Yet, of course, fancying someone might also be based on lust. How do we decide, and organize, which type of sexual desire and practice is related to love and which is not? As William explains:

WILLIAM: It's sort of like lust and a little bit sort of love. I'm not really sure how to explain it. You can't work out a way, you basically can't work out how you're going to be as close to that person as you want to be [. . .].
PJ: OK. So you feel as though you want to be *so* close to somebody . . .
WILLIAM: Yeah, you can't be . . . you need to spend all your time with them, you need to be as close as you can possibly be to that person without actually being them, it's that sort of feeling. You need to spend all your time with them. The point where you want to make love all the time, that's the closest you can be to someone.

Sex provides a vehicle through which a profound level of intimacy is manufactured with another person and is therefore a necessary part of consolidating love (it is fundamental to that process of 'fusing' together). But the crucial factor here is the notion of 'making love' which brings sex and love together, under the rubric of intimate sexual practice, so that sexual desire is not simply lust. Sex actually does *make love* because it operationalizes love in an intimate setting. When making love, sex is purposeful, directed, it aims to consolidate something. It is 'still sort of like lust', as William says, and therefore retains the idea of biological energy but, because it takes place within a framework of love, it is biology put at the service of some greater imperative. Love and sex still maintain a form of analytic separation, but they are consolidated in relation to each other within the broader framework of intimacy. Of course, this seems completely normative because it expresses a normal link we make between sexual desire and love. However, this sexualization of love is a specific characteristic of our modern relations of intimacy, where sex becomes the primary vehicle through which love is consolidated (see Seidman, 1991).

Certain problems can become present in negotiating the balance between love and sex. For instance, how does one know when they are operating correctly in an intimate relationship? How does one get the order right? Does sex verify love or vice versa? What comes first? For Margaret, 'when you're really with the right person sex is different, it's more emotional and it's like, the closeness [...] you've really got to love someone to have that and that's when you know it's really love.' In this sense, a form of sexual closeness, and a particular type of sexual practice, verifies the existence of love. But, as Margaret says, you have to really love someone to have that form of sexual closeness and, once you have that closeness, you know that it really is love. Of course, this is inherently confusing because it appears, on the one hand, that love causes the emotional closeness, yet on the other hand it is the emotional closeness of sex that consolidates love. This problem is further confused, as Margaret explains, by the ways in which 'sometimes you get mixed up between lust and love'. As she goes on to explain:

PJ: What's it like when you get lust and love mixed up?
MARGARET: Difficult, very difficult [laughs]. Because you think, oh it's love but it's just ... you know when you cannot, you want to tear their clothes off them all the time, you cannot keep away from them. You think you love them because you love their body and you just want them, but that's lust. But you can think it's love.

Margaret is describing the same set of problems which Carl detailed above, where sexual desire (as lust) becomes 'mixed up' with love. What Margaret's testimony shows are the ways in which sexual desire is tied to a framework of love so that her understanding of sex is constructed through the way in which she conceptualizes love. She is explicit about how forms of sexual desire can lead her to think 'oh it's love'. It is for this reason, because sexual desire can become confused with feelings of love, that it is often mistrusted. And it is for precisely this reason that Carl would wish to maintain a total distinction whereby he founded a love relationship and then, later, expressed it in sex. This type of sexual expression would be the form of 'emotional closeness' which Margaret describes as the foundation of *really* loving someone. So, whilst sexual desire is fundamental to the expression of love, it is also problematic.

But what is lust if not sexual attraction? The conceptual difference is enormous. Lust is seen to denigrate love and is something which must be managed if intimacy is to be secured. The issue is one of finding the right balance. In Cas Wouters' (1999) notion of the 'lust balance', the social agent attempts to find a way to balance the desire and longing for sex within the institutionalized social conventions which govern expressions of that desire.

For Wouters, at any historical moment people confront the lust balance question: *'when and within what kind of relationships(s) are (what kind of) eroticism and sexuality allowed and desired?'* (1999: 189, italics in original). This is a central question when we are considering how love, as a discursive form, is invoked when people consider having sex, but it also carries with it inherent problems. The greatest problem is the tendency it has to essentialize 'lust' as a stubborn drive that fights to express itself within forms of sociality. As Wouters argues of the lust balance question: 'This question is first raised in puberty or adolescence when bodily and erotic impulses that were banned from interaction from early childhood onwards (except in cases of incest) are again explored and experimented with' (1999: 189). Wouters conceptualizes the 'inner impulses' of our sexual desire as the outcome of our innate and rather stubborn drive to have sex. Love, in this sense, is the foil to sex: a set of social impositions onto the core of lust which moulds our human desires.[4]

If we follow Wouters' understanding of the lust/love balance we are required to accept that sex is an unsocial drive that becomes curtailed by social convention. Yet it is clear, from the data of this study, that sex is constructed conceptually through the negotiation of (hetero)sexuality and not simply because of it; that is, that sexuality and sexual desire are social products which are *produced* in relation to the social contexts in which they take place.[5] How sex is invoked and practised through the relations in which it is situated affects a distinctive view of what sex does, how it happens, and where it takes place.[6] My argument is that this is fundamentally related to the social construction of love which, in providing a normative framework through which sex is negotiated, installs particular ideas about innate sexuality.

For example, in the accounts of people who are attempting to form an intimate relationship we see (along with the idea that making love is important) a fundamental negation of the idea of lust. Consider the following from an interview with Susan where she describes the difference between 'proper love' and other relationships:

PJ: And how was [the relationship with your husband] different?
SUSAN: It was more ... it sort of developed, do you know what I mean, it wasn't like this lust, it wasn't like this lust kind of thing when I first saw him. I wasn't really interested in him ... we were friends to be honest, we were friends throughout college and stuff and he sort of liked me, but I didn't know he did, and it developed later on ... I thought he was a really nice person, I got to know him as a person, he did with me, and then it sort of moved on from there, and it was more of a ... and it developed more into a like companionship ... and the trust and the respect was there, and all that kind of stuff. And that's when I knew it was love sort of thing, 'cause I couldn't be without him. And it was totally different, I didn't need to have like sex to be, to feel love with him, where the first time it was like I thought that's what love was all

about [laughs] that you needed to feel really physically attracted and you had to have like sex if you were in love. But we didn't need to do that.

[...]

PJ: OK. Does sex play a part in falling in love, or is it separate?

SUSAN: I think it's an expression of love, yeah, definitely, but I think it's on a different ... to me I think it's on a different level, do you know what I mean, it's the ultimate way of expressing it.

PJ: So it's an expression of love?

SUSAN: Yes.

PJ: Does it come after you've fallen in love?

SUSAN: I do ... I believe that. Like, if you've developed a relationship with somebody and you love them, and they love you, then I think that you can express it that way as well.

It is clear that whilst sex is an expression of love, for Susan, the absence of an initial lust is also an important mechanism for verifying the existence of love. And Susan is explicit about this: 'I didn't need to have sex to be, to feel love with him.' What Susan is describing is not just a lack of needing to have sex, but an actual negation of that need – it is the lack of sexual desire that actually authenticates love. It is important for Susan that sex comes at a specific point in the 'script' of her relationship: sex too soon would indicate something was wrong and the total absence of sexual attraction would negate the expression of love. Ideas about love therefore delimit sexual practice in relation to the broader principles of heterosexual intimacy. Certain types of sexual expression are produced as desirable whilst lust is relegated to the position of something which must be mistrusted since it symbolizes the absence of 'companionable' intimacy and love. In this sense, love serves as a way of producing and framing forms of desire into legitimate (in this case, feminine) types of expressions (Leonard, 1980; Lees, 1993).

As Phillip suggested to me: sex should not be a departure in a relationship but mark a particular point, 'turning a corner', after love is established. Like Susan, Phillip told me that sex should express a love which existed before sex is enacted; that sex should be a vehicle through which intimacy is expressed. For the people I interviewed this cannot be seen to be a gendered phenomenon. Although convention might tell us that the social construction of love only regulates women's sexuality, this cannot be seen to be a blanket rule. For instance, in Phillip's account we find the exact same response to Susan's feelings about love and sex:

PJ: Do you think sex plays a big part in falling in love?

PHILLIP: No, not really because the first relationship I had when I was sixteen, there was no sex involved with that at all and it was the same, the same feelings initially that I experienced when I was 26 when I met

my ex[-wife], and just developed into a sexual relationship. The sex didn't come first.
PJ: Right. So you . . .
PHILLIP: It was the falling in love first.
PJ: Do you think that falling in love always precedes having sex?
PHILLIP: As far as I'm concerned, yes.
PJ: Is that important?
PHILLIP: Yes.
PJ: Why is that?
PHILLIP: Well I feel I couldn't have a sexual relationship with somebody I didn't love.
PJ: Why?
PHILLIP: The bits don't work [laughs].

What is different about Phillip's account, in relation to Susan's, is that, although they both effect a form of sexual containment through an appeal to love, for Phillip it is the presence of the sexual 'drive' (the very mechanistic model of penile erection) which verifies the existence of love. So, for both Phillip and Susan, love is productive of particular, but different, ways of relating to their own sexuality.

Normative convention might tell us that male sexuality is animalistic and that Phillip's account is an example of something rare. Yet, what is actually being appealed to here is extremely common in all of the accounts provided by the men I interviewed because they all expressed the view that sex within a love relationship was fundamentally 'better'. As we will see in the next part of this chapter, when we consider the separation of sex from love, men and women experience this in fundamentally different ways. However, the point I want to make is that, for both the men and women I interviewed, sexual practice is conceptualized within a hierarchy, and regulated in relation to, the social construction of love. Indeed, the main point I am making is that the social construction of heterosexual intimacy relies on a formulaic principle that sex extracted from love is less valuable than sex which ratifies love. It is the *belief* of the different values of sexual desire – where lust is a mere example of something biological – which underwrites the monogamous ideal of heterosexuality.

I am not suggesting, of course, that forms of sexual activity do not take place outside of a relationship characterized by love. What I am suggesting, however, is that the conceptual idea of love 'does' something to the notion of sex because it delimits forms of sexual expression within a conceptual hierarchy. The 'ideal' of sexual intimacy provides a normative framework through which all sexual activity (although gendered in particular ways) is evaluated. Why sex in an intimate relationship should be considered 'better' is a complicated issue and brings together a range of factors. One contemporary explanation is that an appeal to love allows a negotiation of 'risks' (both social and sexual), such as the risk of sexually transmitted diseases (see, Rosenthal *et al.* 1998). In this sense, a love relationship facilitates a respectable space in which to avoid the risks associated with disease.[7] This was certainly expressed by two of the younger people I interviewed, Elizabeth and Douglas, who both expressed the view that casual sex was undesirable because of the risk of HIV and AIDS which it presented.

But there is a broader point to be made here which is that love affects the ways in which, not only sex is experienced, but also the ways in which we relate to ourselves as beings with a sexuality. Love functions as a mediating principle in the modern constitution of sexuality because it frames a hermeneutic relationship between oneself and one's own libido (where the notion of lust represents a type of libidinal activity which is imagined as a disruptive force that needs to be subjected to constraint and scrutiny). As Michel Foucault often stated: 'sexual ethics imply very strict truth obligations' ([1981] 1997: 182), and it is the intersection of ethics and sexuality which reproduce specific ways of understanding oneself. The crucial point I am making is that, in the relation between self and sexuality, love functions as a salient mediating discursive framework. I do not mean that this injunction is simply the ordering of 'relationships'; it is not simply a question of how sex is placed in a 'script' of a relationship (although that is, as we have seen, important). It is a question of how forms of sexual morality are produced in relation to love; how sex is understood to be more 'proper' when it is at the service of love; and the ways in which sexuality functions through love. This is how morality and truth tie sex and love together. There is a pervasive ethic at work which tempers and moulds the almost hegemonic belief that 'lust' is an animalistic and libidinal drive of humanness; this is the ethic of love. But it is precisely this ethic which produces the types of relation to one's own sexuality which we have seen. It is a way of relating to the imaginary drives of one's own body; a way of imposing a strict and regulated type of 'truth' upon one's self and then using that truth to order one's own practice. If sex requires, as Foucault suggests, a permanent hermeneutics of oneself then that relation is bound up with the principles of love.

Modern intimacy demands a fusion of sex and love because sex, as we have seen, expresses love. In this sense we can argue that intimacy is premised on a specific regulation of sex by love – where 'lust' is transformed into legitimate sexual expression. This view is in opposition to theorists such as Beck and Beck-Gernsheim (1995) and Giddens (1992) who argue that sex and love have been separated into distinct narratives of existence. Coupled with the isolating tendencies of self atomization in 'high modernity' or 'risk society' this separation produces two effects: the first is that the modern 'self' must work far harder to achieve a form of self-fulfilment and happiness because it is 'freed up' from the social constraints of industrial society; and second, as a direct result of this, whilst sexual expression is liberated from the constraints of institutional heterosexuality, there is a need to bring them back together (in the 'pure relationship') so that intimacy may be manufactured. This implies a form of 'choice' whereby the individual chooses an intimate relationship above the mere expression of sex. But this, as I show in the following sections, is fundamentally misconceived because the idea of a separation of the narratives of love and sex is often illusionary and built on a conceptual rather than an empirical divide.

Women and casual sex

Love exerts considerable influence over sexual practice and identity and ideas about love and sex also rely on formulaic models of gender and sexuality. I want to now look at how love and sex work to mutually reinforce each other within the intimate sphere by thinking about how they can (or cannot) be separated from each other. In mapping the limits of separation between sex and love we can understand how heterosexual sexual practice is regulated and how specific forms of sexual expression come into existence. I want to start by looking at how love exerts force over women's experiences and ideas of sex and how that, in turn, produces particular forms of legitimate (and therefore forms of illegitimate) feminine heterosexual sexual expression. Women's accounts of 'casual sex' (that is sex outside of a relationship characterized by love *or* a relationship which is long term) consistently show how normative ideals of love regulate sexual expression. This is not to suggest that women do not practise, or wish to practise, sexual relationships outside of love because, as we will see, they most certainly do. However, such practices are problematized by the way in which heterosexual sexual expression is normatively constructed through love (and in relation to gender).

As Beverley Skeggs (1997) notes, heterosexuality, as a historical and cultural artefact, has produced a set of authorizing discourses which give validity to legitimate and correct forms of sexual expression. 'The heterosexual woman', writes Skeggs, 'is a particular form of woman, not working class or Black, but respectable' (1997: 122). In Skeggs' view it is the normative force of respectability which impels particular forms of sexual expression that conform to a model of legitimate heterosexuality. Skeggs notes that, for the working-class women she interviewed: 'Sexual practice and respectability seem to be at odds with each other, evoking shame in the women's responses (1997: 124). In this sense, the force of respectability works to enforce a particular type of heterosexuality, bound up in women's attempts to behave in ways that are not shameful or, in the end, unrespectable. Yet this operation of regulating heterosexual sexual expression is intimately bound up with love. It is not simply the discourses of sexuality per se which regulate sexual expression. Rather, those discourses intermesh with ideas about love and intimate relationships which, in turn, regulate forms of respectable feminine sexual conduct. Consider the following extract from an interview with Margaret where she describes a 'one-night-stand':

PJ: What about having sex with someone you don't love?
MARGARET: What about it? [laughs]

PJ: Sorry! What's different about it?

MARGARET: Well it's just physical isn't it, it's just a physical thing.

PJ: And what's it like? What are the differences?

MARGARET: Well it's like, when you love someone and you're having sex it's like, you're just, oh, you're so close to them. Physically you're close and emotionally you're close. But if it's just a one night stand and you don't feel anything it's just a one-night-stand and you don't feel anything, it's just pure sex isn't it, it's just physical.

PJ: So what do you feel if you don't feel the closeness? What do you feel like if you're having sex with someone you're not having a relationship with and you're not in love with?

MARGARET: You're just enjoying the sex [laughs] it's just sex.

PJ: And do you enjoy sex as much?

MARGARET: Yeah. Yeah you can still enjoy it just as much.

For Margaret, the experience of 'pure sex' is, as she describes here, different to sex in a love relationship but just as enjoyable. Splitting ideas of 'physical' and 'emotional' experience suggests a definite ability to separate out the discourses of love and sex and gives a form of legitimacy to the experience of 'pure sex' outside of any romantic or love relationship. Access to this type of sexual expression for women (the legitimacy of the 'one-night-stand') relies on a series of inter-connected historical changes which include greater access to more efficient birth-control, the decline of the 'virgin before marriage' narrative of romance, and the effects of changes in women's 'public' lives (in terms of the changing patterns of work and economic status). It seems that what Margaret is describing here is the ability to appropriate a form of sexual expression which is decoupled from the regulation of love.

Yet, as we saw in Margaret's earlier account, love and sex are often in implicit collusion. As Steven Seidman (1991) argues, the relationship between love and sex is a thoroughly contemporary one and is in sharp contrast to, for example, the Victorian conception of love (based on spiritual cleanliness and sexual purity). We have seen that sex is understood to be absolutely central to the notion of intimate love and this is axiomatic to Seidman's historical reading of social change. Yet what this also means is that, far from separating sex from love, sexual expression becomes more securely tied to notions of intimacy. As Margaret goes on to explain, the 'one-night-stand' may be less about 'pure sex' and more about love. I asked her why she wanted to have one-night-stands: 'It makes you feel beautiful and gorgeous and loved. That's why you have one-night-stands I suppose, to feel a bit love I suppose, if there's nobody around.' So there is something more than 'pure sex' in the desire for 'casual' sex where the need to feel attractive and beautiful, and to feel loved and be loved, are framed through this form of sexual practice.

Margaret talked about her experience of one-night-stands a great deal and it became clear that her understanding of sexual expression was completely bound up with issues of love and tied to notions of sexual intimacy. Consider how, in describing her feelings after a one-night-stand, Margaret draws on the discourses of love to position her actions within a broader consideration of sex and intimacy:

MARGARET: I'm thinking back to when I was on my own for about five years and I did have a lot of one-night-stands and sometimes in the morning I just used to think, ughh, I just used to walk out. They were still asleep and I used to just get away, I just wanted to go. I would feel guilty.
PJ: You would feel guilty?
MARGARET: Yeah.
PJ: What would you feel guilty about?
MARGARET: I just knew it was wrong, just to have a one-night-stand. I just know it's wrong but I couldn't stop myself because I wanted to be with someone because I was lonely, very lonely.
PJ: What's wrong about it?
MARGARET: I just don't believe it's right, I don't think it's spiritually right, it's ... I believe you're making a bond between two people and it should only be there when it's something special.
PJ: But you enjoy it?
MARGARET: Yeah, I can still enjoy it, it doesn't affect the sex at all and sometimes you can stay friends [...] But now, when I look back, I can see it was wrong.
PJ: So you think it's wrong because ... are you saying it is wrong because sex should be part of ...
MARGARET: A loving relationship.
PJ: A loving relationship?
MARGARET: Yeah, yeah.
PJ: And what's the guilt like? How do you feel about yourself?
MARGARET: I just think, oh, I'm just disgusted by the amount of men I've had. I just think about it sometimes and I think, god, if anybody knew I would just die. I'm ashamed of it. I often think that, I think I'm so ashamed of my past.

Shame and guilt are, as Skeggs (1997) suggests, the outcome of sexual activity which does not accord with the principles of respectable feminine heterosexual expression. Margaret, as a working-class woman, is 'disgusted' by her own sexual activity because it positions her as unrespectable. Yet this enforcement of sexual respectability is, as we can see, impelled through the relationship between love and sex. Love frames sex in two distinct, yet interconnected, ways. The first is that sex can be seen as a vehicle through which a form of intimacy is attempted. Far from being 'pure sex' (sex only for the sake of sex) the one-night-stand is, for Margaret, a result of feeling 'lonely' and wanting to be 'with someone'. The second, and interrelated, way in which love frames sex is through an appeal to how sex *should* be at the service of love – that sex should be 'special', involve a 'bond' between two people and express something that is 'spiritually' right. What, then, makes Margaret feel guilty and ashamed about one-night-stands is the way that sex fails in two ways: sex neither manufactures the intimacy she desires nor does it express it. Sex does not *make love*.

The subjective effects of this process are the feelings of shame, guilt and disgust. Such feelings are produced through Margaret's reflection upon her own sexual activity which is understood through a normative framework of intimacy (where sex and love, in this case, are not ordered in the 'correct' way). It is precisely because Margaret has had sex outside of a 'loving relationship' which leads to these negative self-reflections (and that is not negated by the sex being 'enjoyable'). What Margaret reveals is the way in which sex and love become that 'horrible ugly mess' in empirical reality when the negotiation of one is not compatible with the other. Because Margaret felt 'lonely' she had sex with men and, in that moment, she attempted to manufacture a form of intimacy. Whether she longed for this intimacy or whether such a desire is a post-hoc result of sexual practice which does not accord with the normative construction of femininity, it is clear that Margaret experiences problems in negotiating intimacy through casual sex. What we can conclude from Margaret's account is that the ability to separate sex from love is, at least, problematic.

The relationship between feminine heterosexual expression and its reliance upon ideas of love can be seen to be operationalized by forms of social and self surveillance. For the women I interviewed, casual sex (or any sex which departed from the ideal of love) was problematic because of the *subjective* and *social* consequences it produced. For several of the women, these were problems associated with their sexual reputation as respectable. When I interviewed Ruth, she told me that she would like to have a one-night-stand and, using the script of a film, told me how she imagines the encounter: 'I would love to meet a guy on a bus and go back to his flat and never see him again.' For Ruth, such an encounter is considered 'exciting' and 'dangerous' because it takes place against a normative version of her own heterosexual sexual practice (she has never had casual sex). But it is also made 'exciting' through the mechanisms which constrain it and these are revealed when I ask Ruth why she wouldn't have this form of anonymous sex:

RUTH: I couldn't bring myself to do it.
PJ: Why?
RUTH: I don't know, there's something inside me. Maybe, maybe I'm just, you hear about people saying 'she's a bit of a slapper, she'll go with anyone' whatever, or 'she's a good girl'. I suppose when I was younger I was a 'good girl', I never went out with or slept with boys, I just didn't. Maybe it's just something that's there in me, I just can't go on a one-night-stand, I just couldn't do it.

The difference between being a 'slapper' and a 'good girl' is extremely important here but the crucial factor is the way that this distinction is described as 'something that's there inside me'. For women, to not be seen as a 'slapper', and to avoid having one's sexual reputation put into question, requires a form of surveillance over one's own sexuality. This type of surveillance is operationalized, as Michel Foucault (1990) suggests, through both an internalization of sexual morality and a continuous hermeneutic surveillance based on monitoring, watching, and caring for the self. Producing oneself as a 'good girl' therefore departs from the principles of what such a personage 'is' – in this sense it is a type of being who does not engage in sexual activity outside of respectable relationships – and requires a form of self scrutiny. As Foucault states: 'I don't think there is a morality without a certain number of practices of the self' ([1984] 1989: 458). It is precisely the ways in which self-surveillance, inscribed into the soul of the subject, relies upon the pervasive 'morality' of heterosexuality which produces a specific way of being – a type of ethics – which the 'good girl' appropriates through a rejection of being a 'slapper'. But crucially, this is operationalized in relationship to the dominant discourses of love. As Barbara explains:

BARBARA: I'm very clear, I'm not someone who would have one-night-stands.
PJ: Why not?
BARBARA: Just, it wouldn't feel right for me, because I know sort of what it would do to me afterwards.
PJ: What would it do to you?
BARBARA: Well, I think, I'm fifty-odd and I have a little thing on my shoulder that says nice girls, nice women wouldn't do that, you know. And it would feel as if it wasn't ... you see, I do see sex as part of an intimate relationship if I'm honest.

For Barbara, who is 51 years old, being a 'nice girl' involves a type of sexuality that is not premised on having one-night-stands but having sex within an intimate relationship. A clear type of self-surveillance is invoked by Barbara when she describes the 'little thing on [her] shoulder' which mediates her sexual expression. From this we can see that there are two central effects produced through the negotiation of sex within the discourses of love. The first is the delimitation around what constitutes a 'nice girl' and the second is the feelings which a one-night-stand would produce ('what', as Barbara describes, 'it would do to me afterwards'). Avoiding these effects – being visible as a 'slapper' and feeling the shame and guilt which Margaret spoke of above – are the points at which forms of heterosexual sexuality are negotiated by the women. And it is, as we can see, the normative force which love exerts over such practices that is crucial.

Is this process differentiated across age? For the younger women I interviewed there is little difference between their accounts and those of the older women. For Susan, who clearly stated 'I don't believe that you can sleep with someone purely for sex', a causal sexual encounter is out of the question. Susan told me that she would never consider a one-night-stand and that if she did experience such a thing she would be worried that she would 'get attached' to the person. For her, sex should only be an expression of love and should only take place in an intimate relationship. The normative force of this interrelationship between sex and love, and the way that such a relationship inscribes and legitimates a particular model of feminine heterosexuality, is apparent in the way that Susan describes one of her female friends who engages in, what she describes as, the 'taboo' of casual sex:

SUSAN: I had my reservations about one lass, a friend. I thought, is she confused about her sexuality or something because she seemed to be a total man-eater [laughs]. She used to go out and pin point a bloke and say 'right, that's him for the night' sort of thing, and I'd seen her take him home and in the morning she's like, 'we had sex'. And I was like, 'ah, I don't believe you'. But she, she used to go for all these blokes but at the same time a lot of people thought she was gay. And I thought, is this like a closet kind of thing. And, is she like, going with all these blokes because she's trying to hide the fact that she's gay, or she is embarrassed about it, or frightened, within herself, you know, having a conflict within herself, that she might be gay.

Being a 'man-eater' and practising casual sex problematizes both the normative relationship of sex and love and the heterosexuality of the subject who acts outside of it. Susan's friend is positioned as having a 'conflict within herself' because she does not conform to the principles of heterosexual practice which suggest that sex is something one does in an intimate relationship. Although the language of 'slapper' is not used here we can see that Susan's friend is positioned through the notion of excess – her sexual practice exceeds what is considered to be normal and thus problematizes her own normality. What is being described here is a pathology of sexuality; a sexuality which is out of control and irrational (hence the question over her heterosexuality). What Susan is asserting is a normative framework for evaluating heterosexual feminine practice and the ways in which that framework relies on ideas of how sex should be enacted. The practice described above is rendered illegitimate by Susan because it seems incomprehensible to her – her belief that sex is something one should do when in love means that casual sex reveals, not a desire to have sex, but a deep psychological or biological problem (sex becomes a way of 'trying to hide the fact'). A socially constructed morality is therefore inscribed into the interiority of the subject; a whole psychology is questioned through the normative force of a particular kind of heterosexuality which appears to be 'natural'.

None of the women I interviewed expressed the view that sex could be practised freely outside of an intimate relationship without problem or issue.

Everyone spoke of the problems that casual sex caused. One of the youngest women I interviewed, Elizabeth, told me that she thought a 'one-night-stand and things is just physical, there's absolutely no love there at all, it's just purely for yourself', indicating the appropriation of a certain discourse of sex free from the constraints of love. But in talking about an experience of a 'one-night-stand' Elizabeth told me that it had been 'horrible' because the person 'didn't feel anything for me' and 'had nothing to do with me afterwards'. Elizabeth felt 'used', 'cheap' and her 'self-respect went down'. Yet she had felt, previous to the experience, that she would be able to 'handle' a one-night-stand and that it would be something that she might enjoy. What made her feel negative about it afterwards?

ELIZABETH: I think it's probably just the whole stigma that's attached to it because everyone, well not everyone, but a lot of people around you, well all my friends, were like 'what have you done that for, you shouldn't do things like that'. And because people tell you that it makes you feel bad. And also the fact that there was no feeling there as well, it was just purely, it was just sex and that was it. And I think that feeling actually after having made love to someone, where you know there is feeling there, it wasn't close. And also the images of some people who have one-night-stands a lot, or that you see in the media and you see around you all the time, they're always portrayed as bad and sort of cheap as well. And so that probably has a knock-on effect and makes you think you shouldn't do it.

Elizabeth identifies three factors which influenced her negative experience of a one-night-stand. The first is the response she met from her peers that, in suggesting that this was a form of practice that was wrong, made her feel 'bad'. The second is that the sex involved no 'feeling' and was not 'close'. This is compared with the types of feeling and closeness that she would associate with 'making love' which were missing from the encounter. And third, Elizabeth identifies the loose conglomeration of symbolic media which represent a particularly trenchant view of women who have one-night-stands as 'cheap'. What this brings together is a clear understanding of the ways in which the social construction of normative heterosexual sexual practice is transferred, through interlocution with others and one's social context, into regulatory practices and subjective feelings. Love is crucial to this process because it provides the discursive mechanism through which reflections on sexual practice are mediated: in all three examples, provided by Elizabeth, it is sex outside of a 'feeling' relationship which is problematic (none of the feelings associated with love, as detailed in Chapter 1, are present). It is therefore important to note, as Skeggs argues, that for women 'sexuality is not an expression of their selves, but an expression of the unequal power relations in which they are located' (1997: 120). And this is something which the women are fully aware of because they know (as several of them told me) that the viability of casual sex for men and women is fundamentally different. The 'double standard' which works to produce women as 'slags' and men as 'jack the lad' is trenchantly operationalized around heterosexual sex. As Elizabeth told me: 'I think [sex] is a very natural thing but I just think because of the stigma that has been attached to it now that it's something that is, not prohibited, but suppressed.' One could dispute the sovereignty and essentiality which Elizabeth accords to sex, but one could not argue with her analysis of stigma. It is precisely this notion of stigma, and the fear of it, which inscribes types of self-surveillance around women's sexuality.

The final point I want to make about the regulation of women's sexual practices through love is about the normative construction of gendered sexualities. Women come to a sexual relationship, not as neutral sexual beings, but with the full history of the social construction of gender mediating their feelings and practices. The women I interviewed had very specific understandings about the gendered differences of sexuality and the ways in which those differences required specific negotiations of sex. For instance, a trenchant view is that men are more sexually driven than women: 'most men seem to be ruled by their willies to begin with' (Ruth), 'they think with their trousers' (Susan), 'in my experience the man is more demanding of sex than the woman' (Patricia). Women are often placed in a strategic relation with men as the partner who must 'fend off' sexual advances and sublimate initial male desire. This is a pervasive 'truth' which acts as a mechanism through which sexual negotiations take place and subject positions consolidated. In dialogic opposition to that view of men, women are often seen to need a more 'emotional' engagement rather than a sexual one. As Ellen described to me, she felt 'exploited' by one partner's desire to have sex with her immediately after they met. For many of the women, an initial distrust of sex is built around feelings that men would simply want to 'use' them and that they will leave once they have, as Susan said, 'got what they wanted'. In this sense, the women in this study feared immediate sexual contact because such behaviour might negate a longer-term relationship (that such an encounter will become a one-night-stand).

We must also recognize, therefore, a fundamental, and contradictory, premise on which female sexuality is built. Women often become the 'gatekeepers' of a male sexuality which seeks to overcome the restrictions placed in its way. Yet, conversely, the woman who does not adequately maintain such restrictions is seen to be undesirable as an intimate or long-term partner. As Alex told me: 'I wouldn't want to go out with someone who had been around.' And, for Douglas, the fact that his current girlfriend has had more sexual partners than himself is something which he finds uncomfortable because, in his opinion, it is men who ought to be promiscuous and not women. The respectable heterosexual woman, the desired object of a love relation, is often desexualized and constructed as chaste. That women who desire an intimate relationship would seek to approximate this subject position is not surprising. To be seen as a 'slag', as someone who would immediately have sex with a man, positions women against the more desirable position of the 'good' sexually ambivalent female.

There is another important reason why women might feel ambivalent about casual sex. As Margaret explains:

MARGARET: I mean most one-night-stands they're not going to bother to please a woman but if you're in a relationship they'll take time to get to know the person, to get to know the woman [. . .]
PJ: So is it that they don't know what to do?
MARGARET: Well some of them don't, no. But if they do know they can't be bothered because they're too selfish. There are not many, it's not very often you get a good lover who'll take the time out to please a woman. Not many men will put a woman before their feelings, and that's the good ones that'll put the women first, like the women have their orgasm first before the man. There's not many men will do that, they just want their end away don't they.

The difference between a 'good' and a 'selfish' lover may be an important factor in the negotiation of casual sex for women. The lack of sexual satisfaction that a 'one-night-stand' delivers is a clear source of disappointment for Margaret. And yet we cannot see this outside of the broader relations of heterosexuality in which it is situated. The ways in which women and men arrive at sexual practices inflects the detail of those practices. It is the belief that men only want '*their* end away' that means that women's needs become constructed through this negotiation. Therefore, in order to have the type of sex in which a considerate male lover will enact a form of sexual practice that is not simply about the act of male orgasm, intimacy must be secured. Specifically, it must be intimacy founded on a form of reciprocity which is less likely in a casual or anonymous encounter. How women consolidate intimacy is through an appeal to love. Love, therefore, organizes sexual activity into types of practices which are more and less desirable, rules out particular acts, and, as such, consolidates the belief that 'better' sex is to be found in *making love*.

Men, love and sex

A male patient of the psychoanalyst Adam Phillips comments during analysis: 'you can't browse people, that's what gays have got over us, they can cruise' (2001: 62). Conventional wisdom tells us that male heterosexual sexuality is confounded by its strategic relation with female sexuality because men must sublimate initial desire under the rubric of 'sexual convention'. In this sense, men must suppress their 'urge' to have sex because of the conventions built around heterosexual practice with women. Thus, the preoccupation with homosexual sexuality arises because of the 'jealousy' of the 'loveless fuck' that gay men have access to. For what is cruising if not the freedom from all social constraints (constraints that are imagined to be imposed by women) organized around love? Even Foucault was, surprisingly, convinced by the argument: 'the modern homosexual experience has no relation at all to courtship' (1983: 149) and 'I think that what most bothers those who are not gay about gayness is the gay lifestyle, not sex acts themselves' (1983: 153). Whether homosexual men practise relationships outside of 'courtship' is an empirical question and one that I cannot address here. As for the question of gay 'lifestyle' and 'sex acts' Foucault is, in my opinion, mistaken in his emphasis because, as I argue in Chapter 4, male heterosexual identity is founded precisely through a negotiation of sex 'acts'.

Nevertheless, the common sense view of sexuality is that it is men who want to practise sex outside of love and that love presents a set of constraints from which to escape. Such a view is premised on ideas about male sexuality as a natural set of desires which are 'blocked' or 'directed' by romantic convention. Thus, theorists like Anthony Giddens (1992) also appeal to male homosexuality as the vanguard of a type of sexual expression which has released itself from the 'shackles' of romantic love. This, argue Bell and Binnie, 'leads him into romanticizing queers' (2000: 127). It is not homosexuality I wish to deal with here, but the notion that there exists a state of sexual activity which is, in whatever way, free from the social constraint instigated by the mediating dynamics of love. Is there a way, in other words, of enacting 'pure sex' outside of the normative ideals of intimacy?

There can be no doubt that men are placed in relation to the discourses of love and sex in different ways to women. There can also be no dispute, as we shall see, that men can appropriate and legitimize casual sex in ways which are profoundly different to women (and can utilize casual sex for different purposes). Yet it would be misleading to argue that men do not appeal to the notion of love as a way of negotiating heterosexual sex. As we saw above, and as the following quotation from Mark shows, love is clearly implicated in ideas about sex for men:

PJ: Would [casual sex] be something that you would ever do?
MARK: No.
PJ: Why not?
MARK: Because I feel it's sacred if you like. It should be for people that are in love. You know, it is a beautiful thing, it's a meaningful thing. And I don't think that it's something that you can take lightly. I'm not a one-night-stand sort of person, where I can just like go to club and score with them and then shag them and then say 'ta ra'. Couldn't do it, never would.
PJ: Why not?
MARK: Because like I say, it's an important thing, it's a beautiful thing, it's a special thing, and it should be reserved for special relationships.

Quite clearly Mark thinks that sex should be at the service of the 'beautiful thing' which is love. Of course, there are several problems with this view, because sex is not something which is *only* reserved for 'special' relationships; that it 'should' be is therefore a conceptual rather than an empirical matter. Throughout his life Mark has experienced casual sex and so, even in view of his ideal opinion of sex and love, it is quite clear that such an idealization does not always 'work'. More generally, men know that sex is frequently not associated with love: it can involve violence, it might be a strategy of domination employed against women, it is often rape, it can be a weapon of war, it is pornography, it is enjoyable and momentary pleasure. So why does love still exert, even in the face of all of these facets of sex, a normative force? How does the normativity of 'beautiful' sex set up certain parameters through which sex is negotiated? It is quite clear that Mark does not wish to 'cruise' for sex, doesn't want to (as he believes he could) go to a club and 'shag' someone and then say 'ta ra'. Yet, what if Mark did want to do those things? Would that imply a sexual expression free from the constraints of love?

To split the feeling and practices associated with sex and love from one another is something which is prevalent in some of the men's accounts (see Lees, 1993, for a discussion of this phenomenon). When I interviewed Peter, we talked about the relationship between love and sex and he was clear about the distinctions he can make:

PETER: When I've been with people and they've talked about being in love with me, during sex, I've found it a turn off. In the sense that I've actually wanted, I've wanted sex for pleasure basically and I've ... it's something, yeah, it's never been, in a sense, I've put sex away from love completely. In fact I don't want the two to have anything to do with one another, I really don't. It's quite cold, but you know, I don't know maybe this will change, but so far I've found a time for intimacy and a time for sex. But in a sense, sex for me has been intimate but, I think also I think I've preferred it with people when it hasn't been based around, when it hasn't basically been based around love, you know, to be honest, pleasure for pleasure's sake.

PJ: So, sex is not a big part of being in love?

PETER: No, I don't think so. I think being in love, or whatever it is, is quite beyond sex to be honest with you, yeah, I think so, for me at any rate.

There are a number of ways in which sex and love are operating here. First, there is a distinct separation of sex from love around the notion of pleasure for the sake of pleasure. It is interesting that, in abstracting sex from love, that such a distinction around pleasure is made (a distinction which is the diametric opposite to the one Margaret made). By releasing himself from all the associated 'commitments' which come with a love relationship, Peter is arguing for a form of pleasure which is directly related to his own gratification ('getting his end away', as Margaret said). Yet there is also the way in which the presence of love can interfere with that sphere of pleasure and can disrupt the experience of it – love can be a 'turn off'. Thus, the analytic separation of sex from love relies on a delimitation of sex *with* love; they are, in one sense, reliant upon each other. As Peter states, there is a time for intimacy (where sex and love are brought together) and a time for sex. He has, he says, experienced sex in a love relationship but he *prefers* having sex with a person he has no intimate investment with. Conversely we find an idealization and reification of love as 'beyond' sex. So the split between love and sex is achieved relationally, but to achieve what?

Peter goes on to explain: 'the person I have been infatuated with I haven't even thought sexually about at all, you know, it's almost like the reverse.' In this sense, there is a reification and idealization of the desired love object outside of sexual desire and lust. Sexual desire, on the other hand, is directed towards objects in which no love is established. Whilst we can acknowledge the fundamental separation of sex from love we can also see that such a separation relies on maintaining boundaries and drawing lines around which relationship will constitute what feelings. It also constructs the desired object in two distinct ways: the 'pure' desexualized woman to love and the sexualized woman to have sex with. What Peter describes is a process that was well-known to Freud when he described how men, but not women, have a tendency to idealize and worship their love objects *through* their desexualization. For Freud, the inability for men to recognize their first love object (their mothers) as sexual can lead them to split love and sex which results, through the repetitive ritual of romantic love, in an idealization of the love-object as unsexual and a sexualization of those objects where they see no love: 'Where they love they do not desire and where they desire they cannot love. They seek objects which they do not need to love, in order to keep their sensuality away from the objects they love.' This results in a situation whereby 'their love consists in a physical *debasement* of the sexual object' and 'the overvaluation that normally attaches to the sexual object being reversed' ([1912] 1991e: 251).

Whether or not we accept Freud's analysis of the cause of this separation of love and sex, the point is that we can identify that such a split often occurs. Yet what is crucial is that there remains a mutual reliance between the two 'spheres' of activity. Even where sex is split from love, it relies on maintaining the distinction. What actually becomes 'pleasure for pleasure's sake' is reliant on keeping sex away from love. And yet, as we can see, we are only ever in a position to judge this type of pleasure when it is compared to other forms of sexual activity which are bound up with intimacy and love. Thus, Peter's description is the opposite of claims about casual sex being free from the restrictions of love or representing an *escape* from the construction of love; on the contrary, it highlights the ways in which sex is reliant on the conceptual notion of love which frames it. 'We must not think', argues Foucault, 'that by saying yes to sex, one says no to power' (1979: 157). This is a crucial point because we need to recognize the ways in which love continues to exert a force over sexual practice even where such practice seemingly departs from it.

When I interviewed Barry, we talked about his sexual experiences before he was married. He told me that when he was younger he had had several sexual encounters that had ended once the women had started to 'force' him onto the 'territory' of love, commitment and a long-term relationship. He was quite candid about the fact that once he had experienced sex with a woman he got bored and ended the relationship. This happened many times and Barry presents it as relatively unproblematic. However, Barry did identify a number of problems associated with such practices when he explained that his experiences of casual sex were less than satisfactory. Although Barry's testimony could suggest an unproblematic appropriation of sex outside of the constraints of love, it is also interesting to note how love acts as a framing device because, in managing the boundaries of the 'territories' of sex and love, Barry is forced to sculpt a form of sexual practice in dialogic relation to love:

BARRY: I think if you're straight into bed with somebody you must miss something. I can't think what it is you miss, you must miss the sort of growth period, you know if you go straight to having it away. And you think because you've had it away you're in love, and you think because you're in love you better get married, or live together, and then you find you've got nothing. I mean in the end, as I say, once you've explored all the sex territory what is there? You know if you're dead lucky you've got other things. But I think what you must have done in the courtship period is explore the other things first, you know. Sex was very important and sexual release was very important, no matter how you did it, but it was, yeah, it's a good thought that, you'd looked at all the angles, because you had to, because you weren't going to have sex, or you agreed that you weren't going to have sex before marriage.

Relating sex to love, in this account, departs from two central beliefs: the first is that sex is very important as a form of release (it is a biological prerequisite of male sexuality); the second is that sex is always 'mixed up' with feelings of love. Sex leads, Barry argues, to feelings of love and to a desire to ratify that love in marriage or living together. Yet, as Barry notes, such an outcome might be based on something inauthentic, a misguided sense of intimacy created by sex. This is why Barry invokes the notion of the 'growth period' of 'courtship' that is seen as an important mechanism for evaluating authentic feelings of love. Such a period is necessary because, as Barry asks, what happens once you've explored all the 'sex territory' and there is nothing left? In this sense, sex is not a neutral form of expression outside of the rubric of love because it is inculcated with other factors of intimacy and of how sex 'works'.

Even when men talked about liking or wanting casual sex, there was still recourse to discourses of love. Whilst the men I interviewed did not identify the same problematic issues with casual sex as those of the women – they do not have to negotiate feelings of shame and respectability – there is a sense in which casual sex is understood to be less enjoyable than sex in a love relationship. As William describes:

WILLIAM: I'd say that I'd probably slept with people and there hasn't been an emotional sort of connection there. Not very often, and I'd probably feel that the physical side of it has never been as good as when there'd been an emotional connection there. But I feel that it can be separated out by men, mostly.

Whilst William believes that men can effect a legitimate separation between love and sex (and this itself constructs a view of both masculine and feminine heterosexuality), he also pays attention to the ways in which the 'physical side' of a sexual relationship is always better when there is an 'emotional connection'. Again, we see a hierarchical relationship around types of sex which is created by the injunction of love. The type of separation which is achieved around sex and love is reliant on a particular model of male and female sexuality. The men I spoke to believed that women are more 'emotionally driven' and that they are more in need of love. Men, on the other hand, were seen as more 'visually' and 'biologically' orientated. As William told me, men can 'go through the motions' of sex because 'it's a bodily need, like eating, sleeping, that sort of thing'. And yet, given that William has also said that sex in a love relationship is better, why would (even with a belief in the biological necessity of sex) he want to 'go through the motions'. What does casual sex offer men?

What casual sex offers men is the ability to practise a type of sexual activity which is, as Margaret described above, concerned only with 'going through the motions' of male sexual pleasure:

WILLIAM: [...] when you're outside a relationship, when it's just perhaps a one-off or something, it's a bit more selfish. Perhaps because you're not emotionally attached, I don't know, maybe you don't care enough, you're not going to see that person again, you don't really care as much if they're getting satisfaction from sleeping with them, but you would do if it was a partner you were looking to have a long-term relationship, or a life together, with. I mean for a lot of guys it's going through the motions maybe. That's my feeling on it.
PJ: Going through the motions...?
WILLIAM: Going through the motions physically for a guy. It's a bodily need, like eating, sleeping, that sort of thing.

However, this conceptualization of satisfying this 'bodily need' is, not only delimited around its relation to love, but structured in relation to issues of sexual performance and self-esteem in different contexts:

WILLIAM: I don't suppose any guy wants to be thought of as poor in bed but I think if it's just a one-off and he's not trying to see her again or have any sort of relationship I don't think he's going to care as much as if he's got an emotional attraction or a relationship as such.

PETER: Maybe I separate the two because I find sex quite an intimate thing, and that, maybe it's because, like your body, sometimes I feel ashamed of my body, and things like that, it's quite private, and so like it's . . . well, you expose yourself physically to someone and you do, you know, you're worried that if you're in love with them and, I suppose, if you don't actually care about them sexually then in a different way, if you just want sex from them, then you probably don't care about how they feel about you, yeah, or how you look.

Whilst these two accounts are slightly different, they focus on the same central theme: the way in which casual sex is a way of negating problems associated with men's own self-worth as lovers. For William, if he has no emotional investment in a sexual partner then his sexual performance is of limited concern because, in never seeing the person again, he can minimize the subjective feelings of embarrassment and shame which he will feel should he 'perform' badly during sex.[8] For Peter, sex can involve a level of intimacy in which he has to expose himself to another person. Such a level of exposure matters more or less in different contexts because, where there is no love involved, he cares less about what the other person thinks. Of course, being able to operationalize this split is important in itself but it is the fact that there has to be a split which is crucial. In this study, men continually expressed the view that casual sex is the 'other' to intimacy and they position it against the type of sex which is experienced in love. For some, as outlined above, it is a form of sexual activity which brings with it its own pleasures – perhaps not the pleasure of 'closeness' but certainly the opportunity to attempt to approximate a particular type of sexual activity (with a particular type of woman). But crucially, for the majority of men I interviewed, casual sex was not conceptualized as a particularly desirable type of activity. In fact, in most of the accounts (with the exception of Peter) men express the view that sex is 'better' when framed by love.

Men may have more of a 'choice' when considering casual sex (they may be able to experience it more freely than women) but it is a choice which is built on a hierarchy. For two of the older men in my study, casual sex was not something that was necessarily a good choice because it denied an appropriation of the more desirable feelings of love:

BARRY: You can do the sex without the mutual grooming, you can do the sex without actually being close, and you can just get up and walk away. Whereas if you're in love you do the sex and you don't want to get up and walk away. You know, you want to stay a bit longer so that there's more sex and more of the feeling of rightness, wanting to be together.

PHILLIP: I feel at the age of 56 I shouldn't be going out and, sort of, on the rampage and one-night-stands, it's just not what a 56 year old does. I'm more sort of laid back and sedate, want to take things at a slower pace. Don't want to take risks any more. Whereas in your teens and twenties you're able to take that on board, the risk factor.

It is the 'mutual grooming' and the feeling of 'rightness' which characterizes the most important aspects of Barry's relationship with his wife. For Phillip, at the age of 56, the idea of one-night-stands is not a 'risk factor' he wants to encounter. Phillip wants a companionable relationship where sex is a fundamental part of, and an expression of, love. Sex itself is therefore felt to involve a set of emotional risks which need to be avoided. But Phillip, although invoking the view that younger men might have one-night-stands, never did this himself. For him, sex has always been an expression of love and framed within an intimate relationship. So, as Barry explains, men *can* do casual sex and 'get up and walk away' but this is framed by another type of more desirable intimate activity. As Jonathan Rutherford argues of male desire: 'The appeal of seduction lies in [the] separation of desire from need: the illusion of pure sex, unencumbered by intimacy or commitment' (1999: 143). And the idea of 'pure sex' is, in terms of these men's accounts, very much an illusion because it is a state which can never really be attained. To want a loveless and momentary experience of sexual gratification is something which some of the men do wish for. But, in experiencing those moments, they enter into a schema of sex which is underwritten by the normative force of heterosexual love and intimacy. They therefore have no choice but to conceptualize sex in relation to love and to assess their practices accordingly.

Pleasure for pleasure's sake is difficult to achieve because, placed in relation to intimate sexual love, it seems to lack something. What it lacks is that set of feelings which were described in the last chapter, that timeless sense of 'fusing' together with another and the whole range of emotions and sensations which arise because of it. Men can separate sex from love but most of the men I interviewed were extremely motivated by the compelling language of love. The result is that men find themselves, like women, in a state whereby casual sex is experienced 'inside' of the rubric of love. Men and women practise casual sex in particular ways and they experience different subjective effects; but both men and women use love as a way of negotiating sex, both inside and outside of 'relationships'. Whilst sexuality is felt to be a natural and normal form of human life, it is continually conceptualized in relation to the discourses of love.

Conclusion

Historical changes in sexual activity are multifarious and it has not been my intent to deal with them here. My data would support a number of theorizations (from changes in the public sphere to the impact of sexually transmitted diseases) about sexual change across recent history. The central issue which has concerned me in this chapter is how love provides a mediating framework through which sex is conceptualized and practised. The discursive construction of love provides a way through which sexual relationships are negotiated and is premised on the axiomatic principle that sex should be a vehicle for establishing intimacy. The most desirable form of intimacy is believed to adhere in the 'best' combination of sex and love, where sex is *making* love. Thus, love not only constrains sex but produces it; it acts as a framework through which different types of sexual activity are conceptualized and enacted.

Ideas about love frame and reproduce forms of sexual activity which are deemed safe and secure or risky and dangerous (and this, of course, is experienced in different ways by men and women). Without love, sex would lose its speculative power and force — for what would be the 'quick shag' and the 'loveless fuck' without the regulation of the sex-love model which deems these casual encounters 'taboo'? That sex *should* be an expression of love means that, when it isn't, it takes on a significant meaning. And, as such, this works to produce heterosexual sex in particular ways under particular circumstances and to delimit the ways in which we relate to each other as sexual beings. Crucially, it produces particular heterosexual subject positions which make available legitimate and delimited feminine and masculine forms of sexual expression. Sex becomes a nodal point in the knot of intimate relations which is neither 'pure' nor 'physical' but enacted under the shadow of the broader relations in which it is situated. This, of course, is a gendered phenomenon and is experienced by men and women in different ways. It is specifically to gender that I now wish to turn in the next chapter, to look at how heterosexual love produces and sustains distinct configurations of gendered subjectivity.

3 The lack of love

Producing heterosexual subjectivities

He makes me feel like a woman.
(Margaret)

'Romantic ideals', writes Stevi Jackson, 'can be deeply embedded in our subjectivities even when we are critical of them' (1999: 119). Yet combining a successful critical analysis of such ideals with a working model of how they are transferred into, and endure in, subjectivities has proved something of a lacuna in sociology. How, for instance, are we to account for the ways in which we may be critical and questioning of the social construction of love, with its ideas of chemistry and power, and experience the disappointments of relationships whilst, at the same time, participate in, and take pleasure from, the practice of loving? 'Here', writes Jackson, 'I find myself confronting what seems to me a major gap in feminist theory – the lack of a convincing theory of subjectivity' (1999: 119). Some feminists (for example de Beauvoir 1997; Firestone, 1972) attempted to solve this 'problem' of subjectivity and love by understanding women as ideological slaves to romance (which served the interests of men who exploited them under the 'cover' of love). Strikingly, women are described as simultaneously oppressed by the patriarchal conditions of heterosexual relationships *and* 'falsely conscious' of these conditions. Under such conditions any heterosexual desire becomes seen, as Sheila Jeffreys argues, as a 'desire that is organized around eroticised dominance and submission', the 'grease that oils the machinery of male supremacy', and the outcome of an ideological system which 'makes its followers loyal' (1996: 76–77). The question becomes: *how* does it achieve this?

This question is taken up by Denise Thompson who, in rejecting the possibility of a reciprocal or equal heterosexual love relationship within contemporary social relations, argues that 'to be heterosexual, all a woman needs to do is fall unthinkingly in with what everyone else does', whereas to be a lesbian 'requires some measure of self-reflection, or at least self-consciousness' (1993: 170). Thompson's argument represents a dubious, but still commonly heard, opinion: heterosexual women are at best duped, at worst stupid. But if heterosexual women lack a form of enlightened consciousness, then it would be difficult, under the rubric of Thompson's argument, to account for Robyn Rowland's opinion of her heterosexual relationship:

> One of the fears in lesbian relationships is the anxiety of merging; the anxiety of not knowing where you end and the other begins [...] I think it is one reason I remain heterosexual: the fear of merging is not part of a heterosexual relationship. Because of the obvious differences – physically and in our approach to the world – separateness is retained.
>
> (1993: 77)

For Rowland, self-consciousness around sexuality is certainly not at issue. Yet she raises some crucial questions about the ways in which we think about ourselves, as gendered and sexualized beings, and how that positions us in relation to the gendered and sexed other. There is an explicit materialization of gender and sex within Rowland's account because 'difference' is secured through a relational and complementary system set up within heterosexuality. But these differences are *desirable* for Rowland; they are not merely 'imposed' upon her because she is 'unthinking' but, rather, something she actively wants. She desires a marked, gendered other in order to consolidate a form of subjectivity which has definite parameters, edges and an 'end'. In this sense, Rowland's sense of self, and her sense of gender, is actively reliant on the 'obvious' differences set up by heterosexuality. But this is not simply a determining mechanism under which Rowland labours as an 'unknowing' bearer of social relations; on the contrary, these are differences through which Rowland consolidates her sense of self and *produces* a subjectivity.

What is interesting here is that, if we take Rowland's account and compare it with understandings of romantic love (particularly the notion of 'fusing' together), we find a significant tension. On the one hand, we have a form of gender difference on which heterosexuality relies and, on the other, a set of discourses which construct love as the mechanism to negate such difference: by making two parts into one whole. As Allan Hunter argues: 'To be in love is to be vulnerable to the opinions, needs, wants of the other who is now no longer strictly other at all' (1993: 162). There is a central tension in Hunter's description of being in love – it is being in a state through which one is continually marked by an other who, through the specific act of loving, one attempts to make one's own. And it is this specific tension that I want to explore in this chapter because it reveals the way in which our subjectivities are enmeshed with the other through the love relationships we enter into and, more fundamentally, that our subjectivities are constructed in relation to marked differences operationalized by heterosexuality. What I want to analyse here is a duality which is present in the social construction of love: the way in which the love relationship both facilitates a materialization of gendered difference *and* is premised on the belief that it can transcend such difference through the fusion of 'two into one'. The social construction of love facilitates the construction of gendered identities *because* it promises to consolidate (complete) them. It is within this dual operation of love that we can find, if not an answer, then an explanation of the problem of subjectivity because we can find what makes heterosexual love so compelling: its promise to both confirm, and to overcome, the gender positions which we inhabit.

The prison of the self

One of the most compelling aspects of romantic love is the potential positive effect it can have on the self. Love is often seen, as Charles Lindholm argues, as 'a creative act of human imagination, arising as a cultural expression of deep existential longing for an escape from the prison of the self' (1995: 57). For Lindholm, modern love is akin to a religious experience through which the subject enters into an ecstatic and sacred union with a beloved as a way of transcending the limits of atomized embodiment. This is a remarkably different way of thinking about the effects of love upon subjectivity than, for example, Rich's (1980) account of love as one of the mechanisms through which women experience a colonization of consciousness within the patriarchal relations of heterosexual sociality. For Rich, heterosexual love is far from a transcending experience, for it represents a process through which women's subjectivity is constrained and delimited. But why then is love, for men as well as women, such an enduring and popular way to experience pleasure and joy?

In Weber's (1948) classic account of romantic love, we find a nuanced approach to the ideas of freedom and constraint. The modern lover, for Weber, uses the romantic process to find a haven from the encroachment of rationality into every other aspect of his/her life but, in attempting to escape into a private sphere, serves only to compound the instrumental rationality of the 'outside world'. For Weber, love is constituted as an ecstatic process which allows the lovers to escape from 'the cold skeleton hands of the rational orders, just as completely as from the banality of everyday routine' (1948: 347). What Weber describes is the dynamic interrelationship between the 'outside' world and, what becomes, the 'inside' sphere of love. This interrelationship can be theorized in a number of ways: for Giddens (1992) the 'inside' of confluent democracy not only resists the broader social relations in which it is situated but is a sphere in which such relations are transformed (certainly not a new idea: see Young and Willmott, 1973); Lindholm describes love as 'the search for ways to escape the burden of loneliness while avoiding confrontation with a cold and indifferent cosmos' (1995: 67) which, as Collins and Gregor argue, means that 'the lovers must protect their world and separate it from the surrounding society' (1995: 72).

Love becomes that sphere in which individuals can retreat from the exterior world and be most at home. Yet, as Barthes (1990) would argue, such a view operates through a 'disreality' which (and Weber would agree) produces only the illusion of escape.

For Marx, the only place the alienated being of capitalism can feel free is in the private sphere of 'personal' relationships.[1] For Marx, like Weber, romantic love does not offer any 'real' freedom but, rather, presents a type of illusionary sphere to which the individual turns as a result of social marginalization and fragmentation. For Sartre (1958), love is an existential 'game' in which human beings seek a lover as a way of discovering their own freedom through the appropriation of the other's freedom. Self-realization is at the heart of love for Sartre, but it remains an essentially unobtainable goal because self-freedom is negated by a possessive tyranny of appropriation instituted in the relationship between lovers. The notion of self-realization through love is central to Hegel's conception of desire. For Hegel, the 'journey' of life is a dialectical process of self-conscious discovery mediated through an unfolding movement between the subject and the objective world. As Butler argues of Hegel's desiring subject: 'Desire is *intentional* in that it is always desire *of* or *for* a given object or Other, but it is also *reflexive* in the sense that desire is a modality in which the subject is both discovered and enhanced' (1999b: 25, italics in original). The sensuous practice of desiring subjects leads to a discovery of the self through the beloved other (a process that Marx would appropriate from Hegel and render into the theory of labouring praxis).

What is central to all these theorizations of love is that the self is a project which is dynamically engaged and engendered, whether negatively or positively, through the interlocution which love enables. Love, as Foucault (1988) would have termed it, is a technology of the self that offers us a way to 'work' on our subjectivities and to affect certain ways of feeling about ourselves. Love retains its power precisely because it offers us a range of opportunities with which to engage with our own sense of being in the world; it is a process grounded around questions of self, questions of existence and organized through our relationships with others. But the ways we work upon ourselves, the manner in which we elaborate our subjectivities, is neither a voluntaristic process nor one that is universally experienced. One of the sharpest points of differentiation is around gender where, as we will see, the 'loving self' is constructed in particular ways. The work on subjectivity, in which active social agents engage, is reliant on pre-existing gendered norms which become manifest, in the subject positions of masculine and feminine, through the appropriation of heteronormative forms of love. So, whilst love can be thought of as a way out of the atomized self, it is also bound within relations of sex, gender and sexuality which allow us to 'be' particular versions of ourselves. Loving, I want to argue, does not unfetter the self, but produces specific subjective positions which adhere to the gender relations which heterosexuality puts into motion.

The law of difference and desire

We cannot underestimate the ways in which ways of loving rely on the binary of masculine/feminine set up through the heterosexual matrix (Butler, 1993). The Lacanian model of how gender is assumed is a useful framework for considering the force of the feminine/masculine binary in the subjectifying process of love. For Lacan (1998), sex difference is produced, not because of innate biological difference, but through language which positions subjects in a strategic relation to the phallic signifier. The phallus is always a signifier and never the actual anatomical difference between biological beings. However, it becomes translated into discrete biological sex through the subject's assumption of the illusion of 'real' sexual difference (organized around the penis). It is within the essentially fictitious world of the phallus (fictitious because the phallus has become the penis) that identity is secured against the other who marks the boundaries of what one 'is' (i.e. with or without the phallus). It is this process – the symbolic law of the phallus which is transferred into *material* sexual difference – which is axiomatic to Judith Butler's theorization of the compulsory regime of performative heterosexuality. For Butler, there is a circular causality in operation within 'compulsory heterosexuality' because, in order to pass as a viable sexed being, the subject must incite and reiterate the symbolic law of sex in order that a specific bodily morphology corresponds to the matrix of heterosexual intelligibility which, consequently, serves only to produce the illusion that the law is 'natural' (that is, that 'sex difference' is a real, physical, biological materiality which defines two original and discrete categories of beings – man and woman). Thus, for Butler:

> the symbolic ought to be rethought as a series of normativising injunctions that secures the borders of sex through the threat of psychosis, abjection, psychic unlivability. And further, that this 'law' can only remain a law to the extent that it compels the differentiated citations and approximations called 'feminine' and 'masculine'. The presumption that the symbolic law of sex enjoys a separable ontology prior and autonomous to its assumption is contravened by the notion that the citation of the law is the very mechanism of its production and articulation.
>
> (1993: 15)

For Butler, it is the operation of the performative articulations of masculine/feminine (themselves rendered through forced interpellation) that sustains, through continual reiteration, both sex difference and the law which regulates it. This is an interesting 'twist' to the Lacanian view of the phallus. Butler introduces a central tension into the Lacanian notion of 'symbolic' law by repudiating the view that such laws are pre-social (and thus opening a space for considering non-heterosexual configurations of desire – an enduring problem in psychoanalytic theory). In a critique which extends Foucault's life-long attack on the 'poor technicians of desire [psychoanalysts] who would subjugate the multiplicity of desire to the two-fold law of structure and lack' ([1984] 2000: XII), Butler retains the concept of the phallocentric law by reworking it as an interpellative function of heterosexuality. 'One can certainly concede', she argues, 'that desire is radically conditioned without claiming that it is radically determined' (2000: 21). In this sense, she argues that the symbolic law of sex/gender differentiation holds neither a pre-social quality nor an extra-ontological trans-historicity, but functions as a *social artefact* which is at the service of the heterosexual imperative. As Lynne Segal (1999) notes, Lacan was instrumental in resolving the biologistic and deterministic phallocentrism in Freud's work and producing a framework in which the phallic 'order' could be conceptualized in symbolic terms. But Segal also rightly points out Lacan's own determinism because of the way in which the phallus becomes a transcendental signifier 'which is unaffected by shifts in social practices and relations across time, place and milieu, not to mention the idiosyncrasies of personal biography' (1999: 181).

As Elizabeth Grosz argues: 'For Lacan, love is an entanglement, a knot, of imaginary gratifications and symbolic desires. It is always structured with reference to the phallus, which, in a sense is the third term coming between two lovers' (1990: 137). The phallus acts as a symbolic 'order' under which lovers proceed: they first imagine a lack which they then imagine can be satisfied by the other (because they each imagine that the other has what they need). Butler's point is that this symbolic law does not have any a priori or ontological existence outside of its forced reiteration through heterosexual convention. In understanding how masculine and feminine subjectivities are established through heterosexual love relations, the Butlerian reading of Lacan is pertinent. As Grosz argues of Lacan's model of the phallic signifier: 'There is no direct, unmediated relation between the sexes' (1990: 137). What mediates this relation is a continual attempt to secure a complementary harmony with the other who one believes to occupy the opposite position to one's own self. Lack, as Renata Salecl argues, 'concerns the subject's very being – both a man and a woman are marked by lack, but they relate differently to this lack' (1998: 148). The difference is, as Segal notes, that the phallus 'constitutes women in terms of lack, and men in terms of the threat of lack' (1999: 182). But Butler's point is that this process is in the 'doing' and has no law outside of its own enactment. The doing, of course, is not a voluntaristic set of actions but consists of a compelled and forced approximation of sexual ontology in relation to the regulatory operation of heterosexuality. Butler's point is that it is *compulsory heterosexuality* which produces the law of the binary masculine/feminine and not *vice versa*. It is the repeated articulation of the illusion of gender which, refracted into the subjectivity of the one who acts, comes to establish forms of material difference which reproduce the relational subject positions within heterosexuality.

What I want to do in the following sections of this chapter is to look at how the normative force of gender is impelled through the heterosexual matrix and, facilitated by ways of loving, becomes reiterated through *subjectivity*. I want to show how this process 'works' by looking at the ways in which love produces immediate and profound effects upon subjectivity which facilitates the approximation of specific ways of being organized around the masculine/feminine binary. Beginning with an examination of the effects of romantic love upon subjectivity, I consider how these effects are themselves produced by the different types of emotional work which men and women engage in both upon themselves and with each other. In order to demonstrate this clearly, and to analyse how masculine and feminine modes of subjectivity are reproduced, I look first at the women's experiences and then, in contrast, move on to the men's accounts.

Women's transformations

For all of the women who took part in this study, love is an experience that produces profound effects upon their sense of self. These effects are not only feelings of joy and pleasure, but are also expressed as matters of self-esteem and confidence. As Patricia explains:

PATRICIA: When I'm in love I feel very important, I feel very attractive, I invariably lose weight. I walk faster, I talk faster. I feel I am more fun to be with, not just with the other person, but in all the other social gatherings. I feel I work harder, I feel that I'm more logical, more clear thinking. It's an enviable state to be in.

Love is an 'enviable state' because it enhances the whole of Patricia's life. It inspires her in both her work and her social life, it alters her relationship with her own body, it affects her mental processes and it makes her feel important. Fundamentally, being in love is a good and positive experience that produces a range of beneficial effects and allows Patricia to be a particular version of herself which she likes. Patricia is currently in a relationship but she does not consider herself to be in love. I asked her how she feels about herself at the moment:

PATRICIA: Disappointed with myself. That I have failed myself in not going far enough professionally. Disappointed in myself in that I haven't got a close loving relationship which ... disappointed in that I am unhappy in the relationship that I've got.

For Patricia, not being in love produces a powerful and profound set of feelings characterized by a sense of 'disappointment' about her life. This is not simply a disappointment with those aspects of her relationship that she finds unsatisfactory but a fundamental sense of personal failure. 'I have failed myself' is the language of how a failure to obtain a 'close loving relationship' becomes refracted into forms of self-beratement and personal unhappiness.

As Wendy Langford (1999) argues, this is the fundamental irony of romantic love because heterosexual relationships are always built on the promise of self-transformation and usually end with the latter reality of self-disappointment (she terms this the 'love-cycle'). For Langford, love is an ideological trick because it *always* promises happiness but delivers what Patricia has described: ultimate misery and despair. Yet even if that is true, it does not negate the fact that the former promise of the 'enviable state' of love continues to exert influence over the one who seeks it. As Patricia comments: 'I keep telling myself that at a certain age you must grow out of it, but I don't think so.' It is precisely because the promise of love remains so tangible that it exerts such a compelling influence (an influence which, for the women in this study, was not significantly affected by age).

It is in the space between assertions about love's 'badness' – where love is seen as an ideological trap which secures women in relationships of inequality (Firestone, 1972; de Beauvoir, 1997) – and the notion that love is a path to freedom (hooks, 2000) that we can find one 'truth' of women's heterosexual love. This is because the process of falling in love, and the relationships formed because of that process, involves forms of both enablement and constraint, pleasure and danger. Whilst romantic love may create the 'hell of mutual alienation' (Langford, 1999: 151) it also retains its primacy as an anti-alienating potential because it offers a way of experiencing forms of pleasurable subjective transformation. We can see this in Patricia's account because, even though romantic love does not *secure* the desired transformation, it continues to hold out the promise. This may be one of the fundamental contradictions in the social construction of love, but it is a contradiction which endures. Love, in offering what Ellen describes as 'an opportunity for you to relate to another human being', provides a mechanism to secure what Victoria describes as 'loads of self-esteem and loads of self-confidence'. Because falling in love continues to offer such an important way to maximize feelings of self-worth, then it remains a viable process in which to enter. That such a process may not be altogether reducible to 'rational' description is not seen as a central problem. As Victoria explains: 'It makes me feel powerful. How does it do that? I don't know, I can't really describe it.' This connects the effects upon the self to the ways in which such effects are constituted, as we saw in Chapter 1, as 'beyond words'.

We cannot underestimate the effects which love produces upon women's sense of self. Love is a process which is compelling precisely because it holds the potential for self-discovery and self-transformation. Below are some examples of the ways in which romantic love is experienced as the basis for self-realization and subjective change:

BARBARA: [I felt] this great sense of well being, nothing niggled me as much, I felt physically well. I held myself, I was holding myself much better, and a great sense of joy, and joy in little things . . .

PJ: Which being in love gave you?

BARBARA: Yes, yeah. And I think made me find parts of myself as well that had maybe been hidden away [. . .] Somehow it just proved that there was someone who could get through that armour in a way that nobody else could [. . .] finding an extra bit of yourself that you didn't know was there.

MARGARET: Yeah. I've got more confidence when I've got a man. I feel completely different. If I'm on me own I feel, oh, I've got to have a drink, you know, to give me confidence and I drink too much then. I don't like being on my own, I get lonely, I feel really lonely. A man just gives me something, I just need a man around me. And as soon as I met this man I felt attractive and wonderful and I lost half a stone, in a month, just being with him. It just made me feel alive again. It's like this feeling inside, it's just wonderful, being in love.

PJ: And that's what . . .

MARGARET: That's what it's all about. It's addictive! [laughs] It's a lovely feeling, I love it. And that's what you keep on searching for, you want that all the time. But of course it wears off, you don't have it like that all of the time.

ELIZABETH: I think it makes you feel a lot more self-confident and it also makes you feel a lot happier as well because, obviously, you think oh yes someone likes me. And you like them back which is nice and they feel nice as well because of that. Because they're happy and you're happy you get even more happier [laughs].

HEATHER: There isn't a word that encompasses it, just, I don't know, I feel as if I, I feel as if I belong, I feel as if I've been a seed that's growing in the ground and all of a sudden I've been rained on, and the sun's shone on me, and all of a sudden I've blossomed. I've learned to see myself in a new light. I'm not as down on myself as I was. Because I did used to be. [Falling in love] was a way of reclaiming myself and what I wanted. But, gosh, I've learned a sense of self that I didn't know existed.

CATHERINE: I don't like myself very much when I'm not in love.

PJ: Why?

CATHERINE: I don't know, I just don't, I don't like my . . . I like, my, I . . . do you know what, I like myself as a person, I love myself as I person, I think I'm a good person, I know I'm a good person, and I wouldn't hurt a fly. But I don't like myself physically, I don't, I wouldn't look at myself and say 'not bad', I'd think 'ughh'. So I don't like myself a lot when I am out of a relationship but when I'm in a relationship and somebody pays me attention and tells me that they love me and that they want to be with me and things like that then that makes me feel a whole lot better. It makes me like myself a little bit more.

The types of feelings expressed above are of powerful and profound types of self-realization and self-actualization which romantic love enables. They are feelings of self-discovery – 'finding an extra bit of yourself that you didn't know was there' – which take place through the appropriation of a heterosexual love relationship. Most of all, they are expressions of the way that falling in love allows these women to experience a sense of joy in their own being. Despite claims from commentators, such as Langford, that such feelings are negated once heterosexual relationships are established, we should not underestimate, given the testimony outlined above, the continuing significance of romantic love's transformative promise. We cannot simply conclude that such feelings of self-enhancement are reducible to an ideological apparatus designed to subject women to forms of exploitation. To do so would be to deny the 'real' pleasure which love gives to these women or to reduce it to a state where pleasure masks other conditions of domination. A question arises: could we not be critical of gender relations within heterosexual love *and* retain an understanding of how love, in its present form, can be genuinely pleasurable?

We need to ask, even when we acknowledge the real material inequalities between men and women in heterosexual relationships, why love retains its compelling effects upon subjectivity. If love really is the 'rain' that makes the 'seed' of the self 'blossom', then it remains 'addictive'. It retains its potency as a process which can offer these women the chance to experience feelings of self-worth, of power and of discovery. As Sue Vice (1995) notes, the desire to be in love continues to be addictive not because of individual 'psychology' but because of the structural resources which it offers for working upon the self and manufacturing a way of being. Such a promise may lead to bitter disappointment but, at its moment of conception, it is perceived in the opposite sense, as a mechanism for securing self-realization. As Gillian Rose argues, the love relationship is one of 'work' allowing the self to be realized in relation to the beloved other and enabling 'the two submerged to surface in a series of unpredictable configurations' (1995: 131). But a central question arises: why *heterosexual* love?

Femininity, lack and the 'something' of love

In thinking about how love enables subjective transformations, the quotations above express examples of why such a process remains a compelling search for many women. A normative ideal of love does seem to hold the key to the prison of the self (to get through the 'armour' of the self, as Barbara said), a way to discover oneself through the beloved other, a way of resolving the dilemma of isolation, and a mechanism for securing forms of ontological security. The reason for this, argues Wendy Hollway (1996), is because love offers the chance to create a mutual state of recognition between lovers which allows for the development of a relationship in which 'safety' and 'bliss' can be experienced. Drawing on a psychoanalytic framework of love, which depicts the desire for the other to be an outcome of early-formed object desire instigated by the original childhood split between infant and parent, Hollway views love as both a 'natural' process *and* one which can resist the inherent patriarchal relations of heterosexuality. Making a distinction between the 'pre-linguistic bedrock of the experiences of both safety and bliss' (1996: 105) and her belief that 'people are never ciphers of their social conditions' (1996: 106), Hollway views the *powerful moral and political force* of love as a way of negating the social construction of contemporary heterosexual relations. Hollway's view is one which imagines the human need to love as an ontology outside of the temporal constructions of heterosexuality (it is, as I argued in Chapter 1, considered to be a universal and essential feature of human existence). For Hollway, heterosexuality is a constructed and cultural process, but the desire for love and intimacy are pre-social.

Are the above quotations by the women expressions of the power of love to offer these essential facets of subjective safety and bliss? Hollway's earlier work may itself be more useful in understanding the subjectifying process of love within the construction of heterosexuality. In her idea of the 'have/hold discourse' ([1984] 1998: 232) she argues that women's subjectivity (and sexuality) is constituted through the demarcation of femininity as 'lack' and consolidated relationally within heterosexuality. In this sense, love becomes a process in which women attempt to reconcile a subjective lack with the other who they believe can complete that lack. If we use the above quotations and read them from this point of view, then we can easily see that the women's sense of self is felt, in various ways, as lacking when they are not in love. Conversely, by entering into love, the self is experienced in an overwhelmingly positive way. So the 'safety' and 'bliss' of love is built on the ideas of fulfilment and self-satisfaction and, importantly, the realization that 'something' is missing when love is not present.

And crucially it is *love* which is desired and not just any heterosexual relationship. In the above quotation, although Margaret does state 'A man just gives me something, I just need a man around me', which might suggest that lack is both experienced and satisfied through simple gender recognition, she is very clear that it is the love relationship which makes her feel 'lovely'. We can see this because Margaret builds a distinction between how that feeling might 'wear off' and why the search to attain it remains compelling. It is *being in love with a man* which gives Margaret the 'something' she requires. This 'something' which love gives to the self is of crucial importance and reveals a nodal point at which heterosexual subjectivity is consolidated. What love gives is 'something' that is perceived to be missing when a heterosexual love relationship is not present. But if this is the satisfaction of a 'lack' then what installed that lack in the first place, what is the 'something' which satisfies it, and why is it specifically a *heterosexual* relationship which produces these subjective effects of joy and completion?

Issues around lack and completion are most clearly expressed by the women in this study through the language of 'becoming whole'. The notion of 'wholeness' and 'completeness' are extremely common descriptions of the subjective effects of being in love. As Heather describes, love has facilitated a form of 'completeness' and removed the lack of 'something' which was missing:

HEATHER: [When I'm] single I just get on with my everyday life, throw myself into friends, family, interests, but there's always the feeling that there's something missing. There's something I want that I don't have and when I'm with someone I feel as if . . . well actually I haven't previously felt as if a jigsaw had been slotted into place, I do now [. . .] It's just as if there is a completeness and a contentment. [. . .] I suppose, a contentment that I am who I want to be now, because I am with someone.
PJ: So there's something missing when you're single?
HEATHER: Yes.
PJ: So you feel complete when you're in love?
HEATHER: Yes.

We can see how subjectivity is constituted through love as both lacking and complete. When Heather is not in love there is, regardless of any other activity in her life, something missing. What heterosexual love offers Heather is both the process to recognize herself as incomplete and the 'tool' through which to work to solve this incompletion: to make the 'jigsaw' of her self 'slot into place'. But what caused this state of incompletion in the first place? Or, more importantly, was there an *original state* of incompletion before the appropriation of love?

We usually think of lack as pre-existing the appropriation of love but the construction of romantic love itself operationalizes forms of subjectivity which create this sense of lack. It is precisely the way that love offers forms of 'completion', and the range of pleasurable and positive effects upon the self which are associated with it, which sculpt the self as less than whole without it. Love is far from a benign social process but itself reproduces forms of subjectivity (through lack and satisfaction). Because femininity (like masculinity) is constructed through heterosexuality as lacking, and women's desire for love is a search to satisfy that lack (by fusing together with the other), then *heterosexual* subjectivity becomes operationalized through love. Love reiterates and reproduces the 'differences' on which heterosexuality is built because, in holding individuals in a specular relationship with the 'other half', love serves to confirm and reiterate a sense of gendered incompleteness. As I argued in Chapter 1, this process is naturalized and essentialized into the chemistry of 'lock and key' fusion built on a complementary system of two halves making a whole. This process of subjective enablement, anchored within the normative binary of masculine/feminine, can therefore be seen to reproduce heterosexuality *through* subjectivity. It is, as Heather states above, a way of producing the self in relation to loving the other (the way in which the 'jigsaw' of the self is put together).

It is the binary of masculine/feminine within the 'jigsaw' of subjectivity which is crucial to the reproduction of heterosexuality. For example, in Victoria's account below we can see that the love relationship allows the approximation of a form of subjectivity which is bound up in an authentication of gender:

VICTORIA: Like I told you before, he makes me feel like a woman, makes me feel appreciated, makes me feel like I deserve to feel.
PJ: You say he makes you feel like a woman, how does he do that?
VICTORIA: [laughs] I don't mean physically!
PJ: No, sure.
VICTORIA: I just mean, like, he's 'you're working your way through life' and 'you've got morals, you know right from wrong'. I don't know whether that's just in general but he makes me feel like a proper human. He makes me feel feminine, he compliments me on nice things, like 'oh you look nice today' and what-not. And then he gets horny and that makes me feel like a woman as well [. . .] I couldn't imagine having a relationship with a woman [. . .] Like I say, my boyfriend makes me feel womanly. I suppose a woman can but my boyfriend's like 'you can bear my children, be a good mother, I want to marry you, I want to take you down the aisle, I want to ask your father's permission, do the whole traditional thing', which makes me feel like a woman.

For Victoria, the heterosexual love relation allows her to become nothing short of a 'proper human'. Her femininity is bound up with the desire for an authenticity that is structured by the heteronormativity of sex and gender difference. As Victoria elaborates: 'At last, someone appreciates me, raw me, pure me, and I don't need to put on an act.' Yet, of course, to *feel* like a woman, which is bound up in feeling authentic, pure, and raw, *is* an act. Such as act is not *pretence* but can be considered, as Butler suggests (1991), as action mediated within an ontological schema in which we 'act out' the gender positions of heterosexuality.

Experiencing the self in ways which are both desirable and 'natural' is intricately bound up in ideas about the complementary other, in notions of 'completeness', and in feeling that the other can give the self the 'something' which at once seems so essential, and completely 'normal'. In other words, it is loving in a way which we imagine will make us 'whole' that we come to reify our own sense of incompleteness through the other half. The implications of this are profound in terms of heterosexuality because love provides a vehicle for establishing an ontology of difference (sex/gender) on which heterosexuality is based. As Lacan argues (echoing a view that can be traced back to Plato), 'lack is what the living being loses, that part of himself (sic), *qua* living being, in reproducing himself through the way of sex' (1998: 205): 'the mystery of love [is] the search by the subject, not of a sexual complement, but of that part of himself, lost forever, that is constituted by the fact that he is only a sexed living being' (1998: 205). Love offers us a search for the other which only compounds the difference on which our search is based. I am not arguing that falling in love does not produce 'real' feelings of joy and pleasure because, on the contrary, such subjective feelings are the logical outcome of the attempt to ratify a 'completeness'. What I would argue is that such a process reproduces the heterosexual matrix in which it is founded and consolidates a particular form of subjectivity (a subjectivity which is 'complementary' to its emotional and physical other) which is felt to be without the 'something' which love can add:

BARBARA: I think it does appeal to me that I would like somebody to come into my life and that goes against the grain because part of my logic says you should never look to another person, you know this is your philosophy, you should never look to another person to make you whole. I actually believe that but then there's a percentage of me which says I am whole-plus, when I was with [my partner]. You know there was five per cent more and that's what I would like.

Losing the self

If love adds 'something' to women's sense of self, then what effect does the loss of love have upon subjectivity? Consider how, even though her relationship was extremely problematic, Barbara experienced its end:

BARBARA: I felt tremendous panic and sort of a desperation to sort of . . . and scared really of letting him go, and this was somebody very important had gone out of my life. So I guess I was holding on very tight, and it was somebody else who said to me maybe the word was, you know, about being abandoned, you know [. . .] I think it was more about once he'd gone, I felt as though there was a massive gaping hole [. . .] I felt there was something missing, yeah, but this was like . . . it isn't just missing, there's a chasm of blackness. You know I have, I have felt very very down.

Barbara's relationship certainly did not constitute the confluent ideal of the pure relationship. She had been involved with a married man who she later found out had been lying to her about planning to leave his wife to live with her. Even in the face of this knowledge, and the belief that he was 'a bastard', the sense of loss was immense. Barbara never lived with this man, she never created a 'family unit' with him and, as a middle-class woman with a professional career, she was not financially dependent on him. She knew, as she told me, the relationship would not work but she was 'holding on tight' for fear of the 'gaping hole' that would be opened by its end. A form of depression ensued once the relationship was over and she now feels as if there is something missing from her life. What is the loss that Barbara feels? The 'chasm of blackness' and the 'gaping hole' that Barbara describes are felt as a profound sense of lack, a 'desperation' and 'panic', which is the opposite to the completeness described in the earlier accounts of the women. When we compare these data, in terms of the capacity of love to produce both affirmative and destructive feelings, we see the way in which subjectivity is being framed and experienced through the heterosexual matrix: where love installs or completes a sense of lack.

When a relationship ends we (both men and women) are affected deeply and, in terms of the data of this study, experience similar forms of loss. The individual may want that 'special person' again, they may feel 'bereaved', or they may feel angry and enraged. Yet, for the majority of women in this research, the loss of a relationship is experienced, unlike for the men, as a profound loss of self. To demonstrate how powerful that loss can be, we can look at the relationship of one woman which was physically violent and abusive.[2] If we were utilitarian we might suggest that a woman who left a violent relationship may find that conclusion a wholly satisfactory one. Yet Margaret, in a similar way to Barbara, but in a physically abusive relationship with her partner, experienced a profound sense of loss when her partner left her for someone else:

MARGARET: I was absolutely shell shocked. I just couldn't believe it. It was like, I couldn't eat, I couldn't sleep. I mean I lost half a stone in a week and I was on sleeping pills and I was having these panic attacks. I just couldn't believe the effects, how it affected me [...] I physically felt like I had lost an arm because he was so close, he was always there [...] It was like a bereavement.

This sense of loss is a common way that women talk about the end of love. Even when people leave, or are released from, relationships which would not conform to the standard 'ideal' of love (relationships which are violent, abusive, unhappy, difficult) there is often a profound sense of loss. We cannot simply assume that if we make a link between the *promise* of romantic love and the disappointment of heterosexual *relationships* that women will be glad or happy when such relationships end. To make such an assertion would both profoundly fail to understand the power of love and also render meaningless the constraints instituted by heterosexuality. It is precisely because there is such a profound level of self-investment in heterosexual love relationships that experiences like Margaret's exist. What is important here is to understand, not just how love leads to relationships which 'fail', but how subjectivity is intimately tied up in heterosexual love; how we 'become' versions of ourselves through the process of falling in love. Our identities are so co-existent with the other that the loss of that person feels like 'losing an arm'.

This form of subjective experience is common in the accounts of the women I interviewed. As Elizabeth and Susan describe, the loss of a partner induced profound effects on their sense of self and identity:

ELIZABETH: I actually think if something does go wrong then you start to look to yourself as to why it's gone wrong and you start to think, you know, that it's your fault and that makes you feel self-loathing, self-loathing is too strong, but it makes you have less confidence in yourself and you start to devalue yourself and then, if it ends, you usually think it's the end of the world.

SUSAN: I know that I've lost my partner now but I feel as if half of me has been cut off, because we were so like, as a whole, you know we were whole, like united, so it's really weird, I can't explain [. . .] It feels like you are half a person and stuff [. . .] I feel awful as a single person now. Like it's totally took away my confidence and my self-esteem, and erm, a sense . . . my identity as well. I feel as if I've lost my identity, I don't know who I am any more.

To not know 'who' you are, to lose your identity and sense of self, means that, during a love relationship, a profound transformation of the self must have occurred. To lose that sense of self, and resulting sense of 'completeness', impacts upon subjectivity by producing forms of introspection which are negative and destructive – 'you start to look to yourself'. The end of a love relationship (or the end of love *within* a relationship) brings with it the end of the promise of fulfilment which was attached to the initial process of falling in love. But what is important is that the end of a love relationship does not return these women to an 'original' state of selfhood. Rather it produces a new set of conditions through which their selves are understood. Such a set of conditions are the opposite to the positive effects of being in love because they induce a sense of being 'half a person'. This experience of being 'half' is the language of lack personified, but it is engendered *after* love and not before it. Therefore, unlike in Langford's (1999) account of the return to an original lack, my view is that love instates the perceived sense of lack by operationalizing heteronormative gender relations between men and women. By positioning men and women in opposition to each other, through what Rowland (1993) describes as the 'obvious differences' of sex, heterosexuality operationalizes two discrete ontological categories. What love promises is a way to solve the lack of the self. It is a lack which functions in the Lacanian sense of a symbolic signifier around sex difference, but this lack is installed, sedimented into the self, in the 'doing' of love. The doing of love operationalizes the becoming of the heterosexual feminine self because it is the vehicle through which the self is felt to be 'more' or 'less' complete.

Men's resistance

Love is paradoxical in its effects upon subjectivity. As Rutherford (1999) argues in *I Am No Longer Myself Without You*: 'The paradox of love is that we discover a new sense of self in the moment we lose our self to another person' (1999: 3). Yet the paradox of this 'self-loss' and subsequent 'self-discovery' is profoundly different for men and women. Whilst feelings of transformation and completeness are ways that women experience subjective change in love, these are not the experiences of men. On the contrary, when we look at men's accounts we find that there is a profound resistance to the notion of self-change which, as a result, comes to produce different effects on male subjectivity. Gillian Rose characterizes female subjectivity in love with the epigraph: 'Love in the submission of power' (1995: 55). For Rose, loving demands a submission to the other which, through dialogic engagement, is the basis for the realization of a new identity. Yet this submission to the other is structured by the pre-existing social construction of sexuality so that gendered subjectivity emerges in distinct ways. To characterize the relationship between loving and male subjectivity we should adjust Rose's epigraph to read: 'love by resisting the submission to power.'

In the Lacanian 'model' of subjectivity, men, like women, seek the other through which to consolidate their self and complete their sense of lack. But whilst women often experience a transformation of self, male experience of love is built on a *defence* of the parameters of selfhood. This is because masculinity, that 'other half' to femininity, is constructed through heterosexuality as a gender that does not lack. As we will see in the following accounts, men do not describe love as a process of subjective transformation because they come to the love relation in a position already characterized as 'complete'. For Lacan, this is because men are symbolically marked as the sex which does not lack: the sex which possesses the 'something' which women describe as gaining through love. Men therefore come to the love relation with a dual purpose: they simultaneously seek to ratify their position as the one who is marked with the symbolic possession of the phallus and, consequently, seek to consolidate their self in relation to the one who is without. For Lacan, this process is a symbolic construction, but it reproduces the materiality of sex difference and is expressed through gender identity. There are two central issues in such a process: the first is that masculinity (like femininity) is constructed relationally through lack and attempts, through love, to realize a symbolic completion; the second point is that, by entering into this process, men 'work' to reproduce a particular (and normative) form of subjectivity.

We can begin to explore the distinctiveness of male subjectivity by juxtaposing how men 'feel' when they are in love with the accounts provided by the women. Where women expressed profound effects of transformation upon their self and identity we can see a fundamental difference for the men:

PJ: Can I just ask you, do you feel differently about yourself when you're single and when you're in a relationship?
GARY: I wouldn't say about yourself, no.
PJ: No?
GARY: No. In a relationship you've got other factors to consider. You've got other people's feelings, other people's lives to consider. When you're single you've only got to look after yourself. How you think about yourself, I don't think about myself as a single person, I tend to always put other people first at the moment. But as me, as a person, I feel the same way I did when I was single.

A relationship, for Gary, instigates new ways of thinking about others but not, he contends, about himself. As a 'person' he feels the same way that he did when he was single. The types of changes which love affects are around Gary's relationship with his partner (and his children) but not, he contends, in his relationship with himself. The difference which Gary notes about being single is that, unlike in a relationship, he only has to 'look after' himself. This is a re-occurring theme in the accounts of the men and appears as the most important aspect of how they experience self-change in love. There is a continual preoccupation with this interplay between the change in looking after 'number one' and the requirement, which love instigates, to think of someone else's feelings. This is accompanied in the men's accounts with the view that they 'feel the same way' about themselves when they are in love. The men's accounts never focus on explicit experiences of self-transformation but on implicit forms of self-consistency. These men do not speak with the same language as the women – they do not talk of love being the 'rain' which makes the 'seed' of the self grow.

The needs of the other: the wholeness of the self

The difference between male and female subjectivity can be elucidated by looking at how men appropriate a particular type of selfhood that is framed within a dialogic relationship with the femininity which they confront. Men's sense of self does change in love, but the change is not the 'transformation' which the women experience. Rather it is expressed as a form of *accommodation* to a partner's needs and desires. This is most clearly visible when men talk about how love demands that they stop being 'selfish' and put a partner's interests first:

PHILLIP: You tend to be, when you're in a relationship, you tend to be less self-centred. When you're not in a relationship you are totally self-centred because you've got nobody else to think about and you tend to become selfish and I think you tend to be less considerate to other people, when you're not in a relationship.

BARRY: Yeah I think, I've been in a relationship longer than I've been single now. Yeah, I think, I think, speaking from this terrific height of thirty-odd years, I think . . . incomplete is not the word I'm looking at, self-centred, I think you might be self-centred. I think being in a good relationship stops you from being too self-centred. You can still be self-centred, in fact I may be [. . .] but you've always got someone there to draw you out of yourself.

Both Barry and Phillip think that being in a relationship stops them being 'self-centred' and encourages them to be more considerate. A love relationship, therefore, demands a specific negotiation of selfhood in order to render it co-operative with a female partner. Love impacts on men's selves because they must 'work' at this form of co-operation. But the result of this is *not*, as Barry makes clear, a form of completeness. For Barry, being single does not represent a lack or incompletion but a form of 'self-centredness' which is given up to the other with whom he becomes co-extensive. What is striking about this is that love becomes a way to *diminish* a sense of wholeness. Men ostensibly become less 'self-centred' because they gain what they lack – the other who, as Barry argues, 'draws you out of yourself'.

Love, for men, cannot produce the type of 'wholeness' of which many of the women speak. Men are engaged in a process which does not accord with the discourses of 'wholeness' and 'completeness' because they begin from a position which is already understood as 'whole' and thus speak of how such a 'self-centredness' has to be changed in order to accommodate their partner. This is because masculinities do not depart from a point of being perceived as 'lack' but, rather, are constructed, regulated and enacted within a heterosexualized construction of gender which positions them as *already-whole*. The idea of utilizing the love relationship as a way of producing 'wholeness' remains essentially outside of the realms of masculinity precisely because such masculinity is not seen to be deficient. There is no language in the men's accounts of love giving them the 'something' of which women speak and yet, by the very existence of their desire to love, there must be 'something' which they 'need'. It is more difficult to show this 'something' in the men's accounts because what love gives them is a way to consolidate that which they imagine they already have. Love offers men a way of existing as 'complete' beings because, in confronting a femininity which they perceive as lacking, they satisfy their sense of wholeness by being the provider of the 'something' required by the feminine other (by becoming less 'self-centred'). But as Lacan (1998) would argue, the belief that men have about themselves as already-always 'whole' is imaginary – they are only whole when they are co-existent with the thing they lack.

Producing a masculine self

We can see how this process works when we consider how men shore-up a version of themselves by appropriating a type of masculinity which the relational engagement of heterosexual love puts in motion. For instance, consider how Phillip describes his feelings about the ways in which men and women relate to each other emotionally:

PHILLIP: Men show their emotions in a different way. They're more, they're trying to be more caring and supportive in a masculine, stronger sort of way. They no doubt have the same emotions but don't show them the same way as a female would. Perhaps the male of the species is supposed to look and be stronger and that's the way we do it [...] Women tend to be softer, more tender. It's sort of the masculine and the female. I think the masculine is strength and the female is softness, kindness, tenderness. These are the opposites of male and female.

In Phillip's account the heterosexual love relationship is enacted around the primary, and complementary, difference of masculine and feminine emotions (which is inscribed through the absolute difference of male and female). What is also clear is that Phillip himself argues that this performance of gender is itself a masquerade. No doubt, Phillip argues, men and women have the same emotions but, because of how the 'male of the species' is *supposed* to look and act, they do not 'show' these emotions in the same way. What Phillip points out is how men are positioned, through the relationality of sex difference within heterosexual love, as a gender in possession of certain attributes: masculinity gives, provides, is strong, it is the gender which tends to the 'softness' of women.

This is bound up in how men feel that they take on a role of 'responsibility' towards their partners. Their sense of self becomes intimately bound up with ideas about what Douglas described as 'looking after' his 'girl'. As Martin describes, the take up of this position is infracted into, not simply his actions towards his partner, but his sense of self:

MARTIN: I've got very strong sort of feelings of protectiveness towards [my wife], like I want to make sure that bad shit doesn't happen to her. I want to help her out as much as possible, make her life easier, I want to care for her, I want to help make her into a better person in lots of ways. And, I suppose ... it's quite interesting, for me personally, I have always seen it very much as I'm very proactive in the relationships that I've been in, in trying to do those things. But I've never really, I've never really seen myself as opening up to being the recipient of, you know, to someone who could do that for me. You know, like I never really see that ... which is quite interesting.

For Martin, the love relationship positions him as the 'proactive' carer, the one who protects and cares for his wife, but not the one who is the 'recipient' of this type of 'protectiveness'. The active construction of a femininity in need of care is dialogically structured by the masculinity which frames it and, therefore, in reproducing a normative model of the feminine/masculine binary, and actively positioning himself within it, Martin appropriates his own gendered position and produces his sense of self through such a construction. The fact that the labour of 'caring' is continually found to be structured as a feminine activity (see, for an example of emotional labour: Dryden, 1999; and domestic labour: Oakley, 1984) is not present in the testimony of the men I interviewed.

Holding on to the self

The differences between men's and women's accounts of how they feel about themselves when they are in love suggests that they engage in remarkably different types of work on their own selves. Intimate relations demand all sorts of emotional work and we commonly think of love as labour-intensive. Commentators on love point out the unequal ways in which emotional work in heterosexual relationships is structured around women's role as primary 'carer' (Delphy and Leonard, 1992); the ways in which men find it difficult to 'express themselves' (Gottman and Levenson, 1986); the ways in which men use strategies of emotional withdrawal to create insecurity in their partners in order to retain power (Dryden, 1999); or, in the burgeoning work on masculinity, how men can 'learn' how to love like women (Connell, 1995). Instead of thinking about how men express themselves *towards* a partner, we must also think about how men's own sense of self is produced. When we do this, what we find is that men have a form of *possessiveness* about their self. We have seen how men experience the changes brought about through love as an alteration in the ways they relate to their female partner; this process is negotiated by 'giving up' the 'self-centredness' they experienced when they were single. Yet what is interesting is that men, unlike women, are also preoccupied with, and actively work at, sustaining the self which they imagine pre-exists the relationships they enter and it is this type of work on the self that constitutes men's labour-intensive emotional work.

For men, love demands a type of emotional work built around a maintenance of the parameters of the self rather than their removal. Whilst this may accord with the cultural construction of masculinity as the essentially unemotional gender (Hearn, 1993), and whilst it may appear that men work towards appropriating this unemotional status as an expression of their authentic gender (Duncombe and Marsden, 1998), there is no doubt that men do engage in work on their selves. But whereas women expound the transformative potential of love, men have an altogether different language. Consider the following account by William as he describes how he felt when he fell in love with his current partner:

WILLIAM: I would say that it shouldn't come to a point where you are ... I don't think a relationship should come to a point where it should dictate everything that you are doing in your life. You're still your own person, your own character. She liked me because of the person I was and I don't think that should be changed by our relationship, I should still be me, the person I was. Obviously certain things would have to change but on the whole I'd still like to think I'm the same character, same beliefs, same principles, and the person that she first met and she found attractive.
PJ: Is that difficult then?
WILLIAM: I think it can be, I think in some relationships if you've got a very strong partner you can surrender your complete character and it's swamped by the wants of the other partner. It becomes secondary in importance.

It is clear from William's account that he is strongly concerned to maintain 'who' he is within the relationship with which he is engaged. Obviously, he says, a relationship changes certain activities and practices within his life, but he is centrally concerned that his 'character' must remain unaltered. We can see that, in light of this, forms of control are instigated around the self which resists what William describes as feelings of being 'swamped' by his partner's needs and desires. Although this is, of course, related to the type of intimate work that men and women engage in with each other (in terms of how they relate to each other) it is also crucially a type of work upon the self. William actively works to maintain a sense of who he is – himself as his 'own person' – as separate from the self he might become if he allows the relationship to swamp him. This is important to William because he does not want his relationship to 'dictate' who he 'is'. In this sense, the process of being in love engages a type of emotional work aimed at sustaining a prior and authentic self which pre-exists the experience of love. Yet, importantly, this sense of self is also affirmed and ratified in love ('she liked me because of the person I *was*' and therefore 'I'm the same character, same beliefs, same principles, and the person that she first met and she found attractive').

Men are not 'cold' or 'hollow' (Duncombe and Marsden, 1998). However, they have a particular relationship with their selves that is characterized by a certain degree of self-possessiveness. William did talk during the interview about how his relationship gives him a type of confidence because it functions 'a little bit like a safety net', 'a security blanket if you like', but that is also juxtaposed with the level of self-engagement he is willing to make in the relationship. William, like all the men I interviewed, engages in a dual process by which he attempts to inculcate his emotional self into a state of 'being in love' whilst wanting to maintain 'parts' of himself which resist being swamped. Wendy Hollway ([1984] 1998) notes this dichotomy and argues that it emerges through the tension of wanting and needing to be loved whilst having to maintain and reproduce a masculine identity.

This dichotomy is highlighted in the way that Carl talks about being in love as both a profoundly emotional experience and also one which demands a form of work to delimit how it affects his self:

CARL: I just think it's [being in love] a whole extra element of life that can be exciting and thrilling and if you're in love you can have an emotional engagement with the world. Just understanding someone that closely is really exciting. It's a journey I enjoy being on.
PJ: Does it add something to life?
CARL: Yeah [. . .] but I think it can be a distraction. I end up thinking I can't do anything with my everyday life [laughs] because it's taking up all my efforts to think about this relationship and work on it, like I need to strike a balance here.
[. . .]
PJ: Do you think it's important to maintain space for yourself?
CARL: Yeah.
PJ: Why?
CARL: I don't know, it becomes all-consuming and it's not the only part of life. If it does become the only part of life it's going to exhaust me and suck my energy out. I'm not going to want to do it any more if it demands everything of me because it's just one part of who I am.

Falling in love is both an 'exciting and thrilling . . . emotional engagement with the world' and also something which can become 'all consuming'. For Carl, love does not instigate a profound alteration to his sense of self because it is just 'one part' of who he is. He recoils from the highly intensive emotional 'work' that he might have to do in a relationship, something which would take up all his efforts, and suggests he needs to 'strike a balance'. One of the ways this balance is negotiated is by resisting the type of self-engagement which we find in the women's accounts. Instead Carl compartmentalizes love as one part of his life in order to maintain barriers to his sense of self in other contexts. Such compartmentalization has been seen as the ways in which men resist emotional engagement with their partners (Weiss, 1990), but it also suggests the type of work they are engaged with on themselves. It is a work of maintaining borders, of retaining a strong sense of individuality, and of withdrawing from the types of self-transformation characteristic of the women's accounts. To not want love to be 'all-consuming' means that Carl does not just simply resist the outward displays of emotional work but engages that work by turning it back upon the self. Jonathan Rutherford (1999) would suggest that this is a process which arises because men do not have the ability, or the available language, to express themselves and become imprisoned by the construction of gender. Yet this is only half the story. Men are not simply 'victims' of gender differentiation, they actively participate in its reiteration. Given the opportunity of emotional engagement from which they withdraw, men can be seen to reinstate the barriers of the possessive self and work to maintain who they are and what their own self is. Masculinity is produced in the constraints of its own emergence and in dialogic opposition to that which it is constructed.

Whilst this type of possessive individualism is common in the men's accounts, it is not always considered by them to be a positive thing. As Peter told me, of his relationship: 'I felt so independent I think I began to realize that things were wrong.' Yet feelings of 'independence' and 'separateness' are common in the men's accounts. It is not simply that men cannot 'let themselves go' because they are male; that naturalizes the *effect* of gendered subjectivities as a *cause*. Rather, the cause of such radically different experiences in gendered subjectivity is heterosexuality itself. Positioned in relation to the discursive construct of gender, constrained in the heterosexual matrix, men re-produce a masculine version of themselves. This masculinity re-enacts the foundational principles of heterosexuality by aligning men with a *normative version* of what it means to be a heterosexual man. We are used to understanding this by looking at how men act 'outwardly' (in social life). We equate types of behaviour with a performative gesture of masculinity and see men manufacture their heterosexuality in public. But men also manufacture and produce a type of self 'inwardly', through a hermeneutic relationship with themselves which is regulated by the social 'rules' in which it is founded. This set of rules is brought to life through an engagement with love where men operationalize a particular form of masculine subjectivity which is built on a tension between how they 'fuse' together with the other whilst maintaining a separate sense of self.

Mark was the only man that I interviewed who talked at length about the ways that love can have positive effects on how he feels about himself. Yet it is clear from how he talks about such feelings that there is no simple link between falling in love and positive self-transformation. As Mark explained to me, even though he recognizes that being in love is *supposed* to affect and transform the self, this is something which he questions and remains cynical of:

MARK: I honestly don't know Paul if love, as such, exists at all. [I asked myself] *what* is love? And I thought long and hard about it and maybes I'm being over cynical or what I don't know, but I think maybe love is to do with self-esteem and it's a reaction to you seeing somebody thinking enough to want to spend the rest of their life with you. You know it's a like 'yes, got them', sort of thing. Maybes not as cruel and heartless as that, but unconsciously I think it's got something to do with that. You know it's like a pride thing, you know, they think enough of

me to want to be with me, it's like a feather in the cap sort of thing. Again, I think it harps back to self-esteem. It's all, I think a lot of it, has got a lot to do with self-esteem rather than like you feeling affection to them. It's like you feeling, as I say, a feather in your cap, or putting a badge on saying 'I'm great, they think the world of me.'
PJ: And how does that feel?
MARK: I think listening to myself telling you this it makes me feel incredibly conceited. It makes me feel like I'm not a very nice person at all.
PJ: Why?
MARK: Because, like, love is meant to be a two-way thing. I mean, true love I think is a two-way thing and I think it is all about me me me here, selfish, and it sounds horrible and I'm quite dismayed with myself.

The normative language of love suggests a highly emotional bond between two people which can instigate 'true love' for the lover and the beloved. But as Mark suggests, love can be experienced as a very selfish emotion, something which is used to put a 'feather in your cap'. Understanding love in this way makes Mark feel like he is 'incredible conceited' and 'selfish'. This is because Mark sees these effects on the self as highly suspect because love should be a 'two-way thing'. This two-way thing would be 'real love'; a process which was not simply the cynical process of allowing him to feel good about himself. For Mark, the equation of love with feelings of self-esteem does not make *him* feel the self-esteem; on the contrary, it makes him feel like he is 'not a very nice person'. It also makes him feel 'dismayed' with how, in expressing such opinions, it makes him 'sound horrible'.

For Mark, the split between how love is actually experienced and a 'true love' which remains illusive results in both a reification of the abstract discourses of love and instigates particular feelings about himself. The transformative potential of which the women speak remains essentially 'outside' of masculine selfhood because it cannot be incorporated into it. Whilst men, like women, feel lonely, isolated, bereaved, and long for love, they engage with love by maintaining a parameter (however fictitious) around a priori versions of selfhood. The discourses of love are therefore appropriated by men in profoundly different ways to women. This is because, as Hollway argues, discourses 'make available positions for subjects to take up. These positions are in relation to other people [but] taking up subject or object positions is not equally available to men and women' ([1984] 1998: 236). Whereas women experience the effects of love upon the self as a form of satisfying 'something' that is 'missing', men reproduce themselves as the ones whose selves are already whole. These are not *real* differences between discrete ontological sexes which pre-exist their enactment. They are the outcomes, the real effects, of the ways in which heterosexuality organizes gender as a relational system through which masculine and feminine subjectivities emerge.

Conclusion

If heterosexual love facilitates the production and assumption of subjectivities which are anchored within the binaries of masculine/feminine, then this *establishes* and *reproduces* gender. The process operates through a form of subjectification whereby subjects 'work' upon their subjectivities in accordance with the principles of their own realization (such principles being structured by the 'law' of sex difference which, in sustaining heterosexuality, is reiterated by subjects in their appropriation of masculine/feminine 'roles'). In this sense we can say that subjectivity is radically conditioned by the foundational principles of heterosexuality which are operationalized within the love relationship. It is therefore important to hold on to the Lacanian view of how sex difference 'works' even when, as Stevi Jackson argues, it often relies on 'dubious methodology', 'unfounded assumptions' and a 'residual essentialism' (1999: 91). I take Jackson's concerns very seriously but, as Butler suggests, the symbolic law of sex does not have any ontological essentiality outside of its performative reiteration. It is in this reiteration that I see the value of the framework because femininity and masculinity are always produced in relation to both the symbolic law of sex and the reproduction of that law in the relations of heterosexuality. The ways that love operationalizes subjectivity is through the duality of both confirming, and promising to negate, difference. In anchoring women within a state by which they feel subjectively transformed, where they feel 'whole', and where the loss of that wholeness would split them in half, love imposes its most compelling effects. In placing men in a strategic relation in which they confirm their normative superiority as 'already whole' beings, who 'give' to the feminine other who 'needs', love frames a normative version of masculinity. Love's compelling promise underwrites heterosexuality's compulsiveness because it sustains the conditions under which 'wholeness' is consolidated and lack is avoided. Love is therefore not a 'natural' process which takes place in a socially constructed set of heterosexual relations. On the contrary, love is a carrier of heterosexuality, a vehicle of gender production, and a mechanism for transferring heteronormative social relations into enduring subjectivities and identifications. It is not what love 'gives' to the self, nor what it 'takes away', but how it produces a way of being through which these effects are experienced.

The symbolic law of 'lack' is the mediating principle of male and female selfhood – women are positioned as in 'need'; men as 'having'. These are the *normative* positions which heterosexuality sets up for assumption in the love process. In 'doing' love, we reiterate these positions and install them as ontological effects. What we think of as 'real' difference is in fact a mirage, an imaginary system through which we locate the other and position ourselves. Anatomical sexual difference (the penis) is what Žižek (1989) would term the 'key signifier' in the 'ideological' field of signification. Such a signifier is forced, suggests Butler (1993), through a heterosexual matrix which constructs the either/or of sex in the positions of the 'complementary genders' of masculine/feminine. What is the effect of heterosexuality seems to be its cause. The central significance of lack is that femininity and masculinity stand as opposites to each other, opposites which come together to make a 'whole'. This is the organizing principle of heterosexuality and, in the experiences of the people in this study, is operationalized through the love relationship. Love is a site at which subjectivities are produced, installed and regulated. In enabling ourselves in love we constrain ourselves in convention. And in constraint we enable ourselves conventionally.

The objections to this type of argument could be numerous: isn't love a practice which can resist heteronormativity by being performed differently by subjects; isn't gender more complicated than this; what about lesbians and gay men; isn't the process too unilateral? Of course, to all of these questions the answer could be 'yes'. Yes, the subjectifying process set up by heterosexual love does appear unilateral and, yes, gender might be experienced in different ways. But whilst these objections may be salient, and whilst they may point to further research in this field, the normative force which heterosexuality exerts over gendered subjectivity, as a dividing practice operationalized in love, is considerable. Love installs, sediments and essentializes feminine and masculine subjectivities and, whatever the individual negotiation around those positions, they remain positions to be negotiated.

But what actually *causes* or *impels* men and women to approximate modes of subjectivity which are heterosexual? The objection might be: even if subjects are placed in a self/other relations through which they attempt to satisfy a lack, then why is this process heterosexualized? The analysis I offer in this chapter is inadequate without an understanding of how heteronormativity works, in direct relation with homosexuality, to sustain coherent subjectivities and identities with unbreakable borders. This is extremely important because homosexuality provides a definite set of parameters through which heterosexual identities and practices are consolidated into the normative positions of masculine and feminine which appear as 'complementary' to each other. It is specifically to this that I now turn in the next chapter where I consider the relational construction of heterosexual intimacies through the containment of the homosexual/heterosexual binary.

4 Haunting heterosexuality
Homosexuality and the borders of desire

PJ: Do you think gay men and lesbians fall in love in the same way?
PHILLIP: I'm sure they do, yes. It's still the same feeling. It's a mutual feeling and building trust, developing a relationship.
PJ: Would there be any differences between the love relationship that say two men might have, than the love relationship between a man and a women?
PHILLIP: No, I think it's exactly the same.

One of the most striking features about how the people I interviewed talked about love and intimacy is that they all said that it was not significantly affected by the sexuality (or 'sexual preference') of those who experience it. When speaking about homosexuality, every person expressed the belief that 'gay men and lesbians' experience love in exactly the same way as heterosexuals: 'love is love', they often said. Such a belief relies on a series of changes in the construction of sexuality, but it also draws upon the specific construction of an imagined universal essence of love. It seems to express what Anthony Giddens (1992) describes as the relationship between 'plastic sexuality' and 'confluent love' in late modernity; those contemporary social relations in which intimate love is 'freed-up' from the restrictions of institutional heterosexuality and becomes available to those outside of 'conventional' heterosexual relationships. But if 'love is love' and there is no difference between homo and hetero types of loving, then why did no-one I interview express the desire to love someone of the same sex? If love really is that 'essence' of being which we all universally share, then why is it constrained around gender?

PJ: [...] Do you think it would be possible for you to be in love or desire someone of the same sex?
BARBARA: No, I don't think so. In fact I'm fairly ... I've never had any ... I mean I have friends, I do have friends who are the same sex and I would use the word love, that I loved them, but that's not to say I would have a physical lesbian relationship with them. But I have very close female friends who I do sort of love. But I've never felt any

attractions towards another woman in terms of wanting a physical relationship.
PJ: Why do you think that is?
BARBARA: I don't know, it just hasn't happened, just hasn't been there really. I have no issue over other people, but not for me.

In this short exchange the relationship between love, gender and sexuality is brought into focus. What Barbara reiterates is a set of simple assertions regarding her sexuality and, importantly, the parameters to her heterosexual sexuality. Barbara is quite certain that a same-sex sexual relationship is not a possibility for her and that, even though she has 'close female friends' whom she 'loves', she rejects the idea that she could have a 'physical lesbian relationship'. As she states, homosexuality is 'not for me'. Yet, whilst Barbara expresses parameters to her own desire, drawn around the non-sexual relationships of 'friends who are the same sex' where she would 'use the word love', she also suggests that a lack of such parameters for other women, women who would develop a 'physical lesbian relationship', is not problematic. Barbara has, as she says, 'no issue' about the homosexual practice of others. The lack of her 'issue' regarding same-sex sexuality for others suggests a comfortable relationship with the 'issues' of sexuality more generally. Barbara does not want a homosexual relationship and she is not particularly concerned about why she doesn't want it or why it has not happened. Such a rejection of homosexuality is achieved in a normalized and modern language of sexual 'preference' and expressed within a conceptual framework of sexuality where a lack of same-sex desire needs little or no explanation – homosexuality is absent and she 'doesn't know why'.

Barbara expresses, some might argue, a progressive and enlightened tolerance of modern (homo)sexuality that can be seen to characterize the Euro-American transformation of sexuality in the late twentieth century. Yet what appears at first to be a series of benign statements in Barbara's account, built on what we commonly understand to be the personal preferences of sexuality, is at second glance far more complex. Although Barbara asserts that homosexuality is something that 'just hasn't been there' in her life, it is quite clear from her account that she is, like most people, fully aware of its existence. In one very simple way Barbara knows she is *not* homosexual, that she doesn't want a 'physical lesbian relationship', because she knows the parameters to her own desire and sexuality. But how do such parameters come about? How does Barbara decide what constitutes a 'friendship' which she can call 'love' and a relationship which constitutes a lesbian physicality? How does 'sexual preference' intersect in the conception of intimacy to close-off possibilities which are outside of the borders of heteronormative practice? How do the construction of such borders constitute, not just her own sexuality, but the 'outside' of that sexuality? And how might that outside function to maintain the boundaries of her own desire? Where does her sexuality begin and the sexuality of the 'lesbian' depart? These questions arise from Barbara's account because she *herself* constructs the boundaries of her own sexuality. In doing this she produces a corporeality to her own sexuality, with a definite 'inside' and 'outside', a set of parameters to her own practice which reflexively come to sustain her own desires. Heterosexuality, in this very important sense, is reliant on homosexuality to give it form.

The homo/het binary

It is this relationship between heterosexuality and homosexuality that I want to explore in this chapter. Specifically, I want to look at the ways in which the distinction created by the modern binary of homosexuality/heterosexuality (homo/het) constitutes a series of *dynamic borders* through which modern sexuality, as both practice and identity, is negotiated and produced. But, importantly, I want to show that the binary of homo/het is inculcated within, and co-extensive with the reproduction of, those modern 'liberalizing' discourses of sexuality and intimacy, which are displayed in the two quotations given above. These liberal discourses – of greater recognition, tolerance and a commitment to 'equality' for homosexuals – are often seen as representative of the disintegration of the strict parameters between homosexuality and heterosexuality. For Jeffrey Weeks, this process is 'an inevitable consequence of the developing cultural acceptance, and social embeddedness, of the lesbian and gay community as part of the growing pluralization of society' (Weeks, 2000: 213). For theorists such as Weeks, a culmination of social changes has resulted in the recognition of same-sex relationships as a viable alternative to heterosexuality. New discourses of intimacy, Weeks suggests, 'are making possible diverse ways of life which cut across the heterosexual/homosexual dichotomy' (Weeks, 2000: 214). Sasha Roseneil agrees, arguing that 'changes in the organization of intimacy are impacting upon the wider organization of sexuality' (2002: 33). She goes on to argue:

> we are currently witnessing a significant destabilization of the hetero/homosexual binary. The hierarchical relationship between the two sides of the binary, and its mapping onto an inside/out opposition, is undergoing intense challenge, and the normativity and naturalness of both heterosexuality and heterorelationality have come into question.
> (2002: 33)

Yet these commentaries put forward by Giddens, Roseneil, Weeks and others rely on a conceptual slippage which moves too easily between an analysis of changes in the deployment of sexuality and speculation about how this is affecting the homo/het binary (which then often results in inaccurate depictions of sexual identities as overly fluid and plastic). The fundamental mistake that these authors make is that, whilst there may be a general social tendency towards recognition of certain forms of homosexual intimacy, this has not necessarily impacted upon the organizing principles of sexuality in any meaningful way. We can see this in a cursory reading of the quotation from Barbara, where the 'diverse ways of life' of which Weeks speaks are fundamentally dichotomized around the binary of 'otherness' ('I have no issue' about homosexuality) and of 'self' (it's 'not for me'). In this sense, the liberal discourses of 'diversity' engendered by changes in the recognition of homosexual sexuality and intimacy have produced two effects: first, the 'toleration' of homosexual practices and identities *has* significantly altered but, second, homosexuality's distinctiveness remains intact (the outside/inside dichotomy is still omnipresent). Therefore, rather than seeing Barbara's words as testimony to a progressive movement towards the removal of sexual difference, or its plasticity, we can see it as representative of an *assertion* of difference and rigidity. The modern history of sexuality is not, we might argue, a movement of incorporation or a disintegration of boundaries; rather the history of modern sexuality is of specialization, of separating out, of producing defined and singular beings.

The great irony of modern sexuality, with its specialization of discrete sexual categories, is that we have come to understand homosexuality and heterosexuality as distinctly separate expressions of individual personhood. As Michel Foucault famously argued, the discursive demarcation of homosexuality and heterosexuality engages a new '*specification of individuals*' whereby the homosexual has become 'a personage, a past, a case history, a life form, and a morphology, with an indiscrete anatomy and possibly a mysterious physiology' (1979: 43, italics in original). But if this personage that Foucault describes belongs to the homosexual, then it also belongs to the heterosexual. If, as Foucault argues, the homosexual as a species was born in the nineteenth century, then so too was the modern heterosexual. Whilst heterosexuality appears as a sexuality outside of time, as a trans-historical mode of sexual expression, it is, as Jonathan Ned Katz argues an 'invented tradition' (1996: 182). It is a tradition which embraces the notion that homosexuality is a domain outside of its own fixed borders and boundaries, an excluded realm on the periphery of heterosexual normativity, and that it is an unchanging type of identity and practice which endures *in spite* of homosexuality. Yet, as Diana Fuss (1991) argues, identity positions and practices are founded relationally, in dialogic reference to an exterior which comes to mark the limits of the interiority it creates. In this sense, homosexuality is both outside heterosexuality *and* inside it. If heterosexual identity positions are manufactured through a disavowal of homosexuality then homosexuality is present at the centre of heterosexual identification; or, more precisely, it forms the nodal point for a series of dis-identifications.

If heterosexuality relies upon homosexuality to provide it with its own borders, it follows that, in order to produce and maintain a heterosexual identity, the subject must negotiate the boundaries with homosexuality with extreme care. As Stuart Hall argues:

Throughout their careers, identities can function as points of identification and attachment only *because* of their capacity to exclude, to leave out, to render 'outside', abjected. Every identity has at its 'margin', an excess, something more. The unity, the internal homogeneity, which the term identity treats as foundational is not a natural, but a constructed form of closure, every identity naming as its necessarily, even its silenced and unspoken other, that which it 'lacks'.

(Hall, 1996, italics in original)

One immediately thinks of Foucault's (1979: 27) assertion that silences are an integral part of the strategies which underlie discourses because silences function to provide ways in which other discourses can be incited, spoken and rendered visible. Maintaining silences in the construction of a sexual identity renders a consolidation of that which is made visible at the expense of that which is excluded. And yet, ironically, in the establishment of a heterosexual identity it is heterosexuality itself which usually remains linguistically silent (whilst, of course, being materially everywhere). Homosexuality, on the contrary, stands as a sexuality which is a permanent feature of spoken and written discourse. Returning to the above quotation by Barbara, we can see that homosexuality cannot be characterized as the 'unspoken', certainly not the 'love that dare not speak its name' because homosexuality is incited into speech by Barbara in order to demark a visible distinction between herself and homosexual practice and, thus, materialize her own sexuality. Homosexuality is used at the nodal point when Barbara's heterosexuality needs to be solidified because, as Hall suggests, it is used to define a margin, an excess, and furthermore, a way to make foundational claims about self and personhood. Barbara's heterosexuality becomes visible to us through the process of making homosexuality visible; her 'self' is dependent upon the other that she is not. Yet interestingly, as Wilkinson and Kitzinger (1993) note, it is heterosexuality which remains silent; the ever present, but unspoken, sexuality which results from the incitement into discourse of its homosexual other. As Halperin (1995) argues, homosexuality constitutes a specific domain of spoken and written discourse, whilst heterosexuality remains foundational, normative and unproblematic.

In view of the invocation and citation of homosexuality in the complex negotiation of the borders of sexual identity, Judith Butler argues:

that heterosexuality is always in the act of elaborating itself is evidence that it is perpetually at risk, that is, that it 'knows' its own possibility of becoming undone: hence, its compulsion to repeat which is at once a foreclosure of that which threatens its coherence.

(Butler, 1991: 23)

For Butler, heterosexuality has the perpetual difficulty of relying upon a homosexuality that it most wishes to disavow. In this sense it must continually re-make itself in relation to the strict parameters which sustain it as a recognizable, but exclusionary, sexual form. Homosexuality is, as Diana Fuss argues, an 'indispensable interior exclusion' to heterosexuality, an 'outside which is inside interiority making the articulation of [heterosexuality] possible' (1991: 3). Yet, because heterosexuality relies on homosexuality to provide it with its coherent form, homosexuality can be seen to 'haunt' heterosexuality; to form, as Fuss argues, 'the spectre of abjection' (1991: 3) which continually rubs up against the ontological boundaries which heterosexuality seeks to solidify. Every time the subject makes a disavowal of homosexuality, ejecting homosexuality from the centre to the outside, homosexuality reappears, troubling heterosexuality, rendering it unstable. Thus, the borders of identity created through the homo/het binary cannot be seen to be stable in any permanent sense. Rather such borders, as Butler argues, must be constantly re-made in view of the knowledge that homosexuality is constantly present in both the interior and exterior of sexual subjectivity. Hence Butler's assertion that heterosexuality constitutes a form of 'compulsive performativity', a necessary form of repeating which demands a constant maintenance of the borders which exclude the other.

Sexual identities are multifarious, complex and cross-cutting. If they are 'plastic' or 'fluid', in the sense that they are continually remade and produced, they are not merely voluntaristic. Regardless of our expression of sexuality, the homo/het binary remains central to the organization of it and maintains divisions between practices deemed homosexual and heterosexual. Yet, what we are witnessing is a profound transformation in the ways in which difference and distinction is managed and deployed. The rise in liberal discourses directed at homosexuality is present in the 'progressive' social and governmental moves to equalize and legitimize same-sex relationships in law. What are also visible are both old and new homophobic and illiberal sexualized discourses. One explanation of this process of social change is that homophobia declines through the instigation of new social and public policies aimed at encouraging sexual and intimate pluralism. Yet a fundamental feature of contemporary sexual relationships is that they, by their very nature, reiterate distinctions. We *may* be a plural society, but we are organized by difference.

Many commentators on sexuality want to abandon ideas about regulation and constraint – the homo/het binary seeming a little old-fashioned in an age of sexual pluralism. Yet, whilst sexual identities and practices appear as the benign and neutral expressions of personal 'preference', the modern social construction of sexuality masks the very real effects of the homo/het binary and the strict maintenance of sexual borders which it institutes. In view of this binary, Diana Fuss argues that what we need is 'a theory of sexual borders that will help us come to terms with, and to organize around, the new cultural and sexual arrangements occasioned by the movements and transmutations of pleasure in the social field' (1991: 5). Yet what we also need is an *empirical* account of sexual borders and how they continue to organize how and who we desire and love. In the following sections I explore some of the ways in which the homo/het binary is expressed and, as a consequence, how heterosexual identities are performatively iterated and 'made'.

Disgust at the parameters of desire

> Our preferences have to be a good cover story for our terrors.
> (Phillips, 2001: 54)

When I spoke to the men in this study about the possibility of them having a same-sex relationship, all of them said that they would not do it. In light of various claims that many of the men had made about same-sex love being 'the same' as heterosexual love, I asked them why they would not consider it? If homosexual love is 'the same' then what would be 'the difference'?

MARTIN: I can't help feeling quite repulsed by the idea to be honest, which...
PJ: What repulses you?
MARTIN: Not falling in love with them, but the idea of male, gay ... it's really, it's a typical male thing really, it's just gay male sex, like I find it very 'ugh, oh no, oh no, that's terrible'. Well not terrible, but I can't help taking a mental step backwards and thinking, ah, shit.
PJ: But you're not repulsed by the idea of men falling in love with each other? It's the sex?
MARTIN: Yeah, yeah [laughs]. Stupid isn't it, it's really ridiculous.

There are a number of things going on here but centrally Martin is repulsed by the idea of gay male sex. Such disgust is, he suggests, a 'typical male thing' (although it cannot be typical for homosexual men). Yet Martin had previously in the interview elaborated a sophisticated liberal attitude to homosexuality and told me that he believed in 'equality' and marriage rights for gays and lesbians. Is that why, in light of his commitment to equality and tolerance, that he finds it 'ridiculous' to have these feelings of repulsion? Shouldn't such thoughts have disappeared within a society of equal 'sexual citizens' which he, and many others, subscribes to? Or are Martin's feelings a rare expression of discrimination and prejudice; the last bastion of bigotry, soon to be wiped out by sexual pluralization? Martin answers this question himself: sexual disgust is actually a 'typical' element of the ways in which heterosexual men talk about male same-sex sexual activity.

Like Martin, most men separated ideas about homosexual sexual acts from the notion of homosexual love; they were never disgusted by the idea of men loving each other yet, in considering same-sex intimacy, 'homosexual sex' provided a central point of repulsion. This is an interesting dichotomy because it reveals a certain ambivalence over homosexual love relationships and an absolute disgust of homosexual sex. How can we reconcile these seemingly paradoxical ideas? What I found was that feelings of disgust were only ever present when men considered *themselves* engaged in a homosexual relationship. I found disgust and repulsion over sexual *acts* to be a nodal point of tension when men considered who *they* might love. In short, in considering the possibility of a homosexual love relationship it is the sex 'act' which becomes the reason for its impossibility.

It is not simply 'gay male sex' which is the point of repulsion but also the specific act of (male homosexual) anal sex. As Mark explains to me:

MARK: I mean, certainly, to a certain extent, it's horrible to have to admit it, but I find the idea of a bloke penetrating another bloke a bit repulsive. But that's the only side that I find repulsive. You know, that's the only element to homosexuality in blokes that I find repulsive, that puts me off. You know the idea of somebody getting shit all over their dick basically, I think it's horrible, I don't think it's natural, I think anal sex is, you know . . . But apart from that I've got absolutely no taboos relating to homosexuality whatsoever.

To claim to have no 'taboos' over homosexuality but to relate, in such strong terms, an absolute horror of homosexual anal sex may seem like two contradictory statements. Yet Mark gives us a clue to how these feelings can coexist by saying that his disgust is 'horrible to have to admit'. Like Martin, who says he finds his repulsion 'ridiculous', there is a certain horror about the feeling itself. Yet clearly, even though they may be horrible to have to admit, feelings of disgust are very strong. For Mark the homosexual sex 'act' is constructed as disgusting, involves the idea of dirt, of mess, of shit (surely the shit is, as Freud's saying goes, matter which is essentially out of place[1]) and is deemed to be 'unnatural'. For Mark, we might argue, anal sex stands at the centre of what homosexuality *is* because it is a nodal point of what homosexuals *do*. Besides everything else – their identities, their love relationships, their intimate practices – homosexuality involves 'a bloke penetrating another bloke'. So, Mark's claim that he has no 'taboos' regarding any other aspect of homosexuality is rendered facile by his central preoccupation with anal sex because anal sex, the 'unnatural' act, comes to constitute what homosexuality is.[2]

In focusing on these 'disgusting' acts, what Mark and Martin are effecting is a delimitation of their own desire and the possibilities for certain intimate practices.[3] Because anal sex comes to stand *for* homosexuality,[4] then the repulsion towards what one imagines homosexuality to *be* becomes an indicator that one is not 'a homosexual'. This is not surprising and the feelings expressed here may be extremely common. For if the act of buggery stands (as it does in law[5]) as the defining moment of enacting homosexuality, and thus by default *being* a homosexual, wouldn't the idea of placing one's penis into the anus of another man be a central point of prohibition? Wouldn't the margin of homosexual anal sex be a line that would be unthinkable to cross? Wouldn't it represent a form of sexual practice which was irreconcilable with one's own heterosexual identity? And what would prohibit a desire of such practice if not the opposite of desire, disgust?

Disgust is intrinsically bound up with sexual desire, providing a boundary to forms of sexuality which are deemed 'outside' of what one associates with normative (and thus not 'unnatural') sexual activity. Yet, this important function of disgust within sexuality is not something we are used to thinking of. As Jonathan Dollimore (2001) suggests, even though we are saturated by the notion of desire, we rarely consider how our own desires are formulated in relation to their boundaries. As Dollimore argues, sexual identities are often seen to be founded through 'indifference' or 'neutrality', the result of some benign notion of sexual 'preference'. Yet, preference conceals a multitude of negotiations through which sexual identity is constituted, not least around the binary of homo/het, and recalls a naturalized and foundational essence which does not elaborate the relationship of desire to its margins of repulsion. Individuals who feel disgust towards homosexual sex are often quick to assert that they have no problems with homosexual 'people'. In this way, their own sexual desire seems to be founded on some abstract notion of 'it's just not for me' but 'live and let live'. Yet, if that were the case, why is disgust expressed so strongly? Disgust, suggests Dollimore:

> can work to protect cultural and bodily boundaries; but often does so in ways which indicate their vulnerability to disruption, and the psychological and social cost paid for securing them. It can be a reaction which consolidates individual identity, or a disavowal which threatens it.
> (2001: 47)

He goes on to argue that disgust:

> reveals so much about ourselves and our culture. At the same time it suggests how little we really know about either. There is something mysterious or at least elusive about the dialectic between desire and disgust, within both the individual psyche and the larger culture.
> (2001: 48)

The disgust and repulsion felt by Mark and Martin isn't simply 'homophobia', although it may render a certain form of homophobia visible, but rather an expression of the dialectic of desire and disgust which Dollimore outlines; a dialectic through which desire is consolidated into a coherent, and in this instance, heterosexual form. In this sense, their heterosexuality is secured through prohibition and erasure of specific acts which are rendered 'outside' of heterosexual desire. Yet, given the rise of sexual liberalism and tolerance for homosexuality, such disgust commonly becomes buried and difficult to speak of. Given that displaying disgust may result in either the charge of bigotry or, perhaps worse, evidence of repressed desire, it needs to be managed with care. Therefore, the liberal language of sexuality, and the type of pluralism which Weeks (2000) and Giddens (1992) identify, can be seen, rather than to *replace* the boundaries of desire, to contribute to *disguising* them. The result is a belief in untroubled individuality, desire free from the feelings of disgust, and a sexuality based on voluntaristic preference. As a consequence, 'the disgusted individual becomes vaguely disgusting' (Dollimore, 2001: 48).

As Dollimore argues, there is something mystifying about disgust, something ambiguous and unreachable about it. This is clear in how William describes his repulsion of gay male sex:

WILLIAM: I don't ... I can't explain it. I think it's probably a gut feeling but the homosexual sex act just makes me feel ... it's not something I like the thought of, full stop. It just makes me feel ... not any outside influences make me feel that way, it just makes me feel ... I mean my nephew, is an actual homosexual but he's always going to be my nephew and I don't judge him by how he feels he wants to have relationships. But it isn't something I feel comfortable, the physical fact of it, with.

William's admission that he 'can't explain' his disgust is interesting. He is quite sure that it isn't any 'outside influences' which make him feel this way but rather a 'gut' feeling. This suggests that sexual disgust is felt as a natural expression of the self, a fundamental property of sexuality which emanates from 'inside'. And yet of course this 'inside' is most certainly dependent on 'outside influences' because the parameters to William's desires can only be set in context with others. We can read this invocation of inside/outside in two ways. First, it can be seen to be a claim which naturalizes sexuality inside the body and produces a pristine core of subjectivity untouched by the outside world. Second, from this basis it is possible for William to make claims about the naturalness of his sexual preferences because they seem to result from a causal chain of biology–sexuality–desire–disgust. And if disgust of gay male sex is something which is 'typical' of all heterosexual men (although this may be a constructed truism), heterosexuality therefore uses that truism to naturalize its causal chain. The 'gut' feeling, if all men feel it, suggests a natural heterosexual feeling towards the unnatural 'act'. We can also see that William, when he talks about 'outside influences', might be distancing himself from homophobic discourses with which he could be seen to be aligned. Look how, even in talking about his disgust, William expresses simultaneously the language of tolerance regarding his nephew who is gay, someone he doesn't 'judge'. Yet this liberal attitude to homosexuality clearly does not extend to himself. His own desire, unlike his nephew's, is trenchantly opposed to the 'physical fact' of homosexuality (which contrasts with the 'facts' of heterosexuality).

The borders of love, friendship and (homo)sexual desire

The prevalence of repulsion about homosexuality among the people I interviewed was certainly not gendered and many of the women expressed similar feelings to the men. What was gendered, however, was the different form the repulsion took because, for the women I spoke to, their disgust was not focused on a particular sexual act. Consider the following extract from an interview with Ruth:

RUTH: I just don't, I just don't feel like having sex with another woman. I'm not saying that, I'm not saying I'd find it distasteful, I just haven't, I just don't really . . .
PJ: Would you find it distasteful?
RUTH: I really don't know, I haven't really thought about it, you know. I sleep with all of my girlfriends, you know they'll come over and I'll say, 'oh don't go in the spare room I haven't made the bed, just sleep with me'. You know, we'll cuddle up at night but that's it, I don't think about snogging them, I don't think about it.
PJ: And if you did think about it, would you find it distasteful?
RUTH: Probably, probably.
PJ: So what would it make you feel like?
RUTH: Sick.
PJ: Yeah? In what sense?
RUTH: Well I don't know I just can't, I just can't, I can't, I just don't fancy snogging another woman.

Although at first Ruth says that the thought of same-sex sex isn't 'distasteful', she comes to admit that the idea makes her feel 'sick'. Yet this form of repulsion is different from the disgust expressed by the men. For instance, Ruth expresses her disgust in a more subtle way because she frames it within a context in which she is already describing a form of intimacy between herself and her female friends. She is marking the distinction between sleeping in the same bed as her female friends, where they might 'cuddle up', and kissing them. I began this chapter with a quotation from an interview with Barbara where she makes a similar distinction between friends whom she feels very close to and forms of physicality which remain prohibited. This type of divide occurs frequently in the ways which women talk about friendship and sexuality. Men do not, generally, talk about friendship in such intimate terms; their distinctions between physical intimacy and friendship seem to be much further apart than those described by the women. Particularly, for Ruth, there is a form of intimate love bound up with friendship which involves physical bodily contact, albeit in a way which is not deemed 'sexual'.

Negotiating the border between love, sex and sexuality is something in which both men and women engage. For women, the border is dynamic, intermeshed with forms of intimacy, but certainly controlled. In the extract below, Patricia describes her feelings about friendship and sexual relationships:

PJ: Do you think it would ever be possible for you to be in love with someone of the same sex?
PATRICIA: No, I've tried to imagine myself in a lesbian relationship and I can't.
PJ: Why do you think that is?
PATRICIA: I'm not attracted to women sexually. I have had some very good women friends. You know I can certainly envisage sharing a house with a woman but it wouldn't be that sort of loving, sexual relationship. Yes, I would say I was fond of certain women, you could say that I loved them, but it wouldn't be sexual.
PJ: You couldn't be in love with them?
PATRICIA: No. And we wouldn't be a unit, ever. You know, from a sexual ... lesbians are a unit. We'd just be two friends living together.

Patricia has a definite view of the distinction between a loving friendship and a 'loving, sexual relationship'. Yet the border is constructed and maintained particularly through the use of the word 'lesbian' and Patricia's understanding of what constitutes a lesbian relationship. Although Patricia has tried to 'imagine' herself in a lesbian relationship, her desire is constrained around issues of attraction. Patricia can imagine herself living with a woman and sharing a house together, perhaps with one of the friends whom she loves, but she cannot imagine this being a 'lesbian relationship'. By invoking 'lesbian', a border is created which marks a point to what is permissible as loving friendship and what could become an undesirable homosexuality. Notice that Patricia first suggests that if she did share a house with another woman it could never be a 'loving, sexual relationship' like that of a lesbian relationship. Yet she adds, about her friends, that 'you could say that I loved them, but it wouldn't be sexual'. So Patricia invokes a distinction between love and sex which can incorporate an intimate form of love towards her female friends but maintain intimacy with certain (sexualized) limits and constraints. In this sense, ways of loving are constrained around the parameters of heterosexuality but, reflexively, shore up those same parameters because, by delimiting *who* and *how* she can and cannot love, Patricia delimits her sexual practice and identity as heterosexual. Patricia's reason for finding a same-sex relationship unimaginable is quite clear: it is the limit imposed between love and intimacy by sex and sexuality.

Although the borders which control same-sex heterosexual intimacy may be gendered phenomena, it would be wrong to suggest that men's friendships were devoid of intimate expression. Men, like women, have to negotiate the sexual boundaries of friendship in much the same way. The central difference is one of visibility. The men I interviewed were more ready to disassociate all forms of intimacy from their same-sex friendships whereas, as we can see, the women have 'higher' levels of emotional and physical intimacy with other women.[6] Although the accounts of friendship from the women I spoke to are littered with reference to intimacy, in a way that the men's are not, I was struck by how Carl described a long-standing male friendship:

PJ: I wanted to ask you if you have ever been in love with or desired anyone of the same sex?
CARL: No, I don't think I have. I've joked about it [laughs].
PJ: You've joked about it?
CARL: Yeah.
PJ: In what sense?
CARL: Well me and Gavin have always, Gavin my friend, we're dead good friends who have outlasted all sorts of relationships and we've always seemed to end up in the same places for the last three years. We've ended up going in different career paths and coming back together and we kind of think ... we cuddle up on the sofa, or whatever, and as we despair in all our relationships with women we say, ah what the hell, why don't we just do it together and just indulge each other [laughs].
PJ: But it's not really a possibility for you though?
CARL: No.
PJ: Why is that?
CARL: Because I'm not gay. I just can't see it.
PJ: Is it about attraction?
CARL: I think there is something about that.
PJ: Sex?
CARL: Yeah, it's attraction and sex.
PJ: So even though that's a joke you couldn't imagine having that relationship?
CARL: Well I can imagine it, but I can't imagine it being ... it wouldn't feel right. I mean I couldn't ... [laughs].

Carl and his friend 'joke' about 'indulging each other' in a manner that is perhaps a safe way of talking to each other about homosexuality. That is not to suggest that they want to have sex with each other; they may 'joke' about it as a way of deliberately maintaining the parameters of their friendship. Yet their friendship does involve a certain amount of intimacy in that they 'cuddle up on the sofa' and lament their failures at sustaining sexual and romantic relationships with women. Indeed the 'joke' actually constitutes a good question: given that they are very close, that they have things in common, and they share a certain level of intimacy, why not have a sexual relationship? We can see that when I ask Carl about attraction he confirms, like Patricia, that this is one of the reasons he could not have a same-sex relationship. He is also made uncomfortable by the suggestion of same-sex

sex. It is precisely because he *can* imagine it that he can't imagine feeling comfortable with it and, at the end of the quotation, we can see that he legitimates this with saying it wouldn't 'feel right'.

Carl also utilizes a very simple performative statement in negating the idea of a same-sex sexual relationship when he says: 'I'm not gay.' In one very simple sense we see how, through a dis-identification, an identification is made. In invoking what he is not, Carl can ontologize that which he is. Yet this performative statement relies on a number of presuppositions regarding sexuality. First, it requires us to recognize that sexualities are discrete categories with causal mechanisms which direct desire. It follows that one's sexual identity becomes established because one is, and always will be, only attracted to a defined gender. Yet we know, from various studies, that sexual practices and identity do not necessarily coalesce very easily and that 'heterosexual men' often have same-sex sex (certainly a truism now but, when first outlined by Kinsey *et al.*, 1948, was a revolutionary observation). Second, the dis-identification which Carl makes relies upon the homo/het binary as the central axis of sexuality. It reiterates the normative idea that when we invoke the name of our sexuality, we are talking about something which pre-exists our enactment of it, because it is inside of us, it drives us. Yet, ironically, the naturalized essence of sexuality, as a pre-existing installation of being, is produced and materialized through its reiteration in language, through its 'naming', and not before it. As Butler notes: 'A name tends to fix, to freeze, to delimit, to render substantial, indeed, it appears to recall a metaphysics of substance, of discrete and singular types of beings' (1997a: 35). Yet what is interesting is that the 'name' which Carl uses to ontologize his sexuality is not the name heterosexual but, on the contrary, homosexual. It is precisely at the moment when Carl invokes homosexuality, placing himself within the homo/het binary, that his sexuality becomes visible.

The parameters of desire and attraction

> The desire of the subject is not transparent: it does not give us the truth of the self from which it emerges.
> (Butler, 1999a: 20)

Issues of love, intimacy and sexual desire may be seen to fundamentally separate out when heterosexuals consider a same-sex relationship. Where, in their own intimate relationships, love and sex are in a symbiotic (albeit vacillating) relationship, in considering homosexuality they are torn asunder: sex is neither the potential for, nor the outcome of, intimacy but the fundamental reason why a same-sex love relationship could never happen. This may seem a simple and unproblematic result of an innate and directional sexuality. Indeed it supports the idea that sexuality is an all-encompassing and once-and-for-all defined way of being. Yet, as Judith Butler argues, to think that we craft our sexualities so that they are forever focused on members of the opposite sex with whom we want to have some kind of genital sex, well 'it's a fairly funny way of being in the world' (1994: 34). Yet, at least as it is publicly expressed and socially constituted, desire and attraction are understood to be highly stable around the homo/het binary. It is one of the most common ways to express the take-up position of a sexual identity because 'who' one is attracted to expresses 'what' type of sexual being one is.[7]

Whether it is a funny way of being in the world or not, the language of attraction (of, for example, 'fancying someone') was a common invocation in the justification for the prohibition of same-sex love. Consider the following:

PJ: Would there . . . has there ever been a possibility when you would have considered a same-sex relationship?
GARY: No.
PJ: No?
GARY: No, never come across that at all. Never had feelings that way. I have a very open mind about it and have never been approached by anyone of the same sex, ever. Which possibly means I've led a sheltered life but, as I say, I have met quite a few gay men in, through my work, especially in the last six, seven years, and it hasn't changed my opinion of them at all. It doesn't appeal to me.
PJ: What doesn't appeal to you?
GARY: I just don't find them attractive basically. I find women attractive . . .

Attraction is used by Gary to legitimate and demonstrate his own heterosexuality. Although he does this in a way which relies on a liberal framework of sexual tolerance – 'a very open mind about it' – homosexuality is not something which 'appeals' to him. His 'open mind' therefore refers to the practices of others rather than to himself, and expresses the modern language of 'personal preference' which disguises the trenchant opposition to an 'open mind' at the heart of the homo/het binary. Not finding 'them', by which he means all men, attractive is an extremely general statement. Yet it is a statement which carries with it the normative weight of the constitution of sexuality and, as such, appears 'natural'. However, the way in which we talk about attraction is often a vehicle for materializing sexuality rather than a result of it. The language of attraction does not automatically express some inner essence of sexuality; on the contrary, it is a way of accomplishing sexual identities. For instance, consider how, in the accounts below, Phillip and Jackie delimit the parameters of their own sexualities by invoking a normative and biological understanding of complementary gendered attraction:

PJ: But [a same-sex relationship] is not something you've ever done?
PHILLIP: Not something I've ever done.
PJ: And why is that do you think?

PHILLIP: [...] I can't see myself in a relationship like I was in a relationship with my wife. I can't see myself in a relationship with a member of the same sex in the same way.

PJ: Why not?

PHILLIP: I don't know. Never thought about it. I couldn't see a physical relationship developing whereas I could see a physical relationship developing with a woman. You know, shapely, attractive, and like the magnets, you know the opposite poles of the magnets. That wouldn't happen to me – I don't think so anyway – with a member of the . . . another man, other men.

JACKIE: I've never fallen in love with a girl and in fact I wouldn't like to because I don't think . . . not that I was taught not to or I'm brain-washed into something, but, I don't know. I think it's only natural that you have feelings towards men I suppose, me being a woman. So I really, I don't know. No, I don't think so, I'm not that way, I like men [laughs]. No, I'm sorry, I don't think I'll ever have a relationship with a woman, no I wouldn't, I love men so much. And I think it is unnatural for me, I think, the way I was brought up.

Both Jackie and Phillip invoke parameters to their sexuality with recourse to a heterosexualized conception of gendered desire. They use different methods to naturalize heterosexuality but the effect is the same: they instantiate different genders as complementary to each other and as the 'normal' basis for intimate relationships. Philip uses the metaphor of 'magnets' to imagine a natural synthesis between men and women (presumably, the same poles of a magnet would repel each other, forcing each other away). In the previous chapter I argued that ideas about 'complementary' genders are essential to naturalized conceptions of heterosexuality. Yet this construction of gender is itself made real through a rejection of what might be 'unnatural' gender relations: in short, homosexuality. We can see this in how Jackie rejects the idea that her 'natural' attraction to men is the result of being 'brain-washed', of having been 'taught' it. Jackie believes she is attracted to men simply because she is a woman, that it is 'natural', and because of how she was 'brought up'. What Jackie invokes in support of her heterosexuality is first the 'law' of gender difference but, second, the idea of *social* parameters instigated by being 'brought up' in a particular way. In other words, claims about 'natural' gender difference are not enough; there needs to be recourse to the notion of the social world and its networks of constraint. 'Nature' cannot ever fully support heterosexuality because to go against nature is a spectre of possibility which is always present.

The interrelationship between naturalized ideas about gender is a crucial factor in the construction of a delimited heterosexual identity and itself raises sociological questions about how we might theorize the relationship between gender and heterosexuality. For instance, is it gender difference which is structuring heterosexuality, or vice versa, is gender the outcome of heterosexuality? Given the examples provided by Jackie and Phillip, it seems clear that, as Judith Butler (1990; 1993) argues, gender is a taxonomy which is created in service of the heterosexual imperative; that is, rather than pre-exist heterosexuality, ideas about gender are negotiated within the heterosexual matrix. It is clear from the ways that both Jackie and Phillip talk about their attractions to the 'opposite sex' that they are invoking the axis of gender as the basis of their heterosexuality. But they also rely upon ideas about homosexuality to establish their conceptions of how gender 'works'. In both accounts, the performative iteration of heterosexuality requires the disavowal of homosexuality to establish claims about 'natural' gendered desire.

Conclusion

If heterosexual identity is constrained through the invocation and maintenance of 'border controls' with homosexuality, then it follows that forms of intimate love, in practice, become prohibited. Ideas and feelings about sexuality exert a productive power over ways of loving, and forms of intimate practices, deemed homosexual: they strangle them. Hiding in the modern language of 'preference', intimate love and sexual desire seem to be the practical outcome of the 'inner' necessities of personhood. What is at work here is a twofold process of hiding the social construction of heterosexuality and establishing a normative and natural sexual identity: first, through a rejection of homosexuality as 'outside' of themselves, heterosexuals establish an ontological validity for their own identities and, second, as a consequence, their own intimate practices are naturalized. As such, in constraining who they love, by erecting borders and boundaries to intimacies not permitted, they become *what* they are and in becoming what they are they delimit who they love. In this very important sense *becoming heterosexual* is reliant upon renouncing the spectre of homosexual intimacy. However, a distinction must be made between a form of renunciation in *practice* and the way that such repudiation structures desire. Although the relationship between sexual desire, and its expression in intimate practices, may appear relatively unproblematic, it needs further consideration. For instance, does the performative repudiation of homosexual desire mean that 'the heterosexual' is a singular and defined desiring being? In the next chapter, and in light of what I have argued above, I want to think about how desire can be thought of outside of the practices and identities to which it is attached.

5 The escape of desire, the constraints of love

Throughout this book I have argued that intimate love is, in various ways, at the service of the heterosexual imperative. Constructed as an 'essence' (which 'connects' two people together in a 'natural' and 'biological' bond), love is interwoven with heterosexual sexual practice, frames the production of heteronormative gendered subjectivity, and intersects in the binaries of sexual identity. Now I want to turn, with a specific focus on three testimonies,[1] to examine how forms of desire 'escape' the constraints of heterosexuality. Specifically, I want to look at forms of ambiguous desire that are produced by the foreclosure of heterosexual sexuality; in other words, at the ways in which the construction of heterosexuality both enables and constrains forms of homosexual desire.

In the last chapter I argued that heterosexuality institutes a range of constraints around identity and delimits practice in specific ways. But, as I showed, heterosexuality does not simply constrain the desiring self but *produces* it. If the 'borders' of sexual identity institute concrete parameters for intimate *practices*, they also create ways of relating to the self, a hermeneutics of desire, which could exceed the limits placed upon practice. There is always a 'gap' between our material enactment of desire, in practice, and the psychic life of our own desires. This is because the desiring self stands at the 'borders' which the delimitation of heterosexuality creates, not simply as the self which is guarded and self-patrolled at such check-points, but as a self which could potentially transgress such borders. Where such possibility exists, a form of agency is present and this agency makes the gap between psychic desire and intimate practice a realm of unstable and unknown possibilities.

In the last chapter I stressed the need for (hetero)sexual subjects to negotiate the borders of homo/het in their everyday lives. But given that I have also stressed the need for heterosexuals to performatively reiterate their heterosexuality through these borders with homosexuality, a homosexuality that continually haunts its other, then it follows that such performative reiteration will be complex, involve ambiguities and perhaps even fail. Whilst I have stressed that sexual subjects are constituted within certain discursive parameters, through which they reiterate and incite the historical conventions of sexuality in order to produce recognizable sexualities, I want to look here at the ways in which such performative reiteration can be characterized less by a process of unilateral subjection and more by tensions within subjectification. In this sense I am concerned to show that, whilst the 'border controls' I have outlined are most certainly invoked by subjects, such controls also produce forms of ambivalence and ambiguity. We cannot suppose that power 'works' in a unilateral way to the exclusion of agency; it is precisely because agency is present that negotiating the homo/het binary is a tenuous and 'weak' process.

The question of agency is crucial to understanding the homo/het binary. Yet how are we to imagine this agency? If we accept that the discourses of sexuality are compulsorily incited, through the homo/het binary, but materialized in a number of ways, then the self might emerge, as Butler argues, 'in ways that can't quite be anticipated' and that might be 'unpredictable' (1999a: 164). For Butler this is because agency is produced at the very moment the subject reiterates the conventions in which it exists. In this sense, the working of power is itself a process which is characterized by a form of indeterminate agency because, at the moment of reiterating conventionality, the subject has the capacity to achieve this unconventionally. Such a view is informed by Foucault's theorization of processes of subjectification, where subjects 'effect by their own means or with the help of others a certain number of operations on their own bodies and souls, thoughts, conduct, and way of being' (1988: 18).

It is this process of 'self-elaboration' which necessarily involves a form of agency that renders the 'compulsory' operation of the homo/het binary fragile. The negotiation of sexuality is never a process of unilateral division, dividing people into permanent and concrete sexualities to be retained for all time. On the contrary, the power of sexuality 'works' through its constant reiteration and performative citation which materializes sexual ontology in certain configurations. But in 'performing' sexuality, and in constructing ourselves as sexual beings and desiring selves, we are forced to negotiate ambiguities and faultlines to our own sexual borders. These ambiguities arise because we might always be more than the terms by which we are named; we always might exceed the terms 'homosexual' and 'heterosexual'. Although we are compelled to decipher ourselves through a regime of sexuality which produces the discrete categories that we come to inhabit, we come to exist as sexual beings through a process of self-understanding which does not guarantee a synthesis between our 'self' and the category of our sexuality. We are often more than the identity that we possess, and our desires and thoughts may not always accord with our social identifications. In the next section I want to explore how heterosexual identity constrains intimate practices whilst, at the same time, enabling types of desire which remain endless and unquantifiable forms of transgressive possibility.

Action constrained but desire retained

When I spoke to some of the people in this study about the possibilities of them considering a same-sex relationship, although they frequently invoked the 'border controls' outlined in the previous chapter, they also spoke about their desires in ways which suggested a definite ambiguity or ambivalence about their own heterosexuality. This was certainly the case in an interview with Margaret when we discussed whether or not she would consider a 'lesbian relationship'. At first Margaret was quite adamant that she would not and when I asked her why she used the common 'border controls' of attraction and friendship to delimit the relationships she formed with women. But I went on to ask her if she could imagine that changing in the future and whether a same-sex relationship would ever be something she would consider?

MARGARET: Oh I've thought about it, yeah. I've imagined the thought, I've thought I wonder if I could ever ... what would it be like, it passes through your head, what would it be like. And I think, oh, it would be quite good because at least a woman knows what a woman likes. I think, oh, it would be nice to try it. But then I don't think I would actually have the nerve to try it.

Margaret has clearly given some thought to the idea of a same-sex relationship. She has considered what having sex with another woman would be like and she has evaluated this against heterosexual sex by comparing how men and women relate to each other's bodies. She thinks it would be 'nice' to try and that it may even be 'quite good'. In this sense, although Margaret has always been heterosexual and had heterosexual relationships, the 'thought' of homosexuality is not absent. As I have argued previously, we can see this as a result of the way in which heterosexuality is constituted by having homosexuality both at its centre and at its margins. Heterosexuality must forever push homosexuality outside itself to maintain its own parameters, yet homosexuality remains forever 'in' heterosexuality as a spectre of possibility ('it passes through your head'). This dual 'function' of homosexuality is expressed by Margaret: it is clear that homosexuality is fundamental to her own sense of heterosexual identification because it is something that she has considered (it is therefore a part of what constitutes her own identity, albeit through a form of negation) and it is also clearly demarked as outside of her sexual *practices*. Yet the boundaries of this 'outside' are not unilaterally fixed. If Margaret relies on the border with homosexuality to maintain a coherent sense of heterosexual identity, then those same borders also function as a transgressive possibility, something that one might cross if one had the 'nerve' to do so. I asked Margaret if she thought she would ever have the 'nerve' to try it?

MARGARET: Oh no, I've thought about it, I thought about what it would be like, yeah, I've thought about it, I suppose it would be quite nice. But not for me.

PJ: Because you haven't got the nerve to do it?
MARGARET: Probably [laughs] yeah.
PJ: So do you think you could ever have the nerve to do it?
MARGARET: If I was very drunk probably [laughs].

So again Margaret reiterates her view that it would be 'quite nice' to have a same-sex relationship but that it is 'not for me'. Yet, her ambiguity over the possibility of transgressing the parameters of her own heterosexuality is clearly invoked around the concept of 'nerve'. If she was drunk, she jokes, she may find that 'nerve'. We need to understand that the potential of 'nerve' is produced as a tangible form of agency around the homo/het binary. Whilst the power of sexuality works through the self to produce delimitations of practice and constraints of action, it also produces this quality of 'freedom' which is expressed by Margaret's idea of a transgressive possibility. For what if Margaret did find that 'nerve'? What if she did act upon her notion that a same-sex relationship would be 'quite nice'? And why doesn't she? One reason she does not act is clearly because the normative constraints of heterosexual practice are installed to prevent such a transgression, invoking feelings of discomfort and a tangible sense of self-anxiety: 'it wouldn't feel right . . . I would just feel, oh I couldn't . . . uncomfortable'. Margaret's sense of unease was tangible during the interview. And yet that unease itself sits uneasily with her own sense of a same-sex relationship being 'quite nice'.

Like most of the other women I spoke to Margaret talked about 'loving' her friends. But she was also quick to delimit that love as non-sexual:

MARGARET: [. . .] I mean, I like to have a close friend who I'm very, very close to. But if it went sexual it would spoil the relationship. We couldn't be friends, it would go over the line. So no, I wouldn't like it.

This 'line', and the notion of 'going over' it, is a tangible point of the borders instituted through the homo/het binary. It is a way which Margaret expresses the tangible constraints to the limits of her own transgressive possibilities. This is the 'line' which would have to be crossed if she had the 'nerve' to do it. But, even though the line is clearly in place and maintained at various points in the self-surveillance of her own intimate practices, we should not underestimate the possibility of the existence of the 'nerve' that might transgress it. This notion of 'nerve', which seems to suggest the possibility of a certain form of freedom, may be pre-requisite in the government of sexual subjects – it may be exactly because we know we can transgress the limits of our own identities that we are careful not to – but, nevertheless, it also provides a point at which transgression could occur. It is this *potential* for polymorphous sexuality which some commentators mistake for the emergence of sexual 'fluidity' in contemporary society. Yet it is precisely because Margaret, like most other people, knows of the possibilities for 'other' sexual practices and identities that she can clearly define her own and, as a consequence, reproduce and maintain the binary through which it is founded. As Margaret shows, when I ask her again why she wouldn't consider a same-sex relationship, the homo/het binary has a tremendous effect upon the organization of subjectivity:

MARGARET: I'm not a lesbian. I mean surely it's something that's in you, that you fancy women or, you know, it must be something that's inside or everybody would go off with everyone else. You're either one or the other and I'm just not a lesbian, so I couldn't fancy a woman.

In reiterating the conventions of the homo/het binary, Margaret invokes a framework, and the evaluative criteria, for understanding her self as a sexual being. She argues that sexuality is 'inside' of you, as a generative biological mechanism which controls desire, and which directs one to the person whom one will 'fancy'. If this wasn't the case, argues Margaret, then 'everybody would go off with everyone else'. And indeed Margaret is absolutely correct because if the binary of homo/het did not institute such a stark differentiation through sexual practices and identities, then we would no longer have a fixated and directional organization of desires. The fact that such a bisexuality is not socially pervasive is testament to the fact that how we feel 'inside' must fundamentally link to the organization of sexuality at a macro level; an organization which asks us, fundamentally, to be 'one or the other'. And in becoming 'one or the other' we must jettison the other to become our own self. Margaret does such a thing through a disavowal of one identity – 'I'm not a lesbian' – in order to make an identification with another.

But as Diana Fuss (1995) points out, the identifications we make may not easily express our identity; our identities may be more than that which we identify with. That is true to the extent that Margaret makes an explicit dis-identification with the lesbian whilst retaining a form of ambivalence over her own heterosexuality. In this sense her identity is ambiguous to the extent that she can retain the idea of a possible future transgression of her heterosexuality. In one very important sense, Margaret's sexual identity is secured and fixed within the homo/het binary; she becomes heterosexual through a disavowal of that which she is not. Given that there are limits to the types of sexual being that Margaret can 'be', she disavows one and, by default, appropriates the other. With this appropriation comes the criteria for containing it, for monitoring it, and for drawing the 'line' around it. But, more fundamentally, after drawing the line around her *practice*, there exists the ambiguity of *desire* which is constrained within the circumference of her own *identity* (a perpetual inside which must always be kept out).

During an interview I conducted with Douglas, the same types of ambiguity which Margaret displayed became apparent. I asked Douglas if he would ever consider a same-sex relationship.

DOUGLAS: Ever consider it? I have considered it. I have considered it because certain people I've found to be attractive. But at the end of the day when I actually looked at it [...] I realized that no I wouldn't really. I have considered it, I've thought about it, I've thought that, you know, it wouldn't be something that really repulsed me at all, but when it comes down to the real nitty gritty, I don't think the real physical drive is there for me, I think it would be more of an emotional thing and more like me just being playful than anything else [...] I think I'd be more physically touchy feely and playful and when it came down to the act I probably wouldn't be able to do it.

The 'act', which Douglas considers to be the real 'nitty gritty' of homosexuality, is a tangible point of control for his own desire; he can't imagine feeling the 'real physical drive' of wanting to have sex with another man. Such a 'drive', and the fact that it is felt to be 'real', or 'unreal' in this case, is therefore one of the ways in which Douglas negotiates his own sense of an embodied sexuality. Yet, even in the absence of this 'real' drive, Douglas is quite clear that he has considered a same-sex relationship and that he has been attracted to other men. The language of being 'playful', of wanting to be more 'touchy feely', is a way of describing an imagined intimacy which would not involve the 'act' he could not do. A homosexual relationship is not, he says, something which repulses him, but it would have to be a relationship founded in an 'emotional' realm for him to be comfortable with it. There is a certain ambivalence at work in Douglas' account of his own desires. Although his own sexuality is foreclosed and shored-up around the rejection of the 'act', there is nevertheless a tangible sense of attraction to other men. In explaining this further to me, Douglas says that 'in my heart, you know, I'm not . . . ' a homosexual. This seems to explain his reluctance over the 'act' (however that act is imagined) as a result of the implied depth of his 'true' sexuality; a sexuality that is described as in the 'heart'.

As I have previously argued, a dis-identification with the 'act' of homosexuality is tied to a refusal and disavowal that one is a homosexual. Yet what would happen if Douglas separated the notion of the 'act' from the 'playful' type of relationship he is describing? Could such a relationship exist that would allow Douglas to transgress the instituted differentiation around the homo/het binary? Or would that be suggesting a type of relationship which was not homosexual? The central issue here is the split between an 'emotional' realm and the physicality of homosexuality. This is created, I would suggest, through the compulsory negotiation of the homo/het binary which does not unilaterally produce a uniformed desiring being. On the contrary, the homo/het binary leaves a certain form of ambiguous desire which exceeds the naming of its own discrete categories. Yet this type of ambiguous desire, which Douglas displays, is still produced through the abjection and prohibition of homosexuality. It is a type of desire which cannot speak as desire because of the threat to identity which it presents; it is a desire which emerges through constraint.[2] As such, we can see the crucial gap between the psychic life of desire and the social enactment of intimate practice. Identifying as heterosexual does not unilaterally remove forms of homo-erotic possibilities from the psyche but, on the contrary, simultaneously produces such possibilities and instils the defined parameters for action, parameters maintained through the self, and by the self, through a constant hermeneutics of desire which legitimates and debars sexual acts in relation to their affirmative or transgressive potential.

This type of constrained, but ambiguous, desire is highlighted by Douglas when he tells me about a friendship he experienced which presented certain difficulties:

DOUGLAS: I mean I've sort of like admired people, for one quality or another, that have been men and wanted to spend a lot of time with them because I found them very attractive as a person, you know. I mean I remember it actually got to the stage once where someone actually said to me 'look, you know, you fancy this lad' you know, and I was 'I don't fancy him'. I remember that was a bit of an infatuation, well not, it kind of was infatuation, but I always wanted to talk to this bloke [...] But that, actually, that stopped, you know, I sort of caught up in terms of being, growing up quite rapidly. It just turned into a normal friendship, you know [...] But it wasn't sexual, it wasn't longing for him or anything like that, it was more of a kind of like, if it was love it was more a sort of admiration I think more than anything else, and infatuation as I say.

There is something more than 'friendship' in Douglas' descriptions of this relationship because, by his own testimony, it eventually turned into a 'normal friendship'. What, then, was it before it became 'normal'? Douglas is sure that he did not 'fancy' the other man and that his feelings constituted a form of 'infatuation'. Such linguistic distinctions are not mere semantics; they are ways of delimiting exactly what Douglas felt, making sure his feelings could not be deemed 'homosexual'. Douglas can be seen to invoke the parameters of desire and attraction which I outlined as a border control to homosexuality. Yet Douglas' account of his feelings is ambiguous and contradictory. He is clear that he did not experience 'longing' for the man or feel 'sexual' towards him; rather, if it were 'love', it was 'admiration'. But Douglas did feel drawn to the other man in the sense that he wanted to spend time with him, wanted to talk to him, liked him a great deal and, fundamentally, felt 'attracted' to him 'as a person'. I am not suggesting that Douglas' account reveals a 'deep' or 'hidden' desire to have homosexual sex or a same-sex relationship; nor am I suggesting that his description is an elaborate way of covering up such feelings. What I would suggest is that Douglas' account reveals the type of ambiguity that is instituted by the homo/het binary. These are forms of desire which exceed the interpellative power of heterosexuality and escape the reduction and directional force of, what becomes, heterosexual subjectivity. It reveals how Douglas is engaged in the activity of monitoring and governing his self through the process of deciphering himself in light of certain truths which compose normative male heterosexuality. His desires are problematized, dissected and analysed in relation to the truths of what his sexuality 'is'. In this sense he is both subject to sexual knowledge and subjectified through it.

Douglas is extremely careful to make it clear that his feelings towards his friend can be demarked from sexual attraction or physical desire. Yet that disavowal of 'fancying' another man is itself problematized by Douglas later in the interview:

DOUGLAS: I was out for a drink with my girlfriend and her mate, who is gay [...] and I remember, I remember actually looking at my girlfriend and looking at him and thinking I'd probably actually – and this is a horrible thing to say – I quite fancy him and I'd rather probably spend the night with him actually. But then when it came down to the sort of like, you know . . . he started, actually, you know, flirting on a bit with me. And it's not that I didn't like it because I thought, well it's a compliment isn't it. But when it came down to the nitty gritty sort of like, you know, he started going a bit too far and I thought, no, this isn't social stigma because I haven't got that over my head, I'm in a gay club, it doesn't bother me. But when it came down to it and it got to a certain extent and I thought, no, it's not working for me, it's not, you know, any woman I would feel, well not any woman, but most women I would feel more given to than this man here, who seems to be taking an interest in me. And it did make me feel uncomfortable, it did make me realize that the thoughts I'd been having about, you know, maybe I should go over to considering that sort of relationship, it made me realize that it wasn't for me.

By Douglas' own account, even though he finds it 'horrible' to have to 'admit it', he did 'fancy' this other man and thought that he would 'prefer' to 'spend the night' with him rather than his girlfriend. Douglas, unlike in his previous account, does not deny a form of sexual attraction to the other man. In this sense, a previous 'border control' which he invoked to delimit his heterosexuality is crossed. However, this border control is re-erected when he describes the other man flirting with him. This man, he says, started to go 'too far' and his flirting made Douglas feel 'uncomfortable'. This sense of discomfort made Douglas 'realize' that he did not want to have a sexual relationship with this man. Such a realization is built on a causal link between 'feelings' and an embodied sexuality, and this link is demonstrated by how Douglas places his 'uncomfortable' feeling within a sophisticated understanding of how such anxiety is produced. It is not an anxiety created by 'social stigma', because the event took place in a gay club where same-sex intimate activity would appear normalized. Therefore Douglas rejects the idea that his anxiety was created 'outside' of himself, stimulated by what other people might think of him. Instead he understands the feeling to be inside himself, to arise from the parameters of his desire (parameters which are felt to result from a natural and innate interiority). Yet such parameters are erected and felt at a particular point in negotiating sexuality. It is at the particular point where the 'nitty gritty' reality of homosexuality appears in its monstrous form that all previous feelings of attraction are negated. Douglas revokes his previous claim that he was more attracted to the other man than his girlfriend; now he would be attracted to most women rather than this man who was taking an interest in him. His initial attraction to the man mutates; the homosexual man is 'going too far', is taking an interest in *him*, and the thoughts he had been having about a same-sex relationship are ejected. The binary of homo/het immediately cuts off those previous feelings of attraction and deems them 'homosexual', thus relegating them to the 'outside' of heterosexuality. What was once 'playful' feelings of attraction are instituted as the 'nitty gritty' of homosexual practice; a practice which Douglas excludes as a possibility in his intimate, sexual life.

Yet, paradoxically, those feelings of attraction and desire remain perpetually present and, as we can see from Douglas' two descriptions above, they exist as an essentially transgressive possibility. Whilst the 'border controls' are invoked, and the sexual self is constrained from acting, the types of feelings that Douglas describes remain. This is the result of a tenuous and weak form of sexual identification which comes to exists after Douglas' negotiation of his own sexual parameters because it is dependent upon a form of agency which is itself unpredictable and volatile. Even though Douglas delimits his own practice through a rejection of 'homosexuality', this delimitation required an active and complex form of negotiation because, just as he was impelled to decipher himself in relation to the normative discourses of sexuality, so too did that same compulsion present a range of non-normative possibilities and feelings. Such possibilities and thoughts remain a permanent feature of the continuous negotiation and repetitious enactment of heterosexuality that Douglas makes. He may feel again that form of attraction (which is not reconcilable with the 'act' of homosexuality), he may feel that ambiguous attraction to another man which seems to exceed the name 'homosexual', and he may have further desires about 'fancying' another man. But in reiterating the border controls of heterosexuality, these feelings are likely to remain negated. So how can we understand a permanent desire which is constrained? How does one reconcile attraction and desire with a feeling that they are wrong and misplaced? And what are the results of such a stark delimitation of desire and practice through the homo/het binary? Even after the process of heterosexual self-cleansing has taken place, what is the residue of such prohibition and marginalization? Might it be, as Judith Butler suggests, 'the archaeological remainder, as it were, of unresolved grief'? (1997b: 133).

Melancholic incorporation

I want to now suggest another way of understanding the operation of the homo/het binary in the formation of subjectivity through the notion of 'loss'. If heterosexual identity is formed through exclusion to a realm which is constituted outside of itself, through the prohibition of homosexuality which is rendered as a corporeal margin of the self, then the subject is founded through a form of loss. Such a loss is forced through the heterosexual subject's need to 'give up' the possibility of homosexuality. But is there a cost to this loss? For Freud, the loss of, or inability to obtain, a love-object was of profound significance and in describing the formation and maintenance of the human ego, he argued consistently that such object loss could produce melancholia. 'A leading characteristic' of such melancholia, argues Freud, 'is a cruel self-depreciation of the ego combined with relentless self-criticism and bitter self-reproach' ([1921] 1991b: 139). He goes on to argue that melancholia results in:

> the ego divided, fallen apart into two pieces, one of which rages against the second. This second piece is the one which has been altered by the introjection and which contains the lost object. But the piece which behaves so cruelly is not unknown to us either. It comprises the conscience, a critical agency within the ego, which even in normal times takes up a critical attitude towards the ego.
> ([1921] 1991b: 139)

The self that is produced through such a loss becomes divided, according to Freud, and results in one 'side' becoming a 'critical agency' to the other. Loss, in other words, institutes a type of subjectivity whereby the ego comes to monitor itself. Yet Freud is clear that such a condition need not result from the loss of a specific person. Melancholia is not, suggests Freud, like mourning; it is not a form of grief that is characterized by a tangible event placed within time, where mourning represents the outcome of a 'known' loss. Melancholia is far more ethereal in that it represents a state of loss which, resulting in the damaged ego outlined above, is often instigated outside of consciousness:

> one feels justified in maintaining the belief that a loss of this kind has occurred, but one cannot see clearly what it is that has been lost, and it is all the more reasonable to suppose that the patient cannot consciously perceive what he has lost either. [. . .] this would suggest that melancholia is in some ways related to an object-loss which is withdrawn from

consciousness, in contradistinction to mourning, in which there is nothing about the loss that is unconscious.

([1917] 1991c: 253–254)

The divided ego which Freud outlines is dependent upon the lost object on which its own melancholia is based. The ego, in this sense, has *incorporated* the lost object; it relies on that which it does not have. For Judith Butler (1997b), Freud's description of an unconscious loss which comes to create a melancholic ego is a useful way of understanding the way in which the loss of the possibilities of homosexual love are psychically sustained. In commenting upon Freud's distinction between mourning and melancholia she argues: 'Melancholy is both the refusal of grief and the incorporation of loss, a miming of the death it cannot mourn' (1997b: 142). The 'miming' of such a loss results, for Butler, from the incorporation of the homo/het binary into the psyche of the subject. When the heterosexual subject is forced to compulsorily renounce homosexual love, when s/he disavows forms of homosexual intimacy, the subject must achieve this without recourse to grief.

Heterosexual subjects lose the experience of homosexual love without knowing it as a possibility; one cannot grieve something that one does not know is lost, something that always seems unliveable. Because both homosexuality and heterosexuality are founded through exclusion, through rendering each other as distinct 'ways of life', then modern sexual subjects do not mourn the loss of the other way of being. Rather, in the formation of sexual subjectivity, the other is sustained 'outside' the self, as something that was always-already external. And this, for both heterosexuals and homosexuals, is the basis for a *celebration* of difference, rather than the source of loss. Yet, for Freud, the self always depends on that which it has lost and, as Butler elaborates, this produces distinct effects:

> The prohibition on homosexuality preempts the process of grief and prompts a melancholic identification which effectively turns homosexual desire back upon itself. This turning-back upon itself is precisely self-beratement and guilt. Significantly, homosexuality is *not* abolished but preserved, though preserved precisely in the prohibition on homosexuality.
>
> (1997b: 142, italics in original)

In this sense the result of the homo/het binary is a melancholic ego which, as Freud outlines, produces a self that becomes split. Homosexuality is a lost object that produces the melancholic ego; that critical agency that turns back upon its own self in the form of self enquiry. We have seen, in various accounts above, how heterosexuality is founded on a critical scrutiny of the self; how sexual subjects are hostile to the idea that there is any component of their own desire which may not accord with their sexual identity. The Freudian view, elaborated by Butler, is useful for showing the residual remains of homosexuality after the homo/het binary is instituted into heterosexual identities. This residue is all that remains of a desire that is lost from the subject. In producing and maintaining the boundaries of sexuality, subjects must 'give up' forms of love, but in renouncing homosexuality they produce psychic 'archaeological remainders'.

When I interviewed Mark we talked a great deal about same-sex relationships and I asked him if he would ever consider having a homosexual relationship himself. At first Mark told me that he would not consider it and invoked the common parameters to his own heterosexual desire (around disgust, attraction, friendship and gender). Yet as we talked he recounted an event from his youth which, in view of what I have just outlined, is significant:

MARK: [. . .] when I was seventeen there was me and a bunch of lads, just lads, and this Tom, up at my friend's caravan [. . .]. And we all got pissed and we were all sort of chilling out in the caravan watching whatever film was on at the end of the night's transmission. And we were just sort of like [indicates tired]. And I can remember to this day, I was sitting next to Tom, and I think just the way we were sat, he put his hand on my knee and started rubbing my knee and I reciprocated, at the time. And I was finding it quite comforting at the time, you know not, it wasn't arousing but it was comforting and it was quite nice. And to this day, from that day forth, I've never let on [. . .] that I remember that happening. I just played on the fact that I was pissed and that. I mean he's never asked me did I remember but I just played on the fact that I was pissed and I didn't know what the hell went on that night, sort of thing. And it's embarrassing to have to admit it but I felt comforted and reassured, not reassured but I felt comfortable when he was, like, rubbing my hand.

This story, which is 'embarrassing' for Mark to 'admit', and which further leads him to ask me if the interview is 'completely confidential', is one which is extremely significant to him. It is a difficult story for him to tell and he is uncomfortable in relating it to me. Yet, given the circumstances of the story, why is it so difficult to talk about it? And, more importantly, why is it such an important memory for Mark? The experience of the hand rubbing is something he has not forgotten; he may not have 'let on' about remembering it but he has retained the memory for 18 years. He associates it with feeling comfortable and recalls it being 'quite nice'. Yet he could not talk about this to his friend. He was unable to discuss the incident and, whilst he is still friends with the other man, he has never been able to mention it to him. What is striking is that this form of touching becomes associated with a homosexual form of intimacy and that, consequently, it becomes a debarred experience which cannot be spoken of. The event might represent a point of transgression, a border crossing, which is outside of the rubric of permissible masculine heterosexuality, one which is made illegitimate through the homo/het binary. But there is also the way in which Mark's friendship is delimited, through the foreclosure of heterosexuality and its prohibition of homosexuality, which instigate a form of loss around the event. He cannot talk to his friend about this reciprocal experience even though he found it pleasant, he is unable to place the event in a legitimate form of communication, and the consequence is Mark's silence.

What Mark is describing is a fundamental loss of the possibilities of intimacy which the disavowal of homosexuality has created. It is the loss of a language to speak, to experience, to enjoy intimacy. Mark's testimony does not reveal a hidden homosexuality, far from it, it reveals the ways in which heterosexuality strangles forms of intimacy and produces exclusions which do not accord with it. The result is that Mark becomes critical of himself and of his past; a past which he later describes as something which he has 'dragged up' and that he would rather 'had stayed hidden'. Yet, even though the event will remain 'hidden' to others, it will remain visible to himself. Indeed, in remembering the event over a long period of time, Mark explicitly identifies the event as something he must hide, a secret he must constantly keep. The event is fundamental to his dis-identification with homosexuality; it remains in his psyche as a representation of the type of intimacy which is 'embarrassing to have to admit'. Yet Mark does not speak of this experience in ways which exhibits disgust or repulsion. Rather, in recounting the story, Mark seems both sad and bemused by the event. There is sadness about the way the reciprocated intimacy has to remain hidden; that he is unable to talk about it; and that it has come to represent something which is deemed to be wrong. He is bemused because he can't quite understand why the event is so important to him, why he remembers it as a secret worth keeping. Yet the importance of the event across his lifetime endures, displaying the results of a foreclosing compulsory heteronormativity which relegates and abjects certain forms of intimacy.

What Mark is describing is how doing heterosexuality debars forms of same-sex intimacy which come to be unrecognizable as legitimate experience. The cost of such a process is that an intimate experience becomes constituted outside of identity, existing as an abject form (the slightest touch) which can never be spoken of. The result, for Butler, is that:

> the man who insists upon the coherence of his heterosexuality will claim that he never loved another man, and hence never lost another man. That love, that attachment becomes subject to a double disavowal, a never having loved, and a never having lost. This 'never–never' thus founds the heterosexual subject, as it were; it is an identity based upon the refusal to avow an attachment and, hence, the refusal to grieve.
>
> (1997b: 139–140)

It is this dual operation of loss, and a refusal to mourn loss, which founds the modern sexual subject within the homo/het binary.

I am not suggesting that Mark was 'in love' with his friend. But what is clear is that the attachment he felt towards his friend, however brief, in a shared moment of intimacy, is debarred as legitimate through the exclusionary force of the homo/het binary. As a heterosexual subject he is both forced to exclude that intimacy and keep it hidden. Same-sex intimacy, in certain forms, therefore constitutes both the 'outside' of the subject and the 'inside'; it is both disavowed and incorporated. Perhaps the consequence of such an exclusionary matrix is, ultimately, a form of sadness which expresses the lost possibility of same-sex love. Perhaps, even though we watch ourselves, scrutinize ourselves, regulate our desires and constitute ourselves as the types of sexual beings that we must become, there is a form of sadness produced which quietly laments the expense of the binary through which we have constituted our self. During an interview with Peter I asked him about his feelings regarding same-sex love:

PETER: I have to be careful here because there is a kind of like [problem in] exploring that side of myself, I think, especially about sexuality and crossing the boundaries from heterosexuality [but] gay love [is] a very romantic, a very romantic thing. It's quite beautiful and so I think it's sad in some ways.

What is interesting is that, even though Peter thinks that gay *love* is quite beautiful, he knows that he has to be 'careful' in crossing the 'boundaries from heterosexuality'. Whilst homosexual love may appeal to him, may even be something he would wish to 'do', he knows it would instigate a series of ruptured borders which will instigate a crisis in his own heterosexuality (hence the need to be careful). The result is, as he says, quite 'sad'. In this sense the exclusionary matrix of heterosexuality produces a form of melancholia 'inside' itself, an expression of all the possibilities it has lost.

Conclusion

The relationship between the formation of identity and the social construction of heterosexuality is, as I have argued in this chapter, organized around delimited forms of sexual practice and experiences of sexual desire. Heterosexual identity is founded on an exclusionary set of practices which are bounded by what becomes illegitimate homosexuality. But forms of desire escape the parameters instituted by compulsory heterosexuality. Whilst transgression across the borders of homo/het may not occur in practice, a desire to cross such borders may be prevalent. It is often asserted that what we are witnessing is the deployment of new discourses and language which express these forms of desire: the linguistic construction of the 'bi-curious' subject being an example. Some commentators maintain that this subject represents a type of heterosexuality which 'comes out' and expresses its desire to transgress the boundaries through which it is founded. Whether or not such a subject poses a serious challenge to the homo/het binary is highly debateable – in my opinion, it does not, since what it represents is a reassertion of such binaries through the exoticization of actual or imagined transgression.

Yet it is important that we recognize the form and potential of the agency I have outlined in this chapter. The history of theorizing heterosexuality has largely centred on the absolute tyranny of foreclosing heteronormative desire and the theft of all homosexual possibilities from (female) subjects (see, for example, MacKinnon, 1982; Rich, 1980). Yet, when we look at how forms of sexual ambiguity are present in the life of subjects, we encounter the ways in which power cannot unilaterally act upon the psyche to exclude, or render impossible, ways of desiring. Power is, as Foucault said, a productive and producing force and makes us more than the names and the reductions under which we labour. But we labour under loss. When we take up a sexual identity, we are forced to renounce the possibility of the other. This dual operation of renouncing and retaining homosexuality (outside and in) shows the way that we are subject to an austere regime of sexuality which constitutes us and confines us in particular ways. What we become is what we are not and what we are not is what we have lost. And what are we then? We are subjects who, confined in the regimes of sexual identity, must delimit and police our own practice. And yet within all the 'categories' of sexual identity the voice of desire remains a constant and permanent feature of transgressive possibility. This is not an 'essential' or 'real' form of desire which resides in some depth of the self. This is a type of desire which is produced as the necessary inclusion to the exclusionary matrix of, not just heterosexuality, but all sexual categories. We think of the psyche as a boiling pot of desire which, if we wish to maintain a singular and defined sexual identity, we must keep a lid on. Isn't it funny that by keeping a lid on it we constantly remind ourselves that the 'trouble' is there?

Conclusion

Writing about heterosexual women's experiences, Carol Smart argues that women who are heterosexual are often 'far from being the dupes of patriarchy, are far from homophobic, are far from accepting male dominance, and are far from seeking their own missing penises' (1996: 177). In other words, as Smart so eruditely puts it, women aren't heterosexual just because they are 'forced' to be but because, actually, some of them quite like it. The main point of this book has been an attempt to examine how heterosexuality is constituted and made through a set of social relations often characterized by pleasure. Whatever else loving is, or whatever intimacy might be, it is usually founded in practices which begin with, and sometimes retain, aspects of joy and gratification. These are practices, and ways of being, which involve active choice. Until we recognize and acknowledge this aspect of heterosexuality, Smart argues, 'feminist theories of sexuality will remain strangely repressed on a most important aspect of the lives of many women' (1996: 77). Just because heterosexual identities and practices are socially accomplished and made, it doesn't automatically follow that by 'doing heterosexuality' women (and men) are the passive instruments of social relations.

This is not to say that heterosexuality isn't a highly composed, organized and institutionalized set of practices and relations. I've tried to show throughout this book that heterosexuality is continually reproduced in both actions and identities in ways which are socially normative. And I have also stressed that heterosexual identities are the result of forms of regulation and compulsion which are organized in relation to the social construction of sex and gender. It is this emphasis on *regulation* which, for some, seems somewhat at odds with the view that heterosexuality can be anything but absolute constraint and misery. But, as I have argued throughout this book, we need to be able to speak of the regulation of desire whilst acknowledging that within such regulation there are choices to be made and pleasure to be gained. It sometimes seems to me that whenever we mention forms of social constraint around sexuality it's as if we are saying that heterosexuality is 'bad' and that heterosexuals can't see the errors of their ways.

Yet isn't it strange that the same doesn't hold true for homosexuality?

It is continually acknowledged in the human and social sciences that homosexuality is a socially constructed sexual category, and that gays and lesbians assume socially available sexual identities, but this never seems to suggest anything disparaging or offensive. After all, homosexual identities and practices are subject to continual forms of social regulation, yet the embracement of them by individuals is usually seen as a cause for celebration. Defining one's self as homosexual and maintaining a life-long commitment to a gay or lesbian identity is often regarded as an expression or condition of self-realization. Yet to become homosexual is, at the very least, to reject heterosexuality. It is to instigate particular controls around one's sexual identity and sexual practices in order to become a version or type of sexual being. In other words, it is to regulate one's sexuality. That, in the case of non-heterosexuals, rarely seems a contentious thing to say.

This is because homosexuality usually appears as an active identity. It is often publicly expressed as the result of an individual 'soul searching' and 'coming to terms' with being gay or lesbian. The process of 'coming out' is, however problematically experienced, usually regarded as a positive way of realizing the truth of one's sexuality. Yet heterosexuality is rarely recognized as something which is actively achieved but, rather, it is regarded as a 'default' way of being. This misses the point that, whilst socially normative, heterosexuality still needs to be accomplished by those individuals who practice it and identify as it. To make heterosexuality, and to become heterosexual, individuals engage in similar acts of self-elaboration as non-heterosexuals. Heterosexuality is an activity and, as I've argued throughout this book, this activity involves both constraint and choice, both compulsion and agency.

We actually know very little about how heterosexuality is 'made' or how men and women experience it. In fact, we know far more about homosexual sexuality. Heterosexuality is certainly the poor relation in the study of sexuality in much the same way that whiteness remains an under-explored category in sociologies of ethnicity. Yet elaborating heterosexual sexuality is one of the most crucial engagements that sociology should make because it is precisely by doing this that we can understand how *all* sexuality is made. Whilst it is most certainly true that making heterosexuality visible requires some effort, it is possible to achieve this. I sometimes wonder whether little work is done on heterosexuality because, in addition to the methodological difficulties it poses, it seems, in comparison to homosexuality, somewhat dull.

In studying intimacy, we need to foreground issues of heterosexuality, however mundane they seem. In the countless studies we have on heterosexual relationships it is astonishing how few of them actually deal explicitly with relations of sexuality. It is inadequate to see 'sexual preference' as a pre-existing foundation on which intimacy is built because we need to think about how, in practising intimacy, we reproduce sexuality. It is difficult to think about how we 'make' sexuality social at a time when sexual preference seems the individual expression of unique subjectivity. Yet we live in a time when our local authorities, and the public policy which informs them, are actively engaged in constructing sexual difference – the 'gay villages' which have appeared in many UK cities stand as expressions of the apparent liberalization of sexual diversity. It is ironic that in making difference more permanent we believe that we are moving towards a greater form of sexual enlightenment, diversity, and fluidity. The discrimination against gay men and lesbians – on a continuum of harassment to murder – is being replaced, some might argue, by the liberalization of pleasure and the deheterosexualization of social life. There is homosexual pressure for parenting rights, for the right to marry, for the rights associated with full citizenship of a community. We are, it might be said, on the road to a plural sexual society.

The central fact remains: our sexual identities, and the intimate practices which depart from them, are constituted across the binary of homosexuality/heterosexuality. We are beings who make, indeed are *required to make*, sexual identifications and we do so using the modern framework of homo/het. We practice intimacy within that binary and, regardless of how we do it, it remains steadfast. The empirical data in this book shows that the political and civil demands occasioned by the liberalization of homosexuality do not, fundamentally, affect the central dichotomy of that binary. I am not arguing that we are forever defined sexual beings who are permanently constrained within sexual categories. I think desire is an inherently complicated matter, and in the last chapter I tried to show that sexual identifications can be characterized as weak. Yet we need to be able to account for the way that, for most people, sexuality is an enduring set of practices and identity which works to close off certain intimate possibilities. If we lose the ability to think about constraint, in our rush to celebrate diversity, then we have no political grounds on which to argue for future change. If we really do want to live in a sexual and intimate pluralism, then we have to address the interrelationship between that which we believe to be most personal (our sexual and intimate desires) and the social constitution of sexuality.

Again, this is made difficult because love seems natural to us and because it is experienced and negotiated in a way which is both profoundly individualized and anti-social. The modern construction of love is premised on feelings which become engendered through the processes of 'fusing together' with another – the all-important 'chemistry' which binds individuals together. What could, in the end, be more natural than love? We love because of who we are – love just 'is'. However, when we love we do so as beings with genders, and with sexualities, and we reproduce the foundations of our own existence. It is through beliefs about the seemingly unsocial 'chemistry' of love that we order our sexual practices in relation to a gendered 'other'. However we form relationships, we do not diminish the modern construction of sexuality, with its specificity of sexual identity categories, because, on the contrary, we re-iterate it, we bring it to life. Rather than postulating 'plastic sexuality' as the basis for our new sexual millennium we should look at how, even where difference and diversity are genuinely pleasurable, the dichotomy of homo/het endures. It endures alongside, and sometimes as a result of, those 'intimacies of choice' which are described as the result of gay men and lesbians transforming intimacy and consolidating identities in loving relationships.

It is entirely problematic to argue for the negation of difference; all we can hope for is that difference itself becomes benign. But the way to minimize the differences set up through the homo/het binary is not to be found in an uncritical celebration of them. Whilst the political expediency of sexual difference as ready-made categories which are personally ours ('I was born that way') cannot be denied, it does not offer us the basis for a genuinely equal sociality. Difference, in the end, is reproductive, not of a social celebration of diversity, but of a foundation for individual and group identification based on exclusion. As Paul Gilroy argues:

> When identity refers to an indelible mark or code somehow written into the bodies of its carriers, otherness can only be a threat. Identity is latent destiny. Seen or unseen, on the surface of the body or buried deep within its cells, identity forever sets one group apart from others who lack the particular, chosen traits that become the basis of typology and comparative evaluation. No longer a site for the affirmation of subjectivity and autonomy, identity mutates. Its motion reveals a deep desire for mechanical solidarity, seriality and hypersimilarity. The scope for individual agency dwindles and then disappears. People become the bearers of the differences that the rhetoric of absolute identity invents and then invites them to celebrate.
>
> (Gilroy, 2000: 103–104)

We need to be able to move analytically between ideas about 'personal preferences', the seemingly individual experience of intimacy and love, and the ways in which such subjective processes are shaped by the conditions in which they take place. If we do this, we can understand how we are made into the types of beings which we are; how we become versions of ourselves at the expense of the outside which marks us; and how we relate to each other in social life. I would like to see sociology take up these issues more generally and, in doing so, to place questions about heterosexuality at the centre of an on-going empirical investigation into those areas of social life that seem relatively unproblematic and, in so many ways, normal. If we do this, if we attempt to look more thoroughly at one of the most important axioms of our social existence, we may be able to make claims, at least in sociology, about diversity.

Appendix
Interview questions

1.
   a. Would you say that you have ever been in love?
   b. What were your first experiences of falling in love?
   c. And of being in love?
   d. Did you have 'crushes'?
2.
   a. When you were younger did you have an idea about love and expectations of it?
   b. What specific ideas did you hold about being in love and falling in love?
   c. Where do you think you got those ideas?
   d. Do you think that your parents/family influenced your ideas about love?
3.
   a. Can you think of any love stories that stick in your mind?
   b. If yes: What do you think makes these love stories special?
   c. Do you relate to these stories in your own life?
4. Was there a first 'proper' love relationship in your life?
5. What have been the key experiences of love throughout your life?
6.
   a. How would you define love?
   b. If there was no word for love, how would you describe it? For instance, how would you tell someone you loved them?
7.
   a. Are there specific stages of romantic love?
   b. Does love follow a 'path'? And what are its key stages?
   c. Does love develop in the same way for everyone?
8.
   a. What part does sex play in falling in love and sustaining love?
   b. Do sex and love always go together?
   c. Is this the same for everyone?
   d. What is the difference between having sex with someone you love and someone you don't?
9.
   a. What do you think of arranged marriages?
   b. Would you ever get married through a marriage arranged by your family?
10.
    a. Have you ever experienced love at first sight?
    b. Do you think that love at first sight is a good basis for a relationship?

	c	and: why/why not?
11	a	Would you say you were friends with your partner?
	b	Do you have the same types of conversations, or share the same thoughts, with your partner as with your friends?
12	a	Do you think that the way that you use the word love is the same way that others use it?
	b	Your partner for instance?
	c	What about gay men and lesbians?
	d	How do you imagine love is different in relationships between two men and two women?
	e	Do you think the experience of love would be different or similar?
13	a	Do you think that gays and lesbians should be allowed to get married in the same way as heterosexuals?
	b	Why do you think that?
14	a	Would the option of a relationship with someone of the same sex ever have been a possibility for you?
	b	Do you think you could ever have been in love with someone of the same sex as yourself?
	c	Would that be a possibility for you in the future?
	d	If so: why or why not?
15	a	Have you always been able to have the type of relationship you would have liked?
	b	If so, why or why not ?
16	a	What has been your experience (if any) of monogamy?
	b	Do you usually want a relationship to be monogamous?
17	a	What are the main differences between being in a romantic relationship with someone and being single?
	b	In what key ways has being in a relationship changed your life?
	c	Are there any advantages to being single?
	d	Do you feel differently about yourself when you are single or in a relationship?
18	a	Can you describe what your ideal relationship would be like?
	b	Who would be your ideal partner?
19		Is love an escape from everyday life? Does love take you away from normal daily living?
20	a	If you were going to have a 'romantic moment' what would you do?
	b	Where do you think it is best to have such a moment?
21	a	Do you spend 'quality' time with your partner?
	b	Do you think it is important to talk about your feelings with your partner? Do they do that with you?
	c	Are there activities you only do with your partner, and other things you do with your friends?
22	a	Do you think the meaning of love has changed during the last fifty years?

	b	How, and in what kind of ways?
	c	Do you think you experienced falling in love in the same way as A: older people (your parents) or B: younger people (your children)?
	d	And: why do you think that is?
23	a	Some people say that the idea of falling in love with one person, and staying together for life, is 'old fashioned' – what do you think?
	b	Was it more common in the past to stay together for life do you think? And why?
	c	Is marriage important you?
24	a	Some people have said that it is too easy to get a divorce or split up from your partner now – what do you think?
	b	Was it more difficult in the past and was that a good or a bad thing?
	c	Why was it more difficult?
	d	Why do people separate so much these days?
25	a	There is a lot of debate about people having a 'traditional courtship' in a relationship and waiting until they are married before they have sex – what do you think about this?
	b	Do you think you are more or less traditional?
	c	How would you describe a traditional courtship?
26	a	How would you describe your class background?
	b	Do you think your class background has played a part in your experience of a relationship?
	c	What do you think the effects of a person's background are in terms of being in love?
	d	Do you think that people need to have similar backgrounds to be able to have a successful relationship?
	e	Do you think that if people love each other they can have a relationship regardless of their backgrounds and each other's families?
	f	What would happen if people had different backgrounds and had a relationship?
	g	Is class less important now than in the past? Why?
27		If you wanted to listen to some romantic music what would you listen to? What record/CD would you put on?
28		If you were going to buy someone a gift to tell them you were in love with them what would it be?
29	a	Have you ever celebrated Valentine's Day? What did you do?
	b	Do you celebrate Valentine's Day now? What did you do last time?
30	a	Is love different for men and women?
	b	Do you think your partner feels the same things about love that you do?
31	a	Do you think that living together with your partner has (or would) affected your feelings for each other?
	b	If live together: How is your house work organized? Do you have a set routine of household tasks?

32 a What do you (what would you) like least about living with your partner?
  b What aspect of your relationship would you most like to change?
33 a Do men and women show their love for each other in different ways?
  b What would you do to show your partner that you loved them?
  c How would they show you?

Notes

Introduction: making love, doing heterosexuality

1 What is interesting to consider, in terms of heterosexuality's invisibility, is the way in which it is simultaneously hidden and constantly invoked through its deployment as 'normal'. For instance, the debate on gay marriage serves as a nodal point for a series of competing discourses which serve, not only to pressure for changes in homosexual legitimacy, but to reproduce heterosexuality as a constructed and delimited category. The result of governmental interventions, both here and in North American, to strengthen and defend heterosexual marriage in law acts not only to exclude homosexuals from marriage, but, ironically, render heterosexuality into public debate. What the 'gay marriage' debate achieves is not only a discussion of the political dimensions of marriage but a series of contentions regarding heterosexuality and, whilst it is rarely framed in this way, a debate about what heterosexuality actually is. This, ironically, can be seen to render heterosexuality as a visible category in need of definition.

2 There is a significant parallel to be made here with the study of whiteness and its construction as a stable and normative racial category. As Richard Dyer (1997: 1–2) notes: 'As long as race is something only applied to non-white peoples, as long as white people are not racially seen and named, they/we function as a human norm. Other people are raced, we are just people. There is no more powerful position than that of being "just" human.' Like whiteness, heterosexuality stands as both a mark of normality and of originality; it appears as the essential mode of sexuality common to humanity. Research on whiteness confronts similar issues to research on heterosexuality, namely a need to problematize the normality of an essentialized category whilst, at the same time, understanding it as a relational construct.

3 The way in which reproduction is invoked in claims about 'natural' heterosexuality is interesting at this historical juncture. In a time when new reproductive technologies have all but taken Shulamith Firestone's ideas (at the time, ridiculed) of disembodied reproduction towards realization (certainly in terms of fertilization and conception), and as a result opened up horizons for a dislocation between heterosexuality and reproduction, the act of 'making children' has become transformed. New reproductive technologies, at the least, reveal 'nature' as malleable and, at most, moves reproduction outside of heterosexuality.

4 To find such analysis we have to go back to the work of an earlier generation of feminists (de Beauvoir, [1949] 1997; Firestone, 1972; Greer, 1970).

1 The essence of love

1 As Jackson (1999) notes, sociology has been engaged with issues of sexuality for the last few decades but has never paid particular attention to love. Similarly, the (gendered) contexts of the cultural construction of 'romance' has received attention (for example, Stacey and Pearce, 1995), but we lack a thorough *empirical* investigation of how romantic love is constructed, experienced and enacted by individuals.
2 There are many sociological studies (outlined in the previous chapter) which, although enveloping heterosexuality and love within their frames of analysis, do not seek to elucidate the foundations of the construction of romantic love. Whilst it is important to connect this construction to its expression in institutions such as marriage, it is paramount that we decide exactly what love 'is' in terms of how it makes individuals feel, what effects it has upon them and how they themselves define it.
3 To consider the question of different societal modes of romantic expression, one should consult the anthropological literature. For instance, in Jankowiak's (1995) edited collection, there are a number of anthropological accounts of the different ways in which romance is expressed within certain cultural contexts. This is not, however, so much a critique of the essentiality of love but an understanding of how love comes to be practised.
4 I would argue for a constructionist understanding of emotionality which accounted for the ways in which feelings become translated into enduring expressions of individual corporeality. It is not possible here to define the long and multifarious sociological and philosophical debate around emotions because such an undertaking would demand a book in itself. However, Simon Williams defines the constructivist position on emotions, as opposed to a hydraulic or biological definition, with five definite criteria: first, that emotions are expressed within delimited *language games* which contain them within frameworks of meaning; second, emotions are expressed within a particular *moral order* which deems certain emotions legitimate; third, emotions are bounded by particular *social functions*; fourth, that emotions are positioned within *narrative* frames through which they unfold in a legitimate story; and fifth, that emotions are enacted through particular *rules* of conduct (Williams, 2001: 46).

2 Making love and regulating sex

1 See Holland *et al*. (1998) *The Male In The Head* for a detailed empirical analysis of young people's negotiation of sexual relationships. This work suggests that although the 'no sex before marriage' narrative has been removed, there is a central preoccupation with questions of intimacy and establishing relationships in the negotiation of sex. Such issues are gendered and I explore this later in the chapter.
2 Intimacy is a buzz-word which currently circulates in academic discourses concerned with sexual relationships: intimate democracy; intimate citizenship; the transformation of intimacy; intimacy as a confluent ideal. Intimacy, certainly in Giddens' (1992) account, is replacing, and is indicative of a shift from, romantic practices to the confluent ideal of the pure relationship. Such a shift is axiomatic, argues Giddens, to broader changes in 'high modernity'.
3 The construction of gendered sexual 'drives' has a genealogy which can be traced, in modern 'scientific' discourses, to the early sexology of Havelock Ellis where men are conceptualized as forceful and active against women's essentially passive nature:

> Force is the foundation of virility, and its psychic manifestation is courage. In the struggle for life violence is the first virtue. The modesty of women – in its primordial form consisting in physical resistance, active or passive, to

the assaults of the male – aided selection by putting to the test man's most important quality, force. Thus it is to that when choosing among rivals for her favors a woman attributes value to violence.

(Ellis, in Bland and Doan, 1998: 109–110)

Here we find the one enduring 'truth' of the gender differentiation of sexuality set up through the heterosexual matrix: that it is essentially men who embody 'lust'. Such a dichotomy endures in contemporary social relations. For example, it has been used to 'explain' the prevalence of heterosexual rape (the 'it just went too far' thesis of the 'red-blooded male') and it is frequently invoked in popular discourse through the inversion of homosexual gender roles: the dual construction of the hyper-sexual or feminized and passive male homosexual, and the spinster lesbian (all of which were invoked by the people I interviewed).

4 This is axiomatic to Freud's view of the formation of the psyche. In *Civilization and its Discontents* ([1930] 1991a) Freud outlines the ways in which the ego is formed in relation to the social and political order in which the subject is situated. In *The Ego and the Id* ([1923] 1991d) he elaborates the manner in which the drives of the Id are sublimated through forms of repression which are essential to make the ego co-extensive with social life. Freud's analysis is therefore both helpful and constraining. It is useful because it argues in the strongest terms that sex is organized and enacted under social laws. But this is problematic because we are left with a strong essentialism of the sex drive which is residual to the Id. It is this drive which becomes translated into the hydraulic notion of an animalistic lust that is constrained through human imposition (an imposition that those Freudian–Marxists of the Frankfurt school wished to remove – particularly Wilhelm Reich and his 'sex-radicals' (see Ollman, 1979)).

5 This is certainly Foucault's classic account in *The History of Sexuality Volume 1* (1979) where he argues that the nineteenth-century incitement into discourse of sexuality constructed a domain of knowledge which, in turn, created a specific dimension of humanness (with an interiority of sex) that has increasingly become reified. This ontologizing of the sexual drives, he argued in his later work (1988, 1990), is linked to forms of self-cultivation through which we are required to understand ourselves in relation to normalized ways of being. Terming this process 'governmentality', Foucault provides a sophisticated framework for understanding the ways in which we relate to ourselves as sexual beings.

6 A useful method for understanding the ways in which sexual practice is enacted within cultural frameworks can be found in the work of Gagnon and Simon's (1973) conception of sexual 'scripts'. The authors argue that sexual conduct is *created* (as opposed to directed) through learning the symbolic order and codes of sexuality within any given social context. As Stevi Jackson argues: 'For them there is no pre-given sexuality which can be repressed; what is sexual is a matter of social definition and becoming sexual is a process of learning sexual meanings of "scripts" and locating oneself within them' (1999: 9). This is certainly axiomatic to Ken Plummer's (1995) work on how sexuality is enacted through the engendering of stories which bring into being, and legitimate, certain types of sexual conduct; a process, he would argue, which is continually changing and being challenged.

7 Respectability is a salient mediating factor for female sexuality and an organizing principle of the relationship between love and sex in the women's accounts. I deal with this later in the chapter.

8 For a discussion of sexual 'performance', specifically in relation to first experiences of sex, and how such experiences are implicated in 'learning' heterosexual identities, see Holland, *et al.* 1996.

3 The lack of love: producing heterosexual subjectivities

1 Marx is explicit that the modern self is experienced through a duality which is created by the illusion of a 'free' realm of personal relationships as opposed to the stultifying alienation of labouring activity: 'the worker feels himself (sic) only when he is not working; when he is working he does not feel himself. He is at home when he is not working, and not at home when he is working' ([1844] 1992: 326). The alienated being of capitalism, dislocated from the social labour which is essential to the production of a free and unfettered consciousness, retreats into the private sphere where he imagines freedom to reside. The appropriation of the worker's labour power dislocates the individual from his/her self – and Marx is very specific that this relates directly to subjectivity: 'it is a loss of his self' ([1844] 1992: 327) – in the public sphere and forces a split between social and private existence. 'The result is', suggests Marx, 'that man (the worker) feels that he is acting freely only in his animal functions – eating, drinking and procreating, or at most in his dwelling and adornment – while in his human functions he is nothing more than an animal' ([1844] 1992: 327).

2 I use this example of loss in a violent relationship because it challenges theories of an egalitarian confluent ideal, situating love as a cultural process that is linked to the wider relations of heterosexuality, and contests love as reducible to a relation symptomatic of capitalism or modernity. I cannot do justice to the issue of domestic violence here (such a complicated and complex problem would demand a book in itself) but as an example of the way in which romantic love produces forms of subjectivity, delimited by gender, it is a powerful reminder that identity is intimately bound by the process of heterosexual love.

4 Haunting heterosexuality: homosexuality and the borders of desire

1 The phrase is often attributed to Mary Douglas but, as Jonathan Dollimore (2001: 176–177) points out, was originally Freud's.

2 Since anal sex is something which men may engage with in heterosexual activity, we cannot conclude that *all* anal sex is deemed to be unnatural. It is the specific act of men penetrating other men which is made unnatural. Perhaps it is the idea of being penetrated, rather than penetration more generally, because this reverses one of the premises of male sexuality, that penetrative sexual 'acts' are something that are 'done to' another rather than 'done upon' one's own body.

3 It is interesting to note that both Mark and Martin expressed forms of desire around ideas of 'lesbian sex'. As Mark told me: 'I've got a fascination with lesbians, you know I'm a red-blooded man, I would love to watch two lesbians shagging.' As Andrea Dworkin (1981) would argue, the 'lesbian' here does not represent a form of homosexuality but instead functions only as a corollary of male heterosexuality (the lesbian confirms the 'red-blooded' status of man rather than detract from it). Thus the distinctions of homo/het are also produced through a distinction between gendered forms of homosexuality. Catherine MacKinnon would argue that this was true of all female sexuality: 'A woman is a being who identifies and is identified as one whose sexuality exists for someone else, who is socially male. Women's sexuality is the capacity to arouse desire in someone else' (1982: 185). In this sense, for MacKinnon, neither the lesbian nor the heterosexual woman has a separate identity but exists only as an extension of masculine heterosexuality (which, of course, is Adrienne Rich's (1980) classic account of the way in which compulsory heterosexuality subjects women's sexuality, however it is expressed, for male erotic pleasure).

4 Indeed, the history of buggery can be seen to change with the instigation of the homo/het binary. Whereas anal sex was a more generalizable 'perversion' before

the era of sexology (for detailed information and specific cases, see McCormick, 1997) it has become, in the rubric of modern sexuality, constructed as a 'particular' practice of a 'particular' person. Anal sex does not define heterosexuality (although it may be one sexual pleasure which constitutes it) but it stands as *the* defining sexual act of the modern homosexual.
5 As Moran (1996) notes, the use of the archaic conception of buggery became the basis for the construction of the 'homosexual' into law in the Sexual Offences Act of 1967 and, as McIntosh's (1968) classic work argues, conflated once and for all the idea of homosexual sex into a homosexual 'being'.
6 There is a burgeoning amount of work on the construction and enactment of masculinities but, in the specific case of the relationship between male friendship, intimacy and sexuality, Michael Messner's (1992) work is interesting for its consideration of how sexuality is delimited through heterosexual male–male relationships.
7 Hence the continual misunderstanding of bisexuality, where the bisexual being is seen to be in 'confusion' or transition. And hence why, with bisexuality, attraction and desire stand as the central problematic to sustaining a bisexual identity: how can a bisexual man sustain a long-term relationship with a woman if he is continually attracted to men; how could a bisexual woman have a same-sex relationship if she desired men? Attraction and desire here mark out sexuality as an either/or position because sexual attraction is supposed to be continually directed at one sex. Of course, the common presumption that bisexuals 'fancy everybody', and need to be having sex all the time, is testament to the fact that a discontinuity in attraction is seen to be dangerous, destabilizing and unsettling. A continuous form of attraction to the opposite sex, on the other hand, becomes the manifestation of a sexuality settled once and for all.

5 The escape of desire, the constraints of love

1 I am using the data from interviews with Douglas, Margaret and Mark because they were the only people who gave detailed descriptions of the type of ambivalence of sexuality that I want to explore here. This final chapter is therefore not built through a comparison across the data set and I am not making any claims that are generalizable to all my participants. I am using these testimonies as a way of raising some further questions about the construction of sexuality and the experiences of desire and intimacy within it.
2 We might think about how homosexual desire and practices emerge outside of normative identity categories by considering the ways in which, under certain contexts, the relation between sexuality and sexual practice is disrupted. The most common disruption is, of course, in contexts where high levels of same-sex segregation take place, such as in prisons, schools or the armed services. Under such conditions the social meanings which are ascribed to particular acts may be re-constituted without disrupting the heterosexual identity of the subject. I am thinking of the ways that, in popular discourse, it is imagined that men deprived of women will engage in sexual activity with each other as the result of satisfying an essential bodily need.

Bibliography

Barthes, R. (1990) *The Lover's Discourse: Fragments*, Penguin: Harmondsworth.
Beck, U. (1992) *Risk Society: Towards a New Modernity*, Sage: London.
Beck, U. and Beck-Gernsheim, E. (1995) *The Normal Chaos of Love*, Polity Press: Cambridge.
Beck-Gernsheim, E. (1999) 'On the Way to a Post-Familial Family – From a Community of Need to Elective Affinities', in M. Featherstone (ed.) *Love and Eroticism*, Sage (TCS): London.
Bell, D. and Binnie, J (2000) *The Sexual Citizen: Queer Politics and Beyond*, Polity Press: Cambridge.
Bendelow, G. and Williams, S.J. (eds) (1998) *Emotions in Social Life: Critical Themes and Contemporary Issues*, Routledge: London.
Bland, L. and Doan, L. (1998) *Sexology Uncensored: The Documents of Sexual Science*, Polity Press: Cambridge.
Bourdieu, P. (1999) *The Weight of the World: Social Suffering in Contemporary Society*, Polity Press: Cambridge.
Bourdieu, P. (2001) *Masculine Domination*, Polity Press: Cambridge.
Bourdieu, P. and Wacquant, L.J.D. (1992) *An Invitation to Reflexive Sociology*, Polity Press: Cambridge.
Brake, M. (1982) *Human Sexual Relations: A Reader. Towards a Redefinition of Sexual Politics*, Penguin: Harmondsworth.
Butler, J. (1990) *Gender Trouble: Feminism and the Subversion of Identity*, Routledge: London.
Butler, J. (1991) 'Imitation and Gender Insubordination', in D. Fuss (ed.) *Inside/Out: Lesbian Theories, Gay Theories*, Routledge: New York.
Butler, J. (1993) *Bodies That Matter: On The Discursive Limits Of Sex*, Routledge: London.
Butler, J. (1994) 'Gender as Performance: an Interview with Judith Butler', *Radical Philosophy*, 67: 32–39.
Butler, J. (1997a) *Excitable Speech: A Politics of the Performative*, Routledge: New York.
Butler, J. (1997b) *The Psychic Life of Power: Theories in Subjection*, Stanford University Press: Stanford.
Butler, J. (1999a) 'On Speech, Race and Melancholia: An interview with Judith Butler', *Theory, Culture and Society (Special Issue on Performativity and Belonging)*, 16(2) 163–174.
Butler, J. (1999b) *Subjects of Desire: Hegelian Reflections in Twentieth-Century France*, Columbia University Press: New York.

Butler, J. (2000) *Antigone's Claim: Kinship Between Life and Death*, Columbia University Press: New York.
Cameron, D. (1990) 'Ten Years On: "Compulsory Heterosexuality and Lesbian Existence"', *Women: A Cultural Review*, 1(1): 17–19.
Cameron, D. (1992) 'Old het?', *Trouble and Strife*, 24: 41–45.
Clarke, C. (1981) 'Lesbianism: An Act of Resistance', in S. Scott and S. Jackson (eds) *Feminism and Sexuality: A Reader*, Columbia University Press: New York.
Collins, J. and Gregor, T. (1995) 'Boundaries of Love', in W. Jankowiak (ed.) *Romantic Passion: A Universal Experience?*, Columbia University Press: New York.
Connell, R.W. (1995) *Masculinities*, Polity Press: Cambridge.
de Beauvoir, S. (1997) *The Second Sex*, Vintage: London.
Delphy, C. and Leonard, D. (1992) *Familiar Exploitations: A New Analysis of Marriage in Contemporary Western Society*, Polity Press: Cambridge.
Dollimore, J. (2001) *Sex, Literature and Censorship*, Polity Press: Cambridge.
Dryden, C. (1999) *Being Married, Doing Gender: A Critical Analysis of Gender Relationships in Marriage*, Routledge: London.
Duncombe, J. and Marsden, D. (1993) 'Love and Intimacy: the Gender Division of Emotion and "Emotion Work"', *Sociology*, 27(2): 221–241.
Duncombe, J. and Marsden, D. (1998) '"Stepford Wives" and "Hollow Men"? Doing emotional work, doing gender and "authenticity" in intimate heterosexual relationships', in G. Bendelow and S.J. Williams (eds) *Emotions in Social Life: Critical Themes and Contemporary Issues*, Routledge: London.
Dworkin, A. (1981) *Pornography: Men Possessing Women*, The Women's Press: London.
Dworkin, A. (1987) *Intercourse*, Secker and Warburg: London.
Dyer, R. (1997) *White*, Routledge: London.
Evans, M. (1999) '"Falling in Love with Love is Falling for Make Believe": Ideologies of Romance in Post-Enlightenment Culture', in M. Featherstone (ed.) *Love and Eroticism*, Sage (TCS): London.
Featherstone, M. (1999) 'Love and Eroticism: An Introduction', in M. Featherstone (ed.) *Love and Eroticism*, Sage (TCS): London.
Firestone, S. (1972) *The Dialectic of Sex*, Paladin: London.
Fisher, H. (1995) 'The Nature and Evolution of Romantic Love', in W. Jankowiak (ed.) *Romantic Passion: A Universal Experience?*, Columbia University Press: New York.
Foucault, M. (1979) *The History of Sexuality, Volume 1: an Introduction*, Penguin: Harmondsworth.
Foucault, M. (1983) 'Sexual Choice, Sexual Act', in P. Rabinow (ed.) *Michel Foucault: Essential Works: Ethics, Volume 1*, Allen Lane and The Penguin Press: London.
Foucault, M. (1988) 'Technologies of the Self', in L.H. Martin, H. Gutman and P.H. Hutton (eds) *Technologies of the Self: A Seminar with Michel Foucault*, University of Massachusetts Press: Amherst.
Foucault, M. (1989) 'The Concern for Truth', in S. Lotringer (ed.) *Foucault Live: Collected Interviews 1961–1984*, Semiotext[e]: New York.
Foucault, M. (1990) *The Care of the Self: The History of Sexuality, Volume 3*, Penguin: Harmondsworth.
Foucault, M. (1991) 'Politics and the Study of Discourse', in G. Burchell,

C. Gordon and P. Miller (eds) *The Foucault Effect: Studies in Governmentality*, The University of Chicago Press: Chicago.

Foucault, M. (1997) 'Sexuality and Solitude', in P. Rabinow (ed.) *Michel Foucault: Essential Works: Ethics, Volume 1*, Allen Lane The Penguin Press: London.

Foucault, M. (2000) 'Preface', in G. Deleuze and F. Guattari (eds) *Anti-Oedipus: Capitalism and Schizophrenia*, The Athlone Press: London.

Fowler, B. (1997) *Pierre Bourdieu and Cultural Theory: Critical Investigations*, Sage (TCS): London.

Freud, S. (1991a) 'Civilization and its Discontents', in *Civilization, Society and Religion*, Penguin: Harmondsworth.

Freud, S. (1991b) 'Group Psychology and the Analysis of the Ego', in *Civilization, Society and Religion*, Penguin: Harmondsworth.

Freud, S. (1991c) 'Mourning and Melancholia', in *On Metapsychology*, Penguin: Harmondsworth.

Freud, S. (1991d) 'The Ego and the Id', in *On Metapsychology*, Penguin: Harmondsworth.

Freud, S. (1991e) 'The Tendency to Debasement in Love', in *On Sexuality: Three Essays on the Theory of Sexuality and Other Works*, Penguin: Harmondsworth.

Fromm, E. (1995) *The Art of Loving*, Thorsons: London.

Fuss, D. (1991) 'Inside/Out', in D. Fuss (ed.) *Inside/Out: Lesbian Theories, Gay Theories*, Routledge: New York.

Fuss, D. (1995) *Identification Papers*, Routledge: New York.

Gagnon, J.H. and Simon, W. (1973) *Sexual Conduct: The Social Sources of Human Sexuality*, Aldine Publishing: Chicago.

Giddens, A. (1992) *The Transformation of Intimacy: Sexuality, Love and Eroticism in Modern Societies*, Polity Press: Cambridge.

Gilroy, P. (2000) *Between Camps: Nations, Cultures and the Allure of Race*, Allen Lane and The Penguin Press: London.

Goode, W. (1959) 'The Theoretical Importance of Love', *American Sociological Review*, 24: 38–47.

Gottman, J.M. and Levenson, R.W. (1986) 'The Social Psychophysiology of Marriage', in P. Noller and M. Fitpatrick (eds) *Perspectives of Marital Interaction*, College Hill Press; London.

Greer, G. (1970) *The Female Eunuch*, Paladin: London.

Grosz, E. (1990) *Jacques Lacan: A Feminist Introduction*, Routledge: New York.

Hall, S. (1996) 'Who Needs "identity"?', in P. du Gay, J. Evans and P. Redman (eds) *Identity: A Reader* (2000), Sage: London.

Halperin, D.M. (1990) *One Hundred Years of Homosexuality*, Routledge: London.

Halperin, D.M. (1995) *Saint Foucault: Towards a Gay Hagiography*, Oxford University Press: New York.

Hearn, J. (1993) 'Emotive Subjects: Organizational Men, Organizational Masculinities and the (De)construction of "Emotions"', in S. Fineman (ed.) *Emotions in Organizations*, Sage: London.

Hepworth, M. (1999) 'Love, Gender and Morality', in M. Featherstone (ed.) *Love and Eroticism*, Sage (TCS): London.

Hochschild, A. (1983) *The Managed Heart*, University of California Press: Berkeley.

Hochschild, A. (1998) 'A Sociology of Emotion as a Way of Seeing', in G. Bendelow and S.J. Williams (eds) *Emotions in Social Life: Critical Themes and Contemporary Issues*, Routledge: London.

Holland, J., Ramazanoglu, C. and Thomson, R. (1996) 'In the Same Boat? The Gendered (In)experience of First Heterosex', in D. Richardson (ed.) *Theorizing Heterosexuality: Telling It Straight*, Open University Press: Buckingham.
Holland, J., Ramazanoglu, C., Sharpe, S. and Thomson, R. (1998) *The Male in the Head: Young People, Heterosexuality and Power*, The Tufnell Press: London.
Hollway, W. (1996) 'Recognition and Heterosexual Desire', in D. Richardson (ed.) *Theorizing Heterosexuality: Telling It Straight*, Open University Press: Buckingham.
Hollway, W. (1998) 'Gender Difference and the Production of Subjectivity', in J. Henriques, W. Hollway, C. Urwin, C. Venn and V. Walkerdine (eds) *Changing the Subject: Psychology, Social Regulation and Subjectivity*, Routledge: London.
hooks, b. (2000) *All About Love: New Visions*, The Women's Press: London.
Hunter, A. (1993) 'Same Door, Different Closet: A Heterosexual Sissy's Coming-Out Party', in S. Wilkinson and C. Kitzinger (eds) *Heterosexuality: A Feminism & Psychology Reader*, Sage: London.
Illouz, E. (1997) *Consuming the Romantic Utopia: Love and the Cultural Contradictions of Capitalism*, University of California Press: Berkeley.
Illouz, E. (1999) 'The Lost Innocence of Love: Romance as a Postmodern Condition', in M. Featherstone (ed.) *Love and Eroticism*, Sage (TCS): London.
Ingraham, C. (1999) *White Weddings: Romancing Heterosexuality in Popular Culture*, Routledge: New York.
Jackson, S. (1999) *Heterosexuality in Question*, Sage: London.
Jameson, L. (1998) *Intimacy: Personal Relationships in Modern Society*, Polity Press: Cambridge.
Jankowiak, W. (ed.) (1995) *Romantic Love: A universal Experience?*, Columbia University Press: New York.
Jeffreys, S. (1996) 'Heterosexuality and the Desire for Gender', in D. Richardson (ed.) *Theorizing Heterosexuality: Telling It Straight*, Open University Press: Buckingham.
Katz, J.N. (1996) *The Invention of Heterosexuality*, Plume/Penguin: New York.
Kelly, L. (1988) *Surviving Sexual Violence*, Polity Press: Cambridge.
Kinsey, A., Pomeroy, W.B. and Martin, C.E. (1948) *Sexual Behaviour in the Human Male*, Saunders: Philadelphia.
Kureishi, H. (1998) *Intimacy*, Faber and Faber: London.
Lacan, J. (1998) *The Four Fundamental Concepts of Psycho-Analysis*, Vintage: London.
Langford, W. (1999) *Revolutions of the Heart: Gender, Power and the Delusions of Love*, Routledge: London.
Leeds Revolutionary Feminist Group (1981) 'Political Lesbianism: the Case Against Heterosexuality', in Onlywomen Press (eds.) *Love Your Enemy? The Debate Between Heterosexual Feminism and Political Lesbianism*, Onlywomen Press: London.
Lees, S. (1993) *Sugar and Spice: Sexuality and Adolescent Girls*, Penguin: London.
Leonard, D. (1980) *Sex and Generation*, Tavistock: London.
Lindholm, C. (1995) 'Love as an Experience of Transcendence', in W. Jankowiak (ed.) *Romantic Passion: A Universal Experience?*, Columbia University Press: New York.
Lindholm, C. (1999) 'Love and Structure', in M. Featherstone (ed.) *Love and Eroticism*, Sage (TCS): London.
Luhmann, N. (1986) *Love As Passion: The Codification of Intimacy*, Stanford University Press: Stanford.
Lupton, D. (1998) *The Emotional Self: A Sociocultural Exploration*, Sage: London.

McCormick, I. (1997) *Secret Sexualities: A Sourcebook of 17th and 18th Century Writing*, Routledge: London.
McIntosh, M. (1968) 'The Homosexual Role', in P.M. Nardi and B.E. Scheider (eds) (1998) *Social Perspectives in Gay and Lesbian Studies: A Reader*, Routledge: New York.
MacKinnon, C.A. (1982) 'Feminism, Marxism, Method and the State: An Agenda for Theory', in S. Jackson and S. Scott (eds) (1996) *Feminism and Sexuality: A Reader*, Columbia University Press: New York.
Marazziti, D., Akiskal, H.S., Rossi, A. and Cassano, G.B. (1999) 'Alteration of the Platelet Serotonin Transporter in Romantic Love', *Psychological Medicine*, 29: 741–745.
Marcuse, H. (1955) *Eros and Civilization*, Sphere Books: London.
Marx, K. ([1844] 1992) *Economic and Philosophical Manuscripts*, in *Early Writings*, Penguin: Harmondsworth.
Messner, M. (1992) *Power at Play*, Beacon Press: Massachusetts.
Miller, G. (2000) *The Mating Mind: How Sexual Choice Shaped Human Evolution*, William Heinemann: London.
Moran, L.J. (1996) *The Homosexual(ity) of Law*, Routledge: London.
Nicholson, L. (1995) 'Interpreting Gender', in L. Nicholson and S. Seidman (eds) *Social Postmodernism: Beyond Identity Politics*, Cambridge University Press: Cambridge.
Oakley, A. (1984) *The Sociology of Housework*, Blackwell: Oxford.
Ollman, B. (1979) *Social and Sexual Revolution: Essays on Marx and Reich*, Pluto Press: London.
Phillips, A. (2001) *Houdini's Box: On The Arts of Escape*, Faber and Faber: London.
Plummer, K. (1981) 'Going Gay: Identities, Life Cycles and Lifestyles in the Male Gay World', in J. Hart and D. Richardson (eds) *The Theory and Practice of Homosexuality*, Routledge and Kegan Paul: London.
Plummer, K. (1995) *Telling Sexual Stories: Power, Change and Social Worlds*, London: Routledge.
Plummer, K. (1998) 'Afterword', in P.M. Nardi and B.E. Schneider (eds) *Social Perspectives in Lesbian and Gay Studies: A Reader*, Routledge: New York.
Reich, W. (1961) *The Function of the Orgasm*, Paladin: New York.
Roseneil, S. (2002) 'The Heterosexual/Homosexual Binary: Past, Present and Future', in D. Richardson and S. Seidman (eds) *Handbook of Lesbian and Gay Studies*, London: Sage.
Rich, A. (1980), 'Compulsory Heterosexuality and the Lesbian Existence', *Signs: Journal of Women in Culture and Society*, 5(4): 631–660.
Rose, G. (1995) *Love's Work*, Chatto and Windus: London.
Rose, N. (1998) *Inventing Ourselves: Psychology, Power and Personhood*, Cambridge University Press: Cambridge.
Rosenthal, D., Gifford, S. and Moore, S. (1998) 'Safe Sex or Safe Love: Competing Discourses', *AIDS Care*, 10,(1): 35–47.
Rowland, R. (1993) 'Radical Feminist Heterosexuality: The Personal and the Political', in S. Wilkinson and C. Kitzinger (eds) *Heterosexuality: A Feminism & Psychology Reader*, Sage: London.
Rutherford, J. (1999) *I Am No Longer Myself Without You: An Anatomy of Love*, Flamingo: London.
Salecl, R. (1998) *(Per)versions of Love and Hate*, Verso: London.
Sartre, J.-P. (1958) *Being and Nothingness: An Essay on Phenomenological Ontology*, Routledge: London.

Sedgewick, E. (1990) *Epistemology of the Closet*, Penguin Books: Harmondsworth.
Segal, L. (1999) *Why Feminism? Gender, Psychology, Politics*, Polity Press: Cambridge.
Seidman, S. (1991) *Romantic Longings: Love in America, 1830–1980*, Routledge: New York.
Seidman, S. (ed.) (1996) *Queer Theory/Sociology*, Blackwell, Cambridge Ma.
Skeggs, B. (1997) *Formations of Class and Gender: Becoming Respectable*, Sage (TCS): London.
Smart, C. (1996) 'Collusion, Collaboration and Confession: on Moving Beyond the Heterosexuality Debate', in D. Richardson (ed.) *Theorizing Heterosexuality: Telling It Straight*, Open University Press: Buckingham.
Spellman, E.V. (1990) *Inessential Woman: Problems of Exclusion in Feminist Thought*, The Women's Press: London.
Spivak, G.C. (1996) *The Spivak Reader*, D. Landry and G. Maclean (eds) Routledge: New York.
Stacey, J. and Pearce, L. (1995) 'The Heart of the Matter: Feminists Revisit Romance', in L. Pearce and J. Stacey (eds) *Romance Revisited*, Lawrence and Wishart: London.
Stein, E. (ed.) (1992) *Forms of Desire: Sexual Orientation and the Social Constructionist Controversy*, Routledge: New York.
Thompson, D. (1993) 'Against the Dividing of Women: Lesbian Feminism and Heterosexuality', in S. Wilkinson and C. Kitzinger (eds) *Heterosexuality: A Feminism & Psychology Reader*, Sage: London.
VanEvery, J. (1995) *Heterosexual Women Changing the Family: Refusing to be a Wife!*, Taylor and Francis: London.
Vice, S. (1995) 'Addicted to Love', in L. Pearce and J. Stacey (eds) *Romance Revisited*, Lawrence and Wishart: London.
Warner, M. (ed.) (1993) *Fear of a Queer Planet*, University of Minnesota Press: Minneapolis.
Weber, M. (1948) *From Max Weber*, H. Gerth and C.W. Mills (eds), Routledge and Kegan Paul: London.
Weeks, J. (1989) *Sex, Politics & Society: The Regulation of Sexuality Since 1800 (second edition)*, Longman: Essex.
Weeks, J. (1999) 'The Sexual Citizen', in M. Featherstone (ed.) *Love and Eroticism*, Sage (TCS): London.
Weeks, J. (2000) *Making Sexual History*, Polity Press: Cambridge.
Weiss, R. (1990) *Staying the Course*, Fawcett Columbine: New York.
Weston, K. (1991) *Families We Choose: Lesbians, Gays, Kinship*, Columbia University Press: New York.
Wilkinson, S. and Kitzinger, C. (1993) 'Theorizing Heterosexuality', in S. Wilkinson and C. Kitzinger *Heterosexuality: A Feminism & Psychology Reader*, Sage: London.
Williams, S. (ed) (2001) *Emotion and Social Theory: Corporeal Reflections on the (Ir)Rational*, Sage: London.
Wittig, M. (1981) 'One is Not Born a Woman', *Feminist Issues*, 1(2): 47–54.
Wouters, C. (1999) 'Balancing Sex and Love Since the 1960s Sexual Revolution', in M.Featherstone (ed.) *Love and Eroticism*, Sage (TCS): London.
Young, M. and Willmott, P. (1973) *The Symmetrical Family*, Penguin: Harmondsworth.
Žižek, S. (1989) *The Sublime Object of Ideology*, Verso: London.

Index

addictiveness, of love 85
'Alex' 20, 44
ambiguities 120–9, 134
anal sex 110–11
arranged marriages 37–8
attraction 52–3, 116–19

'Barbara' 20, 63, 84, 89, 103–4
'Barry' 20, 71, 74, 94
Barthes, R. 23, 79
Beck, Ulrick 12–13, 42
Beck-Gernsheim, Elisabeth 12–13, 14, 42
Bell, D. 1, 12, 15, 68
Bendelow, G. 14
Binnie, J. 1, 12, 15, 68
biological model 26, 30–2, 47–8
Bodies That Matter 10
bodily sensations 30–2
bonding 39–40
borders, of sexuality 104–19
Bourdieu, P. 17, 18
Brake, M. 48
buggery 110–11
Butler, Judith 9, 10–11, 12, 17, 79, 80, 81, 101, 107, 116, 119, 121, 129, 130, 132
'butterflies' 29–32

Cameron, Debbie 7
'Carl' 20, 25, 43, 50–1, 98, 115
casual sex: men 67–74; women 59–67
'Catherine' 20, 25, 26–7, 29, 32, 34, 37, 84–5
'chemistry': of love 36–40
Clarke, C. 9
'click' metaphor 38
Collins, J. 78
'coming out' 136
completeness 86–8, 92

'compulsory heterosexuality' 4, 12
conceptions: of love 3, 25–6
confluent love 3
Connell, R.W. 96
constraints, social 68
cruising 67–8

de Beauvoir, S. 8, 76, 83
Delphy, C. 14, 96
desexualization 70
desire 116–19; ambiguous 120–9
disgust 109–13
Dollimore, Jonathan 111, 112
'Dorothy' 20, 25, 48
double standard 66
'Douglas' 20–1, 29, 38–9, 41–2, 53, 125–8
Dryden, C. 11, 96
Duncombe, J. 14, 96, 97
Dworkin, A. 7

'Elizabeth' 21, 29, 31, 39, 44, 65, 66, 84, 91
'Ellen' 21, 26, 34–5, 52–3
Ellis, Havelock 144
embodiment: of love 30–2
Epistemology of the Closet 9
essence: of love 40–5
Evans, M. 14

'families of choice' 15
Featherstone, Mike 26
female sexuality 66–7
femininity 88, 101
feminism 7–9
fidelity 47
Firestone, Shulamith 24, 76, 83
Fisher, Helen 36
force: of love 23–4, 32–5

Foucault, Michel 9, 14, 16–17, 18, 31, 63, 68, 70–1, 79, 81, 106, 107, 121
Fowler, B. 17
Freud, S. 6, 48, 70, 129–30
Fromm, Erich 23, 24
'fusing' metaphor 38
Fuss, Diana 5, 9, 106, 108, 124
'fuzziness' 29–32

Gagnon, J.H. 6
'Gary' 21, 93, 117
gay lifestyle 67–8
gay male sex 109–12
gendered differences 66
gender relations 6–8, 11–12
Gender Trouble 10
Giddens, Anthony 4, 13, 49, 68, 78, 103, 112
Gilroy, Paul 138
Goode, W. 23
Gottman, J.M. 96
Gregor, T. 78
Grosz, Elizabeth 81
guilt 61–2

Hall, Stuart 106–7
Halperin, D.M. 9, 10, 107
'have/hold discourse' 86
Hearn, J. 96
'Heather' 21, 25, 84, 87
Hegel, G.W.F. 79
Hepworth, M. 14
heteronormativity 2
heterosexuality: ideas of 4; invisibility of 6; study of 4–6; theorists 6–12
Hochschild, A. 14, 30, 35
Holland, J. 12, 48
Hollway, Wendy 86, 98, 100
homo/het binary 9–10, 105–9
homosexuality 103–19, 124–9, 135–6
hooks, bell 23–4, 28
Hunter, Allan 77

identities, sexual 108, 111; changes in 20th century 4–5
Illouz, Eva 1, 14, 45
individuality: of love 29
Ingraham, C. 15
interviews: methodology 16–18
intimacy 49, 52–9, 67; studies of 12–14
Intimacy 23
intimate love 3
invisibility: of heterosexuality 6

'Jack' 21, 40, 48
'Jackie' 21, 32–3, 36, 118
Jackson, Stevi 1, 9, 11, 15, 23, 24, 26, 27, 28, 51, 76, 101
Jameson, Lynn 16, 49
Jankowiak, W. 45
Jeffreys, S. 11, 76

Katz, J.N. 10, 106
Kelly, L. 9
Kinsey, A. 116
Kitzinger, Celia 5, 8–9, 107
Kureishi, Hanif 23

Lacan, J. 80, 89, 94
Lacanian model 80–1, 92
'lack' 86–7, 91–2, 101
Langford, Wendy 13, 25–6, 83, 91
language: of love 25–6, 36
Lees, S. 56, 69
Leonard, D. 14, 56, 96
lesbianism 6–9, 76–7, 122–4
lesbian sex 113–14
Levenson, R.W. 96
Lindholm, Charles 13, 27, 78
loss: of love 89–92; notion of 129–33
love: addictiveness of 85; biological process 26, 30–2, 47–8; conceptions 3, 25–6; defining 25–6; embodiment of 30–2; expression of 49–59; feeling of 27–8; as a force 23–4; individuality of 29; language of 25–6; loss of 89–92; power of 32–5; studies of 12–14; theorizations of 78–9; trans-history 40–5; universality 40–5; *see also* confluent love; intimate love; romantic love; sexual love
love–sex relationship: historical 48–9
Luhmann, Niklas 1, 13–14, 23, 28
Lupton, D. 14, 27
lust 50–9
lust balance question 54–5

MacKinnon, Catharine 6, 134
Male in the Head, The 12
male subjectivity 92–6
Marazziti, D. 2, 3, 30
Marcuse, H. 24
'Margaret' 21, 34, 44, 54, 59–60, 61, 67, 84, 90, 122–4
'Mark' 21, 29, 35, 68–9, 99–100, 110, 131–3
marriages: arranged 37–8

Marsden, D. 14, 96, 97
'Martin' 22, 28, 29–30, 38, 39–40, 49, 52, 95–6, 109
Marx, Karl 79
masculinity 92, 94, 95, 99, 101
McIntosh, Mary 9
melancholia 129–33
metaphors 27–8, 36–8
Miller, Geoffrey 2, 47

Nicholson, Linda 7–8
Normal Chaos of Love, The 12

Oakley, A. 96
obsessiveness 33–4
one night stands *see* casual sex

'Patricia' 22, 37, 82, 114
Pearce, L. 1, 46
'Peter' 22, 33, 69, 73, 133
'Phillip' 22, 25, 35, 38, 56–7, 74, 94, 95, 103, 117–19
Phillips, Adam 67, 109
'plastic sexuality' 13, 49, 138
Plummer, Ken 9, 11, 18
pluralism, sexual 137
possessiveness, of self 96–100
power: and feminism 7–9; of love 23–4, 32–5

qualitative interviewing 16–18
'queer' theorists 9–10

'radical Freudians' 24
Reich, W. 24
reproduction 47–8
reproductive need 26
repulsion 109–13
respectability: and sexual practice 59
Revolutions of the Heart 13
Rich, Adrienne 4, 6–7, 12, 78, 134
romantic love 1, 23; biological model 2–3; 'butterflies' 29–32; as a social construction 3
Rose, Gillian 85, 92
Rose, Nikolas 24, 31
Roseneil, Sasha 105
Rowland, Robyn 77, 91
'Ruth' 22, 25, 62–3, 113
Rutherford, Jonathan 28, 74, 91–2, 98–9

Salecl, Renata 81

same-sex sexual activity 109–16, 122–9
Sartre, J.-P. 79
'Scott' 22
Sedgewick, E. 9–10
Segal, Lynne 81
Seidman, S. 9, 49, 54, 60
self, sense of 78–9, 82–5, 86, 89–92; men's 93–100
self-esteem 82
self-surveillance 63, 66
sensations, embodied 29–32
sex, casual: men 67–74; women 59–67
sex difference 80–2; biological 8
sex–love relationship: historical 48–9
sexual ambiguities 120–9, 134
sexual attraction 52–3, 116–19
sexual chemistry 39
sexual desire 52–9, 116–19
sexual identities 108, 111; changes in 20th century 4–5
sexual love 3
sexual performance 73
sexual pluralism 137
sexual practice: as expression of love 49–59
sexual reputation 62–3
sexual satisfaction 67
sexual violence 9
shame 61–2
Simon, W. 6
Skeggs, Beverley 4, 12, 59, 61, 65
Smart, Carol 5, 9, 135
social constraints 68
'spark' metaphor 37, 38
Spellman, E.V. 7
Spivak, G.C. 7
Stacey, J. 1, 46
Stein, E. 7
study: participants 20–2
subjectivity: men 92–6; women 82–5, 91
'Susan' 22, 55–6, 64, 91

theorizations, of love 78–9
Thompson, Denise 9, 76
'tingles' 30–2
transformations: men's 92–4; women's 82–92

universality: of love 40–5

VanEvery, J. 9, 11
Vice, Sue 85

'Victoria' 22, 38, 88
violence 9

Wacquant, L.D.J. 18
Warner, M. 9
Weber, Max 13, 78
Weeks, Jeffrey 4, 15, 49, 105, 112
Weiss, R. 98
Weston, K. 15
Wilkinson, Sue 5, 8–9, 107

'William' 22, 33–4, 53, 72–3, 97, 112
Williams, S. 14, 30
Williams, S.J. 14
Willmott, P. 78
Wittig, Monique 8
Wouters, Cas 50, 54–5

Young, M. 78

Žižek, S. 101

eBooks

eBooks – at www.eBookstore.tandf.co.uk

A library at your fingertips!

eBooks are electronic versions of printed books. You can store them on your PC/laptop or browse them online.

They have advantages for anyone needing rapid access to a wide variety of published, copyright information.

eBooks can help your research by enabling you to bookmark chapters, annotate text and use instant searches to find specific words or phrases. Several eBook files would fit on even a small laptop or PDA.

NEW: Save money by eSubscribing: cheap, online access to any eBook for as long as you need it.

Annual subscription packages

We now offer special low-cost bulk subscriptions to packages of eBooks in certain subject areas. These are available to libraries or to individuals.

For more information please contact webmaster.ebooks@tandf.co.uk

We're continually developing the eBook concept, so keep up to date by visiting the website.

www.eBookstore.tandf.co.uk